Cambridge Opera Handbooks

Hector Berlioz
*Les Troyens*

CAMBRIDGE OPERA HANDBOOKS

This is a series of studies of individual operas written for the opera-goer or record-collector as well as the student or scholar. Each volume has three main concerns: historical, analytical and interpretative. There is a detailed description of the genesis of each work, the collaboration between librettist and composer, and the first performance and subsequent stage history. A full synopsis considers the opera as a structure of musical and dramatic effects, and there is also a musical analysis of a section of the score. The analysis, like the history, shades naturally into interpretation: by a careful combination of new essays and excerpts from classic statements the editors of the handbooks show how critical writing about the opera, like the production and performance, can direct or distort appreciation of its structural elements. A final section of documents gives a select bibliography, a discography, and guides to other sources. Each book is published in both hard covers and as a paperback.

Books published

Richard Wagner: *Parsifal* by Lucy Beckett
W. A. Mozart: *Don Giovanni* by Julian Rushton
C. W. von Gluck: *Orfeo* by Patricia Howard
Igor Stravinsky: *The Rake's Progress* by Paul Griffiths
Leoš Janáček: *Kát'a Kabanová* by John Tyrrell
Giuseppe Verdi: *Falstaff* by James A. Hepokoski
Benjamin Britten: *Peter Grimes* by Philip Brett
Giacomo Puccini: *Tosca* by Mosco Carner
Benjamin Britten: *The Turn of the Screw* by Patricia Howard
Richard Strauss: *Der Rosenkavalier* by Alan Jefferson
Claudio Monteverdi: *Orfeo* by John Whenham
Giacomo Puccini: *La bohème* by Arthur Groos and Roger Parker
Giuseppe Verdi: *Otello* by James A. Hepokoski
Benjamin Britten: *Death in Venice* by Donald Mitchell
W. A. Mozart: *Le nozze di Figaro* by Tim Carter
W. A. Mozart: *Die Entführung aus dem Serail* by Thomas Bauman

# Hector Berlioz
# *Les Troyens*

*Edited by*
IAN KEMP

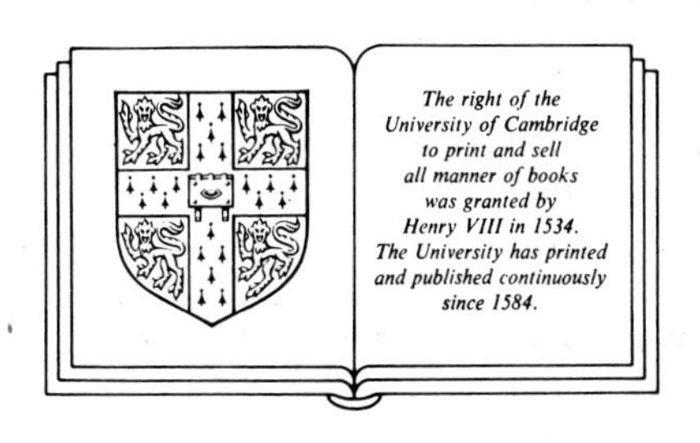


CAMBRIDGE UNIVERSITY PRESS

*Cambridge*
*New York New Rochelle Melbourne Sydney*

Published by the Press Syndicate of the University of Cambridge
The Pitt Building, Trumpington Street, Cambridge CB2 1RP
32 East 57th Street, New York, NY 10022, USA
10 Stamford Road, Oakleigh, Melbourne 3166, Australia



First published 1988

Printed in Great Britain at
the University Press, Cambridge

*British Library cataloguing in publication data*

Hector Berlioz, Les Troyens. – (Cambridge
opera handbooks).
1. Opera in French. Berlioz, Hector 1803–1869
Troyens, Les
I. Kemp, Ian, *1931–*
782.1′092′4

*Library of Congress cataloguing in publication data*

Hector Berlioz Les troyens / edited by Ian Kemp.
p. cm. – (Cambridge opera handbooks)
Discography: p.
Bibliography: p.
Includes index.
ISBN 0 521 34280 5. ISBN 0 521 34813 7 (pbk.)
1. Berlioz, Hector, 1803–1869. Troyens. I. Kemp, Ian.
II. Series.
ML410.B5H3 1988
782.1′092′4 – dc19 88–2719 CIP MN

ISBN 0 521 34280 5 hard covers
ISBN 0 521 34813 7 paperback

ME

*For Sian*

# *Contents*

# *Illustrations*

# *Acknowledgements*

Obviously this book could not have existed without the goodwill and collaboration of its seven other contributors. To them I would like to say thank you – for their expert individual chapters, for submitting so graciously to my persistent and irritating requests, mostly for their tactful understanding that I asked them to contribute so that I could learn and steal from them.

My thanks are also due to several others for their generous help and advice: Pierre Citron, H. Robert Cohen, April FitzLyon, Jonathan Foster, Harry Jocelyn, Francesca Kemp, Richard Macnutt, Michel Pazdro, James Thompson, Lynne Thornton, T. J. Walsh, William Waterhouse, John Webb, Michael Wood. Michael Anderson of the Reid Music Library in the University of Edinburgh, Nicole Wild of the Bibliothèque de l'Opéra, Paris and Ruzena Wood of the Music Department of the National Library of Scotland were unfailingly helpful. I have also received expert help and advice from Michael Black, Penny Souster, Victoria Cooper and Lucy Carolan of Cambridge University Press and invaluable financial assistance, enabling me to visit Paris libraries, from the University of Manchester. The illustrations are reproduced by kind permission of the following institutions and individuals: Figs. 1, 2, 3, 7, 8, 9 and 13, the Bibliothèque Nationale, Paris; Figs. 6 and 12 No. 5, the Musée du Louvre, Paris; Fig. 4, Mr. P. Fischer; Fig. 5, Opera North; Fig. 10, Scottish Opera; Fig. 11, Covent Garden.

To Winnie and Charles, big Alison, little Alison, Christine, Alistair, beloved Alex, Marjorie and Geoffrey I offer gratitude for humouring my enthusiasm for Berlioz and giving it something solid to rest on.

Ian Kemp

# 1 *Les Troyens: mostly questions*

**COLIN DAVIS**

We count the beginning of our civilization from the destruction of a small walled city in Asia Minor. Now we face the destruction of that civilization, of the world perhaps. The Greeks with their superior technology bamboozled the Trojans with a wheeled, wooden horse. We have come beyond the wheel, and the horse: to what?

The destruction of Troy will never lose its fascination. Berlioz, in choosing the subject of the Trojans for his greatest work, has ensured that we can enjoy, or experience rather, the ritual in the opera house. For ritual it is: the characters are more than themselves, they are symbols:

Cassandra – to whom no one listens, for whom excruciating knowledge has shorn away all possibility of personal pleasure.

Coroebus – in love, and seeing only that, in reality, which reflects the infatuation he wishes to nourish.

Andromache – symbol of the silence born of unspeakable suffering.

Aeneas – the egomaniac Hero, chained to the mast of a great idea, for which he must sacrifice everything and everybody, typical of those deluded by calls from 'Destiny'.

Dido – 'widow Dido', passionate, vulnerable queen, who, with Aeneas's help saves her land and her honour from the exigent Iarbas, only to lose her heart and give her life for the Man of Destiny.

Hylas-Palinurus – the archetypal sleepwalker whose poetical mind is as far from reality as are the minds of most of us dreamers.

And over all the little flame of civilization, which so comfortably illumines all upon which it shines, threatened by forces beyond its control, particularly that which we now call nature, or evolution, embodied in Paris and the Three Women, Triple Hecate. A vision of the destruction and renewal brought about by history? And now – for us? After two world wars we have experienced no renewal. . .

What is clear is that the opera must be performed in one evening. 'Carthage', relaxed and erotic, cannot stand alone without the equal and opposite aggressive and hysterical 'Troy'.

*La Prise de Troie* is condensed to such an extent that nothing can be left out. *Les Troyens à Carthage* is, by comparison, leisurely, almost tropical in its sensuousness. Is the opening scene displaying Dido in all her glory not a little too long? And the ballet? Certainly royals of all time have had their entertainments; but Berlioz has not given us a realistic opera: one senses the demands of gestures and fashions of nineteenth-century Paris. And is not the garden scene over-extended? Too many *divertissements*, which add little to the atmosphere of intoxicated love that Berlioz has so masterfully established? Court custom fulfilled, impatiently waiting for the moment when 'we' may retire? But that raises the problem of the *Chasse royale et orage*: before the garden scene or after? Fore-play or after-play? The answer doesn't help to present that wonderful tone poem in the theatre. A materialistic presentation? Naiads, dryads, fauns, rude old uncle Silenus, and all other acceptable representations of the *Erdgeist* rapturously applauding the goings-on-in-the-cave, which we have all heard about but perhaps never seen? Or an interlude in which the scene changes either to the garden or to the harbour?

And what to do with Narbal and Anna? Their duet has little effect in the theatre and appears only to delay that which we know is going to happen, without adding anything to the ritual.

The last question-mark is of course the final scene. Priests mumbling a forgotten rite, Anna and Narbal presiding, before Dido's farewell and suicide (wonderful!) and then the vision of the foundation of Rome, triumph of the Hero and History and defeat of the human in the individual. 'Fate' appears to triumph even though we know that Aeneas must go down, as Napoleon and Hitler went down after him; the Hero ascends the mountain of corpses, once his friends, his family and his lovers, to his own execution. But how portray this? Are we not once more up against Berlioz's Imagination, which prefers the freedom of the Dramatic Legend or Symphony to the material restrictions of the opera?

Yet is it not this same Imagination which gives Berlioz his eccentric power and *Les Troyens* its greatness?

# 2 *Biographical introduction*

**IAN KEMP**

Berlioz never heard *Les Troyens*. He never heard the work he knew was the culmination of his whole output, never knew that after a century of misunderstanding and maltreatment it would finally be performed as he had written it and vindicated as a towering work of art. It is difficult to think of any other work with a history so poignant.

In his early years he might have thought all this a little sentimental. Virgil, after all, had died before the *Aeneid* was even complete. What does it matter so long as a masterwork *exists*? Shortly before completing his own opera Berlioz wrote to a friend in a similar spirit: he didn't care whether it was produced or not; the main thing was that his 'musical and Virgilian passions' had been gratified. But the main thing was that it *should* be produced. He spent the next five years in a dignified but futile attempt to have it produced at the Paris Opéra, eventually accepting that the fruit of his passions would have to be cut in two and served up incomplete, and in an inadequate theatre. He made the last three acts into a separate, five-act opera, *Les Troyens à Carthage*; this was performed at the Théâtre-Lyrique in 1863. He also made the first two acts into a separate, three-act opera, *La Prise de Troie*, which he never heard. But he resigned himself to this division, even referring to two operas in his will. Perhaps the most eloquent testimony to his real feelings is to be seen on his manuscript. The title page of the autograph full score is proudly and lovingly written: *Les Troyens / Grand opéra en cinq actes / Paroles et musique / de / Hector Berlioz*. But it was altered, first to '1re Partie Des Troyens' and then to 'La Prise de Troie / Opéra en trois actes', both in strictly functional handwriting. The handwriting for the second title page, 'Les Troyens à Carthage / opéra en cinq actes / avec un prologue', is perfunctory, irritated. Berlioz was sixty, disillusioned, contemptuous of the vanities and cruelties of mankind. He had ceased composing. It is not overstating the case to say that the fate of *Les Troyens* broke him. Why did that Fate to which he had paid ample tribute in his opera play with him so wantonly? What had happened?

In the original final chapter of his *Memoirs*, written in 1854, Berlioz revealed that for three years he had been 'tormented' by the idea of an enormous opera, knowing all too well that unless he suppressed his intense creative excitement at the prospect of composing it he would lay untold miseries in store for himself. At that time he had good reason to believe that he would hold out, for he *had* resisted the temptation to write a fifth symphony. In one of the most moving passages in the *Memoirs* he pleads with his reader to forgive him for not having composed the symphony he heard in a dream – because the costs involved would have prevented him from supporting his paralysed, dying wife. That was in 1852. Two years later Harriet Smithson was in her grave, and Berlioz himself felt on the 'steep slope that leads with ever-increasing swiftness to the end'. To attempt the opera would be as foolish as ever and would in any case leave him exposed 'not only to the antagonism which my critical ideas have aroused but also to the equally violent opposition provoked by the style of my music'.

There was no denying that Berlioz's music was exceedingly challenging, even if it could conveniently be pigeonholed as the product of a fevered imagination. But his *feuilletons* in the *Journal des Débats* – a newspaper whose liberal sympathies made it hardly the best platform from which to court the necessary presidential or imperial favour – were too elegant and sharply focused to be disregarded in this way. In print, Berlioz was surprisingly generous towards composers, especially young composers; his remarks about the management of opera houses could be less than prudent. In a review of Gounod's *Sapho*, for example, of 7 January 1852, he commented that the times – and by implication, productions at the Opéra – were of 'machineism, mannequinism (and of neologism) and industrialism more or less disguised under the pretext of art'.[1] Later that year he returned to this theme, when reprinting, as the 'Ninth Evening' of his book *Les Soirées de l'orchestre*, an earlier attack on the Opéra. Five years after that, by which time he was deep in the composition of *Les Troyens*, he could be so uncircumspect, in a review of Thomas's *Psyché*, as to repeat the Ninth Evening's chief findings and say of the one place for which his work was designed: 'The Opéra mistrusts composers not in possession of a well-established reputation for mediocrity.'[2]

Berlioz had been in an impossible position. He could not betray his artistic ideals; the practicalities, the politics, the taste of Parisian musical life at the time were diametrically opposed to him. Most of all, if he felt himself 'burned up', at the same time he was 'still burning and filled with an energy that sometimes flares up with terrifying force'.

A hint of this energy can be observed in the main body of his reviews of *Sapho* (that in 1852 was the second; the first was on 22 April 1851). He was evidently so stirred to see the young Gounod in his first opera returning to classical subject matter and to the dramatic methods of Gluck that he was impelled to write at disproportionate length – providing Gounod with an extended composition lesson, here with unstinting praise, there with harsh criticism, everywhere with the enthusiasm of a composer at last in the company of another with whom he could discuss true artistic priorities. In fact *Sapho* is a pallid work. But might it have been the spark that lit up the creative fires of *Les Troyens*? By 1857, with *Sapho* and now even *Psyché* to support him, he could counter a friend's objection to the unfashionable non-historical text of his opera by saying that 'antique subjects have become new again'. Certainly Berlioz borrowed from *Sapho* the idea of a trio for two flutes and harp which he was to use in *L'Enfance du Christ* and it was this work, completed in July 1854 (having been left, in 1850, with only one of its eventual three parts, *La Fuite en Égypte*), that marked the recovery of his appetite for composing after a silent period of three years. At all events the *Memoirs* chapter gives the impression that however reasonable his objections to writing the opera, he protests too much, that he is beset by a kind of deadness in the face of so mammoth an enterprise, that he is waiting for his suppressed creative powers to erupt and overtake him.

The situation was not unpromising. He no longer had the emotional and financial burden of Harriet. In October 1854, seven months after her death, he had married Marie Recio, his mistress for over twelve years ('it was my *duty*'[3]), and if she provided little of the feminine understanding he needed, she did create some domestic stability. His public career was proceeding tolerably well. Concert tours in Germany and England brought wide acclaim; the cabal against his first opera *Benvenuto Cellini* at Covent Garden in 1853 may have hardened his resolve not to write *Les Troyens*, but the 'Berlioz Weeks' promoted by Liszt in Weimar in 1852 and 1855, which included successful performances of the opera, must have weakened it; *L'Enfance du Christ* (which had proved that he could write his own librettos) and his *Te Deum* also had successful first performances in 1854 and 1855 respectively. And in 1854 he had written his cantata *L'Impériale*, a gross attempt to curry favour with Napoleon III, which nevertheless indicated how desperate he was to prepare the ground. (In 1856 he got a gold medal from the Emperor for it.) All that Berlioz now needed was some sort of fillip and this came when for at least the second time he discussed his project, and his continuing reluctance to embark on it, with Liszt and his mistress, Princess Carolyne Sayn-Wittgenstein, during a third 'Berlioz Week' in Weimar in February 1856. The Princess threatened never to see him again unless he stopped playing the faint-heart and started straight away. 'Milder words than these would have been enough to decide me.' Berlioz began work on the opera in April 1856 and two years later libretto and music were complete – though he continued to make alterations until 1863.

The part played by the Princess in the composition of *Les Troyens* – encouraging, cajoling, supporting – was to be readily acknowledged by Berlioz, who found in her a kindred intelligence and the *confidante* he needed. He was probably unaware that her interest in his work was also an attempt to generate a challenge to Wagner (then writing *Der Ring des Nibelungen*), whom she mistrusted and whose influence on Liszt she resented.

The events leading up to its eventual 'performance' make for depressing and somewhat confusing reading. At first he was confident enough, marshalling his resources as on the eve of a successful military engagement. Even during composition he had given readings of his libretto to select audiences of potentially influential sympathizers, as well as to friends whose opinions he respected. He set great store by these readings, using them chiefly to promote the opera but also to test out the effect of his design and his text. In order to articulate correctly the emphases, inflections, silences, he at one time considered asking the famous actress Rachel to read passages for him, so seriously did he take his commitment to expressive fidelity. Rachel – her real name was Élisabeth Félix (she died in 1858 at the age of thirty-six, before Berlioz had finished his opera) – was the leading figure in the revival of the classical repertory and the classical style of acting in French theatre during the 1840s and 50s, and Berlioz's sympathy with this development could account for the most interesting of the surviving descriptions of his manner of delivery at readings – that of Wagner, who after one in 1858 wrote that it was 'curiously dry and theatrically affected'.[4] (Wagner's aesthetic attitudes had of course diverged widely from Berlioz's by that time and his description also reflected his dismay at what he took to be the backward path Berlioz was following in the opera.) In general, reactions to the readings were encouraging. When he had finished the music Berlioz was ready to launch his assault on the fortress of the Opéra.

His plan was simple – to bypass the administration and make a direct approach to the Emperor. Berlioz hated soliciting in this way but he saw in it the only means by which he could overcome the opposition he encountered at the Opéra – from the director, Alphonse Royer, and the conductors there. In any case the Opéra was an imperial theatre or, as Berlioz put it, 'a kind of private theatre of the Emperor where the only new works performed are those by people *adroit* [his italics] at slipping in somehow or other'.[5] He can be imagined hoping that Napoleon III would draw parallels between Berlioz reading *Les Troyens* to his Emperor and Virgil writing the *Aeneid* for Augustus. Accordingly, on 28 March 1858, he drafted a letter to the Emperor, explaining his position and requesting permission to read him the libretto. The letter is printed in his *Memoirs*. His first setback was a request by the Comte de Morny, the Emperor's half-brother, not to send it. (It should be remembered that Berlioz's election to the French Institute in 1856 gave him some sort of access to the Emperor and his entourage.) A few weeks later he met the Emperor at an official reception and was warmly invited to arrange what he thought would be a private audience, which finally took place in the autumn, in the company of forty-two others. Berlioz now presented his libretto, with the result that it was passed on to subordinates, who were expert at parrying his enquiries. Rumours circulated that *Les Troyens* lasted eight hours and required resources twice as large as those at the Opéra. Berlioz himself was perfectly well aware that his opera could not be scheduled quickly, not least because of casting difficulties. All he wanted was a commitment to it and a date. But he began to realize that his imperial strategy was not so adroit, and he now paid more attention to mobilizing public pressure, largely through his readings, which would keep the opera in the musical press and introduce new recruits to his band of influential sympathizers. Also, in August 1859, he arranged discreetly publicized performances of excerpts – on the 6th with piano, in the tiny Salle Beethoven in Paris (Cassandra's aria and the duet from Act I, the mezzo-soprano being his future Dido, Anne Charton-Demeur), and on the 29th, with orchestra, in a concert at

Baden-Baden (the items above and the duet from Act IV, the mezzo-soprano now being Pauline Viardot). All this served to bring Léon Carvalho into the picture – Carvalho the impresario at the Théâtre-Lyrique, who was eventually to mount *Les Troyens à Carthage*.

The astute Carvalho had in fact already, in the summer of 1859, invited Berlioz to prepare and supervise a new production of Gluck's *Orphée*, with Pauline Viardot in the title role, returning to the Paris stage for the first time since *Sapho* eight years earlier. Apart from the attraction of Gluck, and indeed of Viardot (her artistry and musicianship profoundly impressed Berlioz, and led not only to some valuable comments on *Les Troyens* and help in the revision of its piano score but also to a passionate, if short-lived attachment to her[6]), what this meant for Berlioz was that the unexpected and eventually legendary success of *Orphée*, first performed on 18 November 1859, put him firmly in the operatic limelight. It gave public proof of his artistic judgement and professionalism, and of the financial success of an opera based on a classical subject. For his part, Carvalho had needed no such evidence of Berlioz's worth, for in September 1859 he had proposed that *Les Troyens* should be the opera to mark the opening of his new Théâtre-Lyrique, then scheduled for the beginning of the 1861–2 season.

Under Baron Haussmann's schemes for the replanning of central Paris, the two principal theatres in the Boulevard du Temple, the Théâtre-Lyrique and the Cirque Imperial, were to be demolished and rebuilt in the Place du Châtelet[7] (where they still are, under different names, the Théâtre de la Ville and the Théâtre du Châtelet). The Théâtre-Lyrique was privately financed and the order for its rebuilding was recognition of its vital status as the third 'French' opera house in Paris (the others being the Opéra and the Opéra Comique), as well as of the enterprise of its director and quality of its productions. Berlioz waited some months before responding to Carvalho, hoping that the success of *Orphée* would force the hand of the Opéra. But it did not and he eventually accepted Carvalho's proposal. He had sound reasons for doing so. Carvalho was enthusiastic about *Les Troyens*; the Opéra treated him with little less than contempt; Carvalho had shown himself to be a colleague Berlioz could respect, and he had also shown commercial acumen and artistic integrity by interlacing opéras-comiques with lavish and successful productions not only of Berlioz's beloved Gluck but also of Weber and Mozart (*Oberon* in 1857, *Les Noces de Figaro* in 1858 and *L'Enlèvement au sérail* in 1859) and of Gounod (the première of

*Faust* in 1859), as well as with less successful productions of *Euryanthe* (1857) and other Weber operas. Berlioz was still concerned about casting, though in Viardot he had a possible mezzo-soprano who could double as Cassandra and Dido. On 16 January 1860 he signed a contract with Carvalho[8] and shortly afterwards it was officially announced that *Les Troyens* would open the new theatre. Then, on 1 April 1860, Carvalho resigned; his expensive productions had taken him to the brink of bankruptcy.

The new director, Charles Réty, although he mounted a *Fidelio* inherited from Carvalho (it was a failure and exposed Viardot's declining vocal talents) and although he did not entirely ignore the plans for *Les Troyens*, had other priorities. So, in a way, did Berlioz. In the autumn of 1860 he began writing the libretto and music for *Béatrice et Bénédict*, commissioned for another new theatre, at Baden-Baden. This third opera, which occupied him until September 1862, would help keep his mind off *Les Troyens*.

Meanwhile the Opéra was involved in lavish preparations for a new production of Wagner's *Tannhäuser*. With its disastrous failure in March 1861 Berlioz was entitled to feel that it was now the turn of the older, French composer. And indeed it was, but only in the supremely ironic role of supervisor of his 1841 version of Weber's *Der Freischütz*, which the Opéra, following the lead of the Théâtre-Lyrique, hoped would with Berlioz's help restore their fortunes after the disaster of *Tannhäuser*. Berlioz in fact began rehearsals for *Der Freischütz*, but a month later that opera was abandoned in favour of *Alceste*, Berlioz being offered full author's rights for his work on the production. He needed the money, but he withdrew from the project when he discovered that he was supposed to adapt rather than restore Gluck. This was hardly the climate in which he could have expected a change of heart about his own opera but suddenly, in June 1861, he was told by Royer that *Les Troyens* was definitely accepted for production at the Opéra, on the authorisation of the Minister of State. Pressures from all sides seemed at last to have yielded their rewards. Réty at the Théâtre-Lyrique graciously withdrew his claim. There were only two drawbacks: Berlioz would have to cut a scene in Act I (that involving the Greek spy Sinon; see p. 52), which, in order to be accommodating, he did; and he would have to wait until two other new and as yet unwritten operas were produced, by Gounod and Gevaert. (Gounod's *La Reine de Saba* was a fiasco in February 1862 and Gevaert, a little-known Belgian composer, never had an opera performed at the Opéra.) He expected a delay of the best part

The Paris Opéra and the Théâtre-Lyrique – respectively, where Berlioz wanted *Les Troyens* performed and where part of it, *Les Troyens à Carthage*, was performed.

1 The Paris Opéra (Académie Impériale de Musique, rue Le Peletier) in c.1850–60. A performance of Meyerbeer's *Robert le Diable* (1831)

2 The Théâtre-Lyrique in 1869. A performance of Ernest Boulanger's *Don Quichotte* (1869)

of two years before *Les Troyens* was produced but was nevertheless very satisfied, even going so far as to have the vocal score, which he had had privately engraved, printed in readiness for the production. And to put the Opéra in good humour, he agreed to return to *Alceste*: Viardot would be taking the title role and although he would have to submit to transpositions to suit her voice, at least she was singing and he would be in a position to prevent other alterations.

*Alceste* was first performed on 21 October 1861 and was almost as successful as *Orphée*. In February 1862 Berlioz reported that as a consequence Royer had been ordered to put *Les Troyens* into rehearsal immediately after the Gevaert opera had been performed; this was due to have been in September, so Berlioz calculated that his own opera would be performed in March 1863. But nothing happened. The Gevaert did not materialize and neither were there any signs of preparations for *Les Troyens*. The Opéra had reverted to its customary inertia. In part this was due to another factor bedevilling Berlioz's fortunes, the insecurity of Royer's position. Berlioz may have had little respect for the ineffectual Royer but it was Royer who had promised that *Les Troyens* would be produced. When eventually, in December 1862, Royer was replaced, it must have been difficult for Berlioz to know whether to bemoan or applaud the news. To confuse matters Réty, in October 1862, had resigned from the Théâtre-Lyrique, and been immediately and unexpectedly succeeded by none other than Carvalho, who was re-appointed in precisely the month that was to see the opening of the new theatre. This took place a year later than planned, not with *Les Troyens* but with a gala concert followed, on the next night, by an opéra-comique, *La Chatte merveilleuse* by Albert Grisar. Nevertheless Carvalho was still anxious to mount *Les Troyens*. For his part Berlioz had still not given up hope that the Opéra might do so. In January 1863 the papers printed a rumour that he had been appointed musical director and conductor at the Opéra.[9] He was never to find out what was behind it but all the same he wrote that month to the new director, Emile Perrin, in a last attempt to keep the Opéra to its promise, at the same time attempting to scotch some of the more flagrant rumours circulating about his work: it had nine roles, not twenty-two; it lasted not eight hours but no longer than Meyerbeer's *Les Huguenots*. When after a month, he still had no reply, he agreed to Carvalho's proposals and burnt his boats with the Opéra.

The Théâtre-Lyrique was too small (the stage of the new theatre was even smaller than that of the old one) and casting difficulties were not yet resolved; but Carvalho had promised Berlioz everything he wanted and was not, as Berlioz thought, a man to break his word. In any case at that time there was no question but that the whole opera was to be performed. But difficulties emerged. None of the new productions in Carvalho's first season was a success, the best of them being Mozart's *Peines d'amour perdues* (an adaptation of *Così fan tutte*). Even though the theatre had been granted a state subvention at the end of the previous season, the restrictions attached to it, the disappointing receipts, and Berlioz's own insistence that the expensive Charton-Demeur be engaged as Dido meant that Carvalho could not present *Les Troyens* as he had wished. In May 1863 Berlioz was obliged to take the critical step from which fatal misunderstandings were born – to agree to a production of only the Carthaginian acts, preceded by a specially written prologue briefly recounting events in Troy. Nevertheless he threw himself into the rehearsals with genuine enthusiasm, accepting with relative good grace Carvalho's requests for alterations and economies, not to mention his decision that the opening night should be brought forward a month in order to recoup some of his losses in the first part of the season, even though this meant that the opera would be underprepared. Berlioz wanted to see at least part of *Les Troyens* before he died.

The first of the twenty-one performances of *Les Troyens à Carthage* took place on 4 November 1863. Neither the Princess nor Liszt came to see it – and neither Viardot nor Rosine Stoltz. (Both of them had wanted to sing Dido and never forgave Berlioz for not letting them do so: their voices had gone.) But the remainder of the musical élite of Paris did, among them Meyerbeer, who went several times 'for my pleasure and instruction'. What pleased Berlioz most was that his son Louis had arranged leave from the merchant navy in order to see the opera and to be with his father. Louis attended the entire run of performances. He collected sixty-four press reviews,[10] some fulsome in their praise, some offensive, the great majority favourable. Even Scudo, the most virulent of Berlioz's critics, accepted that 'if he has failed, he has failed magnificently'.[11] Critical approval earned the opera a *succès d'estime*. But it was never a box-office success. Carvalho had increased ticket prices in an attempt to recover some of his exceptionally high expenditure, but houses were rarely much better than half-full and when they got worse he was obliged to announce the production's closure. After the final performance, on 20 December, *Les Troyens* was quickly overshadowed by the phenomenal success of Carvalho's next production, Verdi's *Rigoletto*, and went into limbo – a condition encouraged by Berlioz himself, who would authorize neither a revival nor a production of *La Prise de Troie*. He no longer had the stomach for the cuts and compromises of the Théâtre-Lyrique.

Yet his initial reaction to the production had been of intense pleasure. He saw the first four performances and wrote enthusiastically to his friends of the opera's success and especially of the singing of Charton-Demeur; he received countless unsolicited tokens of appreciation which moved him profoundly. Disillusionment, bitterness, resignation did not set in until a few weeks after the première when, after a spell in bed suffering from exhaustion and a recurrence of his intestinal neuralgia, he returned to the production and began to realize what had actually happened to his opera. On the opening night it had 'still needed three or four strenuous general rehearsals'; Carvalho's 'theatre was not large enough, his singers were not good enough, his chorus and orchestra were small and weak'; his staging 'in some places was irrelevant and in others positively ridiculous'. Carvalho's theatre had in fact accommodated about 150 people in some scenes and Carvalho himself had been the only director with faith in the opera – of which Berlioz was well aware. But alterations to his *mise-en-scène* wounded him deeply; and in addition to cutting nearly half his original conception he had had to submit to (and even approve, because the singers were poor) several cuts in the remainder. Most of these are acknowledged in the often exasperated comments he added to his autograph score, when 'tending its wounds' after the performances and preparing it (as he hoped) for publication. The performances did however yield one major benefit, for the royalties provided him with the financial security which enabled him to give up his position on the *Journal des Débats*. His last *feuilleton* therefore was the appreciative, prescient one he had written on 8 October 1863 about Bizet's *Les Pêcheurs de perles*, ironically the opera whose failure had caused his own to be launched before it was ready.

During the composition of *Les Troyens* Berlioz had the idea of putting on a grand series of concerts containing all his works except the opera – so that it, when it was produced, could be revealed as the culmination of his whole output. In the event, the Théâtre-Lyrique performances created a legend to the opposite effect: Berlioz's career had ended in a rather pathetic shudder. Of course, many of his contemporaries thought otherwise and even Wagner, who for reasons of his own considered Berlioz's art to be misdirected, had to admit that Berlioz's gifts 'far surpassed those of all his rivals'.[12] But it was not until a century had elapsed, that is, not until the fitful and usually misleading attempts to salvage the work in the interim had been eclipsed by the Covent Garden production of 1957 and the Scottish Opera and Covent Garden productions of 1969 that the legend was corrected and Berlioz shown to have been right: *Les Troyens* is indeed the summit and summation of his art. The question may be repeated. Why had Fate dealt with him so cruelly?

Part of the answer lies in the opera's length and in its staging and casting demands. These should not be minimized – even though it lasts no longer than *Les Huguenots* (according to Berlioz's calculation, already mentioned) and was in any case designed for the lavish resources of the Opéra. Berlioz's apparent deference to the canon of the Opéra in the heyday of 'grand opera' concealed a reactionary element, namely his reversion to classical, mythological subject matter when the vogue was for the 'historical'. This cannot have improved his chances and neither can his dramaturgy, which is not so intricate nor so crafty as that of grand opera's chief librettist, Eugène Scribe. Whatever the Opéra may have thought about that, *Les Troyens* suffered however from one, overriding fault. It was the work of Berlioz. As he had written, his music provoked violent opposition – and, we might add, indifference. It was weird, tuneless, unpredictable, and exceedingly difficult and expensive to perform. Its composer's artistic beliefs made him too uncomfortable a figure to be admitted to the inner sanctuaries of the musical establishment and his genius aroused jealousy, which was another time-worn reason why he was excluded. The influence of his supporters was negligible. No prudent Opéra director, aware furthermore of the failure of *Benvenuto Cellini* in 1838, would want to get involved with *Les Troyens*.

The opera's posthumous fortunes are less easy to account for. Bad luck, jaundiced ears or plain conspiracy hardly explain why it was neglected for so long, nor why its 'discovery' should have taken place when it did. Certainly, while vocal scores were seriously misleading and the full score remained unpublished, there was little to challenge the 'tradition' born in the Théâtre-Lyrique of a monster so unwieldy that it had to be split in two and trimmed to size. Ignorance thus contributed to the idea that the composer of *Les Troyens* was unprofessional and artistically insecure. But even those who did know something about the opera regarded it as uncharacteristic of

3 Théâtre-Lyrique, 1863: design by Philippe Chaperon for *Les Troyens à Carthage* (*Les Troyens*, Act III)

4 Covent Garden, 1957: the Act I finale

the true Berlioz and to represent a capitulation or, worse, a failing of creative energy. It did not correspond with the received picture – of a composer who, coming from nowhere and leading nowhere, was a brilliant radical, intent on transforming everything he laid his hands on. The deeply conservative streak in Berlioz fitted uneasily with his radicalism. It was this latter however which invited comparison with Wagner. Of all the reasons why *Les Troyens* made so little headway in the later nineteenth and earlier twentieth centuries comparison with Wagner may be counted the strongest. In such a contest Berlioz was bound to be the loser, simply because the genius of Wagner was extraordinarily in tune with the instincts and ambitions of the time, which in musical terms was dominated by the Austro-German aesthetic anyway. Wagner's colossal impact on Western culture dwarfed everything else; his emotional power was overwhelming. By contrast, Berlioz seemed contrived; he lacked depth, vision, focus. To later generations, with experiences of one and then a second world war behind them, the situation would not be so simple. The Wagnerian aesthetic would be viewed with suspicion. Berlioz's unique combination of passion and detachment would be heard with fresh ears. There would be smiles of understanding when it was realized that his ally in operatic theory was not Wagner but Mozart; that he had criticized Wagner – for ceding musical control to the dictates of a dramatic idea, thus forfeiting what to Berlioz was the vital element of *sensation* (by which he meant not only an appeal to the senses but respect for the ear, which needed light and shade, as it were, an accommodation with everything that makes up the psychological totality)[13]; and that he had defended his position with a music of his own, prodigiously inventive, supremely capable of 'appealing at one and the same time to the imagination, the intellect, the feelings *and* the senses'.[14] In short, a climate had emerged in which Berlioz's music in general and *Les Troyens* in particular could be welcomed.

The rediscovery of Berlioz took place pre-eminently in English-speaking countries. It was the culmination of a long process, promoted, as far as *Les Troyens* is concerned, by the Glasgow production of 1935 and by the advocacy of Beecham in particular, whose plans for a production in the 1939–40 season at Covent Garden were thwarted by the Second World War but who conducted an influential BBC studio performance in 1947. Major evidence of a general reassessment of Berlioz's stature came with the publication, in 1950 in the USA, in 1951 in Britain, of Jacques Barzun's pioneering biography, which corrected the record on countless aspects of

Berlioz's music, career and personality and which has been the source of Berlioz scholarship ever since. The 1957 Covent Garden production of *Les Troyens* not only revealed the splendour of the opera for the first time but stimulated a wider interest, which was to reach a climax in 1969, the centenary of Berlioz's death. This year saw the publication of David Cairns's classic translation of the *Memoirs*, the publication, for the first time, of the full score of *Les Troyens* in Hugh Macdonald's edition for the recently launched *New Berlioz Edition*, and the Scottish Opera and Covent Garden productions of the opera, which presented the work complete for the first time (the one in English, the other in French). These were its final vindication. What set the seal on that and carried the opera across the whole world was Colin Davis's recording of his Covent Garden performances, first released in 1970. Over a hundred years late, Fate, after all, had redeemed itself. And even in France:

> Relying purely on received opinions, with a wilful blindness that has persisted, to be precise, for one hundred and seven years, France has always refused to accept that *Les Troyens* is a great masterpiece, the high point of its composer's genius. . .According to the official view that we used to be taught, *Les Troyens* was an operatic 'monster', fruit of the old age of an artist in decline, its occasional beauties set in an ocean of feebleness, and in any case humanly impossible to perform or to listen to in one evening. These judgements, these summary convictions, repeated ad nauseam – till recently even by the most enthusiastic Berliozians – were in fact based not simply on incomprehension but first and foremost on a liberal measure of pure ignorance. What a confession!. . .We have here one of the most astonishing musical scandals of all time.[15]

# 3 *Synopsis*

## IAN KEMP

*Les Troyens* is a 'number opera', a sequence of discrete, though often linked musical units. The actual numbers in the synopsis below are Berlioz's own; here and elsewhere in this book, they are given for convenience of reference. Berlioz did not allocate numbers particularly consistently and they are therefore an unreliable guide to the real units of his design. These are indicated in the layout below, which also indicates the broader dramatic groupings.

Berlioz's French titles for the separate numbers are retained, since English equivalents can be misleading. A *Chœur* is simply a 'chorus', though the style and substance can vary greatly. An *Air* is generally in a single, moderate tempo, its lyricism more concentrated and less obviously tuneful than an Italian 'aria', which in any case is in at least two tempi. The same considerations apply to *Duos*, though with less force, and to the *Quintette*, *Septuor* and *Ottetto*. *Récitatif* covers a much wider range than is suggested by 'recitative' – from straightforward *recitativo secco*, designed to effect narrative connections, to what is more like a fast *Air* (No. 7), and including mixtures of recitative and arioso (No. 15). This last type of *Récitatif* could equally well have been called *Scène*, a term which can be translated as 'scena' (a section of much richer musical and dramatic substance than a recitative), though Berlioz's instinct to enlarge the boundaries of existing genres means that he can also apply it to a number containing an extended orchestral section not unlike a melodrama (beginning of No. 12). In his libretto Berlioz used *Scène* in another, though traditional, sense, to indicate changes in the number of characters on stage. The English word 'scene' can mean either this, or the stage setting in which 'scenes' take place. For this latter Berlioz used the traditional *Tableau*. The distinction between *Ballet* and *Pantomime* is that in pantomime feelings are expressed and action is conveyed through mime as opposed to dance (No. 6), though again in Berlioz's case the term can have a much wider meaning (No. 29). By *Entrées* (Nos. 20, 21, 22) he meant processions.

Stage directions given below in italics are Berlioz's own. The characters appearing in each number are indicated in square brackets. Details of characters and names, along with others mentioned in the libretto, are given in Appendix A.

## Act I

*The stage represents the site of the abandoned Greek camp on the Trojan plain. To the spectator's left and at some distance inside Troy, the citadel. To the right, the Simois with a mound, Achilles's tomb, on one of its banks. On the horizon the peaks of Mount Ida. Downstage a rustic altar and nearby a raised throne.*

1 *Chœur* [Chorus, a Trojan soldier] A crowd of Trojan soldiers and people is surging across the plain in delirious excitement celebrating what they imagine to be the departure of the Greeks after ten years of siege. They dance, play games, breathe in the air, examine remnants of weapons, are terrified at the thought that they are standing where Achilles pitched his tent – until a soldier reminds them that Achilles is dead. Eventually they go off to the banks of the Scamander to see the enormous horse the Greeks have left behind as an offering, the Trojans imagine, to Pallas. The stage clears, revealing the isolated figure of Cassandra.

Within two bars the listener is swept into the inimitable sound world of Berlioz – chattering high winds, cornets and horns in octaves, a tiny point of reference (three oboes), cross rhythms, swerving diminished sevenths, lucid choral textures, accumulating musical invention. *Les Troyens* has begun. The excitement of this short opening chorus does not become genuinely dramatic until its second section, where Berlioz introduces some frantic dance music and shows, notably at the mention of Achilles when the winds shiver with fear and the harmony starts to lurch wildly, that the Trojans' rejoicing is bordering on the irrational. The irony of Cassandra, the sole clear-minded person among them, is thus set in sharp relief.

2 *Récitatif et Air* [Cassandra] Cassandra cannot forget her vision of the ghost of Hector pacing the ramparts, watching darkly over the straits of Sigeum. In the *Air*, 'Malheureux Roi' ('Unhappy king'), she ponders its meaning. Priam, at this moment leading his crazed people out of the city, will die with the rest, because no one will listen to her warnings. Even Coroebus thinks she has lost her reason. They love each other, yet she will never know the happiness of marriage: her own fate is sealed. As for Coroebus, he must leave Troy.

3 *Duo* [Cassandra, Coroebus] Coroebus comes to persuade her to join in the celebrations. She tells him to go. In a *Cavatine*, 'Reviens à toi' ('Return to your senses'), he tries to calm her by treating her as a child: look, the blue, cloudless sky – it will give you peace. For Cassandra the sky is full of menace, and her vision of the destruction of Troy, ending with Coroebus's death, now forms with terrifying clarity. He repeats his attempt to calm her. Wearily, she appeals to his sense of filial duty: he should return to his father, who needs support in his old age. Coroebus retorts that if such ills should really befall them, his father would certainly not want him to abandon his betrothed. For a third time, and with increased urgency, he tries to reassure her: 'Mais le ciel et la terre' ('But the sky and the earth'). Now he points to the evidence on earth as well as in the sky that the war is over: the breeze, the sea breaking on the headlands of Tenedos (where the Greeks are hiding), the flocks and their shepherd, the birds. Cassandra thrusts this all aside. In the *allegro* she implores him to leave that night: 'Quitte-nous dès ce soir' ('Leave us tonight'). But his passion for her is so great that he cannot and will not. Finally Cassandra accepts. She kisses him. 'Envious death will prepare our nuptial bed for tomorrow.' In distraction Coroebus pulls her away with him.

Berlioz now introduces Cassandra, in the process laying out something of the scale and pacing of the opera by having her on stage for over twenty minutes in situations which advance the action not at all. What they do is reveal her character. She is compassionate, passionate, quick-thinking, and driven by that demon of prophecy which colours everything she is and yet which is not strong enough to ride over her love for Coroebus: only when he is dead does she become really decisive. For all its classical form and poised vocal style her music is charged with a vividness of orchestral detail that speaks of life lived at the nerve-ends. Not surprisingly, much of this detail surfaces in later parts of the opera. The scale that introduces her in the *Récitatif* reappears several times (see Ex. 10.3), as does the ominous motif in the bass at her words 'Tu ne m'écoute pas' ('You [the people] will not listen to me') in the *Air* (Ex. 10.9); the chilling sounds of the stopped horn accompanying her account of Hector's ghost recur, greatly intensified, when the actual ghost appears in Act II (Ex. 10.1); her measured chromatic scale at the same point also recurs in the ghost's scene, or when dreams or strange mental states or even clouds and smoke are evoked; the motif associated with Coroebus, heard first in the *Air* and then elaborated when Coroebus enters in the *Duo*, is inverted when Cassandra announces his death in Act II; the chromatic appoggiaturas, heard when she realizes she can no longer dream of tenderness, recur in various forms, notably when Dido realizes the same (Ex. 11.7, bars 47–9). Such concentrated musical substance, together with the *Air*'s slow tempo, demands release in a section of fast music, an expectation which Berlioz duly fulfils in the *allegro* of the *Duo* but which he first uses to hold his listeners' attention while introducing the character of Coroebus and elaborating that of Cassandra. This opening part of the *Duo* alternates set pieces from Coroebus (the *Cavatine*, repeated, and a third, untitled movement Berlioz could have called *Air*) with dramatic recitatives from Cassandra: in an audacious inversion, Berlioz alternates bland and irrelevant appeals to reality with electrifying revelations of the visionary. This is a dangerous tactic, for however appropriate dramatically, Coroebus's music could easily have sounded second-rate by comparison; it remains just persuasive and original enough to hold the balance. The *allegro* takes over a motif heard in Cassandra's recitatives, representing her love, her need to be rid of her love and her agonizing knowledge. Inner conflict to this degree obviously cannot be expressed in settled harmonies and Berlioz here writes a characteristic example of a theme harmonized differently on each of its (four) appearances, clouding it further with another fingerprint, a rhythmic motif in the bass register (see Ex. 9.1B), different patterns underlying each of the theme's appearances. When Cassandra relents, the inflexibility of Berlioz's strophic design is loosened, eventually breaking out into one of those tiny, highly-charged orchestral codas which are to be a feature of the opera. Here it is lit up by a sudden flash of colour and carried forward by (again typical) syncopated accents.

4 *Marche et hymne* [Chorus; Ascanius, Hecuba, Cassandra, Polyxena, Aeneas, Coroebus, Priam, Helenus and Panthus enter and remain until No. 10] The Trojan royal family and dignitaries, with some of the populace, assemble in solemn procession to lay their offerings at the altar in thanks to the gods for their supposed deliverance: the royal children, Hecuba and the princesses, Aeneas and his warriors, finally Priam with his priests.
5 *Combat de ceste: Pas de lutteurs* [Dancers] There are dances and public games (a wrestling match: see Appendix A).
6 *Pantomime* [Andromache, Astyanax (silent roles); Cassandra, Chorus] Andromache and her son Astyanax, both dressed in white, come to offer their prayers. Astyanax lays flowers at the altar and is

blessed by Priam and Hecuba. The widow and child slowly return to the city.

The choral prayer of No. 4 is conventional in type but very unconventional in language. Berlioz creates the effect of a vast people at its private ritual by conceiving a theme which stretches right across the accepted divisions of male and female voices, which is equally wide-ranging in harmony and which, in the second of its two massive paragraphs, is accompanied by the extraordinary sounds of an array of triangles imitating ancient sistra (see Appendix B). The *Combat de ceste* is brilliantly original in rhythm and orchestral colour, in every respect a calculated foil to the *Pantomime*, which is a poignant, extended melody for solo clarinet accompanied by strings. This is a comparatively rare example of an instrumental solo in Berlioz (he usually scored his melodies for combinations of instruments), though solos are in fact quite typical of 'grand opera'. He makes no attempt to introduce 'Trojan' accents into Andromache's grief, being content to portray it as universal and timeless.

6a *Scène* [Sinon, Priam, Cassandra, Chorus] At this point Berlioz had written the scene, later cut (see p. 52), in which the captured Greek spy Sinon is brought in and allowed by Priam to relate his complicated story. Sinon says he hates the Greeks because Ulysses, with the connivance of Calchas, had singled him out as a sacrifice to the gods, in order to obtain fair weather for their return to Greece. But he had escaped. Priam asks the meaning of the wooden horse. It was made, says Sinon, as an offering to Pallas in atonement for the blasphemy committed by Diomedes when he stole the Palladium from Pallas's temple in Troy. Calchas had ordered that the offering should be so large that it could not be got into Troy, for if it was, then Troy would be victorious over the Greeks and the whole world. Priam forthwith commands that the tower at the Scaean Gate be broken down so that the wooden horse can be pulled into the city through the widened gap. Cassandra's protests are scorned.

It is easy to understand why Berlioz cut this scene (see p. 9) – less easy to understand why he then apparently destroyed all but two pages of its full score. (The whole of it survives in piano score: see NBE, pp. 875–86.) The scene fulfils several important functions: as the first number containing real dramatic action it loosens the tight formality of the act thus far and allows it to breathe; it shows Cassandra in a public context; it provides the complete explanation

5 Opera North, 1986: the Sinon scene in Act I

of why the wooden horse was welcomed into the city, in the process according Priam a significance proper to his status (otherwise he is disturbingly remote); and it also establishes Virgil's subtle dramatic motif of the gullible ruler, which will be echoed in Act III when Dido welcomes the Trojans into her city. The 1986 Opera North production, using Hugh Macdonald's orchestration, demonstrated that the scene's restoration strengthens the act.

7 *Récitatif* [Aeneas] Aeneas rushes in with the news that the crowd is thronging back towards the city, panic-stricken because Laocoön, having hurled his javelin into the horse and urged the Trojans to set it on fire, has been attacked and devoured by two monstrous sea-serpents. [Berlioz here seems to have forgotten that Aeneas entered in No. 4. It can perhaps be assumed that Aeneas has been given the news by a messenger.]
8 *Ottetto et double chœur* [Ascanius, Cassandra, Hecuba, Aeneas, Helenus, Coroebus, Panthus, Priam, Double Chorus] Everyone is frozen with horror: Pallas has avenged sacrilege.

Aeneas's vocal entry is a particularly skilful piece of dramaturgy. He is the one principal character to remain throughout the course of the opera, yet in Berlioz's scheme of things his role is less vivid than Cassandra's (or Dido's). Accordingly his entry is arresting, but not elaborate enough to pre-empt the importance of Cassandra. It is a fast, brief melodic statement, set high in the voice and coloured in the orchestra by a particularly realistic imitation of sea-serpents (pedal notes in the trombones). There is a stunned silence. The huge ensemble that grows out of it is at once the act's turning point and the epitome of its static, monumental character. There is no stage action. Everything is expressed in the music – an organic development from disorientation (a strange fugal exposition for the octet, the entries a tone apart, and punctuated by choral cries of horror a tritone away), to gradual realization of the enormity of what has happened (through a second fugal exposition on a new theme, leading to a section with the voices now in unison) and finally to a collective acceptance of it (a new lyrical theme voiced by Cassandra and answered by the rest). Berlioz's final cadence incorporates a clinching reference, in the trombones, to the sea-serpents.

9 *Récitatif et chœur* [Aeneas, Priam, Chorus] Priam commands that the horse be brought in immediately and, led by Aeneas, the Trojans go off to do so.

10 *Air* [Cassandra] Cassandra is again left alone: she cannot watch the pitiful rejoicing of a doomed people. Memories of its past glory, of her now vanished dream of happiness, of Coroebus and Priam, reduce her to tears.
11 *Final: Marche Troyenne* [Cassandra, Double Chorus] In the distance the 'sacred choruses of Ilium', the Trojan March, bring her back to reality. Cassandra witnesses the huge procession in a state of helpless terror. Its route strewn with flowers and its progress accompanied by dancing children, the sounds of the 'flutes of Dindyma', 'Phrygian trumpets', 'Trojan lyres' and by hymns to Pallas, it gradually passes across the plain. There is a moment of anxiety as a clash of arms is heard from inside the horse but the Trojans consider this a good omen, since Pallas Athene was an armed war goddess, and they disappear into the city, ordering a flame to be lit at the summit of the citadel. For Cassandra flame means fire, the axe – weapons that can destroy the horse. She vainly warns that it is a deadly trap and bitterly mocks the gods for what she calls their 'worthy exercise in omnipotence'. Silence: the horse is in the city. She leaves to her death.

The act now gathers momentum, reflecting the Trojans' release from care and submission to emotional abandon. Berlioz's own position is that of both participant and observer: he sustains a level of musical excitement that, extraordinarily, is poised between ecstasy and dread, while at the same time controlling operations with the keenest of intellects. The numbers are no longer self-contained, but open-ended, carefully shaped to merge into each other. In Cassandra's *Air* surging melodic invention and the agony of impending loss once again bring her to the forefront, so that when the strains of the Trojan March are heard in the distance, her own situation creates a supremely theatrical counterpoint to it. The erratic yet persistent emotional shocks that seize her are voiced in the orchestra, superimposed across the March, a crescendo from off-stage and then on-stage instruments and chorus as the procession slowly files past on its way to the city. The eventual diminuendo of the March dramatizes the continuing presence of Cassandra. 'Va mourir sous les débris de Troie!' ('Go to die beneath the ruins of Troy'). In another of those orchestral codas which contain extreme complexity within the tiniest of spaces, Berlioz reveals his, and his audience's intimations of exaltation, catastrophe and inevitability.

## Act II

### *Tableau 1*

*A room in Aeneas's palace, dimly lit by a lamp.*

12 *Scène et récitatif* [Aeneas, Ghost of Hector; Ascanius (silent)] Sounds of distant battle. Aeneas, partly armed, is asleep on his bed. Ascanius, very frightened, comes out of an adjoining room. He approaches his father but dare not disturb him and runs away. The crash of a collapsing building wakes Aeneas, who now sees the bloodstained ghost of Hector standing before him. Hector tells Aeneas that the walls of Troy are in the hands of the enemy and that flames and smoke are driving across the city; but Aeneas has been entrusted with the city's children and gods and he must seek Italy, where he will found an all-ruling empire and where the death of a hero awaits him. Hector vanishes.
13 *Récitatif et chœur* [Aeneas, Panthus, Ascanius, Coroebus, Male Chorus] Aeneas is joined in quick succession by Panthus, who is holding the sacred images of Troy, and Ascanius, and then by Coroebus with a band of armed men. Encouraged by Coroebus, Aeneas leads his men in an attempt to reach the citadel, whose defences have not been breached.

Act II begins where Act I left off – with what amounts to an orchestral tone poem, its fateful, menacing atmosphere now making explicit the disaster that has befallen Troy. The little parenthesis for Ascanius (still with orchestra alone) exemplifies an important aspect of Berlioz's compositional philosophy: however cosmic the events surrounding them and however exalted their behaviour, his characters will always be confronted by the prosaic, the actual, and thus will prevent the composer from retreating into the purely symbolic. Aeneas ultimately, may be larger than life and may even acquire symbolic status; but this is in spite of himself. Berlioz's characters are real – not symbols or types. (The reality here is that Berlioz knew that when he was writing *feuilletons* his own son was frightened of disturbing his irascible father.) As if to demonstrate that an essential part of the real is the imaginative, Berlioz now introduces Hector's ghost, in sounds which could be called surreal or super-real (Ex. 10.1). To the accompaniment of other-worldly harmonies in cellos and basses and sobs in the horns Hector slowly intones his message, in the process descending a complete chromatic scale. After this period of suspended animation, the warriors appear, reality breaks out and the *Tableau* moves with lightning speed. Berlioz's music in No. 13 is a prime example of genius operating at fever pitch, a breathtaking sequence of images and events leading to a battle hymn, 'Prêts à mourir' ('Ready to die'). Berlioz tantalizingly provides just one brief stanza of the hymn, takes breath and then provides the necessary, culminating, final stanza, capping that with a lurid cadence unique in even his output (a swerve to the Neapolitan minor) and a blazing orchestral coda which sweeps along to its own dreadful cadence – a dark hovering as the scene changes.

## *Tableau 2*

*Inside Priam's palace. At the back, a gallery with a colonnade and a low parapet overlooking a square far below. Between the columns Mount Ida is visible in the distance. The altar of Vesta-Cybele, with its sacred flame.*

14 *Chœur – Prière* [Female Chorus with Polyxena, who remain until end of act] Polyxena and a group of dejected Trojan women are praying at the altar. Sounds of distant battle.
15 *Récitatif et chœur* [Cassandra, Female Chorus] Cassandra arrives and announces that Aeneas and his men have relieved the citadel, gained possession of Priam's treasure and are marching towards Mount Ida. They will see a new Troy rise in Italy, where destiny calls them. Coroebus is dead. Cassandra too must end her life. But first she exhorts the women to uphold their Trojan honour and not submit to Greek slavery. To the horror of a few she points to the parapet, to her dagger and to their girdles.
16 *Final* [Cassandra, Greek Chieftain, Female Chorus, Male Chorus] Most of the women resolve to die with Cassandra. A small group of dissenters is hounded away in shame. As the women prepare themselves for death a Greek chieftain rushes in brandishing his sword but is so astounded by the sight before him that he does nothing. More Greeks invade the scene, demanding the treasure. Cassandra scorns them. She stabs herself, followed by Polyxena. As some women climb the parapet, a second detachment of Greeks come in to announce that Aeneas and his men have escaped with the treasure. Crying 'Italy', the women motion towards Mount Ida and then leap from the parapet, stab themselves, strangle themselves.

Muffled sounds of battle linger on from *Tableau* 1, in which respect Berlioz's *Prière* is already a far cry from the norm. (A 'Prayer' was a stock type in nineteenth-century opera, usually an excuse for a slow tune in *bel canto* style.) Its most individual characteristic is its tone, which summons up a desolate landscape where prayers are urgent but futile, an aimlessness deriving particularly from Berlioz's unsettled modality (see p. 58). Its through-composed form confirms the impression of a movement waiting to find some purpose. This is achieved with the arrival of Cassandra (although it must be said that the couple of bars marking her actual entry are oddly pedestrian, one of just two weak moments in the opera: the other is the music accompanying her approach to the faint-hearted women later in this *Tableau*). Cassandra is now authoritative and decisive. Berlioz structures her explanations and exhortations, and the women's responses to them, in a continuous patterning of recitative and arioso sections, each generating a fresh one and thus a sense of direction which soon demands the stabilizing objective of a rounded melody. The finale starts with precisely that, a superb tune for the chorus, 'Complices de sa gloire' ('Sharers of her glory'), whose orchestral colouring of harps immediately lifts the temperature by several degrees. This hymn to death is the equivalent of the battle hymn in *Tableau* 1, and is treated in a similar way. There is a lull, while Cassandra disposes of the faint-hearted women, and then the tune returns, this time in a brighter tonality and, miraculously, extended and completed. The confusion on stage only serves to heighten the mystery of 'life enflamed by death'. Berlioz's orchestral coda underlines the appalling truth that what has happened was right. As a whole Act II provides a fascinating example of how Berlioz can use tempo relationships to control dramatic momentum. The four tempi of *Tableau* 1 all lock into one another – one beat of the first *andante* almost equalling one bar of the succeeding *allegro* (Ascanius), which exactly equals one beat of the second *andante* (Hector's ghost), which almost equals one bar of the final *allegro assai*, which in turn exactly equals one beat of the opening *andante*. Similarly with *Tableau* 2: with the exception of two short sections in freer tempi, all the eight sections following Cassandra's entry are geared to the same pulse, which thus can equal one beat of a 4/4 *andante*, one bar of a 3/4 *allegro con fuoco* or one bar 'alla breve' of an *allegro assai*. These gear changes lend tight coherence to a succession of episodes which might otherwise split apart.

## Act III

*A spacious hall decorated with greenery in Dido's palace in Carthage. To one side, a throne surrounded by trophies of agriculture, commerce and the arts; to the other and backstage, a tiered amphitheatre upon which is seated a very large number of people.*

17 *Chœur* [Chorus] There has been a violent storm but now there is brilliant sunshine, a circumstance the Carthaginians interpret as the gods' blessing on the festival Dido has commanded.

The contrast between the setting for Act III and those for Act II is one of Berlioz's most carefully calculated effects. It is of course reinforced by the musical contrast, and by that between the breezy confidence of the Carthaginians here and the agitation of the Trojans in No. 1.

18 *Chant national* [Chorus Leaders (eight voices), Main Chorus, supplementary Large Chorus; Dido enters with Anna, remaining until the end of the act, and Narbal, who remains until No. 24] Upon the arrival of Dido with her suite the people of Carthage stand and sing their national anthem in homage to their beloved queen.
19 *Récitatif et Air* [Dido, Chorus (tutti)] Dido reminds them that seven years have passed since she had to flee with them from Tyre, in order to escape the tyrant who had murdered her husband. Now a new city has been built, its lands are fruitful and its sea-trade thriving. All that remains is for her people to become a nation of heroes in war, for Iarbas seeks to impose marriage on her and will have to be resisted. The Carthaginians vow to defend her and drive the savage Numidian back to the deserts. Dido then assures them that she has appointed this day to celebrate not war but the arts of peace, and she commands the builders, the sailors and the farm-workers to come forward and receive tokens of the city's gratitude.
20 *Entrée des constructeurs* [Procession of builders] 21 *Entrée des matelots* [Procession of sailors] 22 *Entrée des laboureurs* [Procession of farm-workers] In turn the various groups process before her. The leader of the builders is given a silver set-square and an axe, the leader of the sailors a rudder and an oar.
23 *Récitatif et chœur* [Dido, Chorus (tutti)] Dido gives the leader of the farm-workers, a vigorous old man, a golden sickle and then places a crown of flowers and ears of corn on his head, thereby singling out the 'greatest of the arts, the art which nourishes men'. The Carthaginians acclaim this special honour and in a new version

of their anthem, now expressing their determination to defend their queen by becoming a nation of heroes, they all process in front of her and file out.

Carthage is celebrating its success; Berlioz is conjuring up a picture of his ideal city, which is directed by a benevolent autocrat and where everyone has his place and is appreciated. The order in this scheme of things is reflected in the musical design, a closed form, ABCA, framed by the two appearances of the National Anthem and centred on the twin supports of Dido and her people. The antiphonal phrasing of the splendid National Anthem is carefully designed to accommodate the massive forces on stage (in addition to the normal opera chorus, plus a semi-chorus drawn from it, Berlioz asked for a supplementary chorus including children, making a total of two or three hundred voices), which means that although it is a better tune than any of its rivals it lends itself no more readily to co-option by an emergent nation than does its counterpart in Act I, the Trojan March. The key dramatic moment is obviously the introduction of Dido into the opera. Berlioz allows himself room to provide music relaxed enough to establish her royal assurance, and to distinguish her from Cassandra, even though their voice types are the same. Dido's *Air*, 'Chers Tyriens' ('Dear Tyrians'), is in two broad stanzas. She is radiant, proud and, at the climax of the stanzas, even capable of some Italianate ostentation. Her rapport with her people is reflected, between the stanzas, in their eager appropriation of her melodies and conversion of the National Anthem into a revolutionary hymn. The builders enter with a flourish, the sailors seem a little drunk (their *Entrée* is the most engaging of the orchestral *divertissements* in the opera), the farm-workers weary with their heavy loads – though they get the best rewards.

24 *Duo* [Dido, Anna] Left alone with Anna, Dido confesses that despite the prosperity of Carthage she is sometimes overwhelmed by feelings of sadness. Anna sees this as a need for love but Dido, pointing to Sychaeus's ring on her finger, invokes a curse on herself should she betray the sacred ring which forbids all new love in her heart. Nevertheless Anna has aroused feelings of dangerous delight and Dido entreats her husband's forgiveness for her weakness and prays that his memory will purge her thoughts.

Having first presented the public face of Dido (the opposite of his method with Cassandra) Berlioz now, in an exquisite duet, discloses her private self, her femininity and vulnerability. Of all the music in the opera this is the most beautiful. It is a Berliozian beauty, wistful, as if something has been lost for ever and yet with that sharp edge which keeps it alert and ready to gather energy. Its first section shows Berlioz's melodic prodigality, a luxurious stream of phrases any one of which would have served a lesser composer for a whole number. Its concluding section shows his melodic discipline, a single, haunting melody, seemingly endless, though in fact classically proportioned, the longest, perhaps, ever written. What contributes most to its special flavour is diminished-seventh harmonization of the chromatic inflexions in the melody – a characteristic fingerprint of Berlioz, who used diminished sevenths lovingly and respectfully, to mould expressive curves rather than to make dramatic emphasis (lest, as may be deduced from his comment about Wagner's use of them, the chords should 'escape and gnaw at the furniture', LT, p. 161).

25 *Récitatif et Air* [Iopas, Dido] Iopas announces the arrival of a deputation from an unknown fleet which has narrowly escaped the storm. It asks to be admitted before her. Dido graciously agrees and, when Iopas has gone, reflects that, having herself experienced the dangers of the sea and the suffering it can bring, she cannot be indifferent to the sufferings of others.
26 *Marche Troyenne* (*Dans le Mode Triste*) [orchestral; Dido; Aeneas, Ascanius, Panthus and eight Trojan chieftains, led by Iopas, enter and remain until the end of the act] Ascanius is at the head of the Trojans. Aeneas is disguised as a sailor.
27 *Récitatif* [Ascanius, Dido, Panthus] Ascanius asks for a few days' shelter for his unhappy people and lays precious gifts at Dido's feet, offered on behalf of his leader. Dido asks the name and country of this leader. Ascanius finds it difficult to answer the questions because he is so proud of his father that he might break down when speaking his name. So firstly he presents the gifts (thoughtfully chosen to appeal to a woman) to Dido, describing them one by one – Iliona's sceptre, Hecuba's crown, Helen's veil – thus making it clear that her visitors are Trojans. 'Our leader is Aeneas, I am his son.' Panthus then steps forward to save Ascanius any embarrassment and explains that Aeneas's divine mission is to seek Italy, where destiny holds a glorious death for him and the happiness of giving a homeland to his people. Dido, for whom the deeds of Aeneas and the Trojans are famous, asks Panthus to tell Aeneas that her harbour is open to him and that he is welcome at her court.

Dido's full-voiced 'Errante sur les mers' ('Wandering over the seas'), more like an arioso than a true *Air*, effects a controlled transition from the tone of the duet to that of anticipation as the Trojans arrive. Their minor-key March makes it plain what their situation is; and after so much singing, purely orchestral music signals a turning-point in the opera, as well as creating the sense of anticipation. Just as the Trojans' infiltration of Carthage seemed gradual and adventitious, so Berlioz plays down the significance of their arrival. He proceeds in a tone of charming, self-conscious formality, as Ascanius, to a courteous orchestral reference to the Carthaginian anthem, delivers his recitative. Dido finds her position reversed, for having shortly before presented gifts, she now is receiving them. In her own contribution to the scene she adopts her gracious style of the beginning of the act. Berlioz is sustaining this somewhat unreal atmosphere in order to break it dramatically with his finale.

28 *Final* [Narbal, Dido, with off-stage male voices of Main Chorus; Aeneas, later with Dido, Ascanius, Anna, Iopas, Narbal, Panthus, Trojan chieftains and Chorus (tutti)] Narbal bursts in with the news that Iarbas and the Numidians have launched an invasion and are slaughtering sheep, devastating fields and threatening the city. The Carthaginian soldiers are fighting valiantly but have no more weapons. At this, Aeneas thrusts aside his disguise, announces himself to Dido and offers to fight alongside the Carthaginians. Dido proudly accepts. Aeneas rallies the assembled company, puts on his battle armour, orders Panthus to rouse the Trojan fighting men. He bids farewell to his son, entrusting him to Dido's safe keeping. The people of Carthage rush in carrying scythes, axes and slings, only a few of them with real weapons. Together with the Trojans they move into battle.

With the news of the Numidian invasion, there is an abrupt change of mood. The principal theme (a complex of motives in the orchestra, treated like a concerto ritornello) rushes about without any clear sense of purpose. But it is exhilarating as well as impetuous, suggesting that the invasion is as much a game as a threat to the innocent Carthaginians. Berlioz reserves his real *coup de théâtre* for the revelation of Aeneas. 'Reine! Je suis Énée!' – a marvellous moment in which, in just ten bars, Berlioz provides Aeneas with as dramatic an entrance as in Act I, allows him to settle matters and show the music no less than the Carthaginians what should be done.

His rallying song is broader and more assured than was his battle hymn in Act II but it is treated in a similar way: a first stanza, a lull and then a culminating final stanza involving the full performing resources. The lull, Aeneas's farewell to Ascanius, comprises another instance of the compositional philosophy mentioned earlier (see p. 26). Of course, this also demands that musical impetus should not thereby be squandered, so the music here is not an insertion but organic, developing from tenderness to heroism. Similarly, the excitement of the final stanza spills over into the orchestral coda. And in turn the coda generates its own identity, a cautionary, destabilzing phrase in the bass which, as we learn in the next *Tableau*, signals the passion developing between Dido and Aeneas.

## Act IV

### *Tableau 1*

*The stage represents an African forest. Morning. At the back, a very high rock. Below and to the left of it, the mouth of a cave. A small stream flows along the rock and runs into a pool bordered with reeds and rushes.*

29 *Chasse royale et orage* [orchestral; off-stage Chorus; Ascanius, Dido, Aeneas (silent); water nymphs, hunters, wood nymphs, fauns, satyrs, silvans (dancers)] Water nymphs are glimpsed for a moment. They disappear and then are seen swimming in the pool. Royal hunt. Hunting calls sound in the far distance. The water nymphs become frightened and hide in the reeds. Some huntsmen pass by with dogs on leads, and then a single huntsman who seems alarmed by the approaching storm. He seeks shelter under a tree and goes towards the spot from which he can hear hunting calls. The sky darkens; rain falls. The storm intensifies. Soon it becomes terrifying: torrential rain, hail, lightning and thunder. Repeated hunting calls amidst the tumult of the elements. Ascanius gallops across the stage on horseback, followed shortly afterwards by other riders. Other huntsmen on foot scatter in all directions. Finally Dido and Aeneas appear, striding against the storm, she costumed as Diana the huntress with bow in hand and quiver on shoulder, he in semi-warlike costume. They are both on foot. It is almost completely dark. They enter the cave. At once wood nymphs, their hair dishevelled, appear at the top of the rock and run about shouting and gesticulating

wildly. The word 'Italy' can be distinguished from time to time in the midst of their cries. Dancing fauns appear. The stream swells and becomes a rushing torrent. Several other waterfalls form on various parts of the rock and add their sounds to the uproar of the tempest. Satyrs and silvans dance grotesquely with the fauns in the darkness. Lightning strikes a tree which splits and catches fire. Pieces fall on stage. The satyrs, fauns and silvans collect the flaming branches, dancing with them in their hands, and then run off with the nymphs into the depths of the forest. The stage is slowly covered with clouds. The storm abates. The clouds lift. [In his stage directions for the simplified orchestration made for the 1863 performances Berlioz replaced the clouds with a return of fine weather and of the water nymphs.]

As an orchestral tone poem of astonishing originality and vividness the Royal Hunt and Storm is the most familiar single number in the opera. The scenario above, a conflation of Berlioz's summary at the head of his full score and of the descriptions he added over the relevant bars, illustrates how precise is the correspondence between it and the music, or, in other words, how his mingling of ballet, mime, action, spectacle and music comprises one of the most ambitious scenes ever conceived for the opera house. The essential dramatic event is drawn directly from Virgil: Dido's passion for Aeneas ignites when, out on a hunt, they make love in a cave, while sheltering from a storm. Only after that has happened does she forget everything else and luxuriate in her passion. Berlioz *had* to represent this supreme moment in some way and at this point. Why he chose to do so orchestrally and visually was doubtless for the same reason that he rejected voices for the love scene in *Roméo et Juliette*: all-too-human voices and words would have restricted full expression of the sublimity of the subject. What 'full expression' actually means is of course open to speculation. But the *Chasse royale* does not have to be understood just as a piece of descriptive music faithfully following its scenario. The overt sexual symbolism in that already suggests that the music represents more than a hunt and a storm and it can indeed also be heard from the beginning as a representation of Dido and Aeneas's love-making (see p. 155). Berlioz's subtitle of *Intermède symphonique* (Symphonic Interlude) is as prudent as it is discreet. It indicates that, momentarily, the opera is lifted out of its realism into the realm of the purely imaginative.

*Tableau 2*

*Dido's gardens by the sea. Sunset.*

30 *Récitatif* [Anna, Narbal] Anna and Narbal are waiting for the arrival of Dido, when the lavish diversions she has planned for the evening will take place. Narbal is uneasy. Anna cannot understand why, since Iarbas and the Numidians have been defeated. Narbal explains that it is Dido's indulgent living and neglect of her royal calling that disturb him. In turn Anna explains, to Narbal's astonishment, that Dido is in love and that her love could not be given to a man more valiant than Aeneas, nor could Carthage want for a more magnanimous king. Narbal protests that Aeneas's fate calls him to Italy.
31 *Air et Duo* [Narbal, Anna] Narbal sees a dark future for Carthage while Anna sees only its triumph.

The first two numbers of this *Tableau* bring the opera back to the real, rather ordinary world of court life with an explanation of the political effect of the love of Dido and Aeneas. That Anna and Narbal can only reach stalemate is a warning of the inertia that will soon cripple the city. The main function of the numbers however is to provide a foil to the remainder of the act, whose sensuousness would otherwise seem gratuitous. Anna and Narbal pace around each other in tones respectively skittish and ponderous. Berlioz's musical solution to this impasse is to have a *Récitatif et Duo* (his numberings and titles are somewhat misleading) in which two different types of music are first juxtaposed and then, in the final section of the *Duo*, superposed (*allegretto* 3/8 over *larghetto* 9/8): a compositional sleight-of-hand he was very fond of.

32 *Marche pour l'Entrée de la Reine* [orchestral; Dido, Aeneas, Ascanius, Iopas, Panthus, two Trojan chieftains and Chorus enter and remain, with Anna and Narbal, until No. 37] Dido takes her seat on a dais, with Anna and Narbal beside her.
33 *Ballets* [Dancers] (a) *Pas des Almées* (b) *Danse des Esclaves* (c) *Pas d'Esclaves Nubiennes* [with four contraltos]
34 *Scène et Chant d'Iopas* [Dido, Iopas] Dido grows tired of the dances and the dancers are ushered away. She then leaves the dais for the more intimate environment of a couch and commands Iopas to sing for them. He does so, accompanied by an Egyptian harpist.

Berlioz now effects a subtle transition. The theme for Dido's entry music (the Carthaginian anthem) indicates that she is queen but its orchestral colouring (including three harps playing harmonics) indicates that her eyes are alive with other matters: thereby Berlioz has already introduced that atmosphere of enchantment which will be sustained for the rest of the act. His treatment of the ballets as a means towards this end, rather than a necessary evil to be got over somehow, is especially skilful. The very fact that they must be passively watched contributes to it, as does the absence of singing, but the main reason why they are so integral a part of this *Tableau* is simply that their music invites the listener to enter into a world of pure hedonism. The opening dance of the almas (see Appendix A) is languorous and voluptuous, its drooping phrases continuously unwinding to reveal new ones. The phrases of the dance of the slaves are thrusting and virile, thus making the dance a nicely balanced complement and the two together a satisfying pair – as is confirmed with the apparently conclusive climax to the second one. Then, as if to encourage indulgence, Berlioz adds a little treat, a third dance. This dance of the Nubian slaves (see Appendix A) is exotically flavoured, flat in contour (so it doesn't diminish the effect of the others), and it re-introduces singing (an oriental 'language' Berlioz invented himself), which means that it also effects a link with the next event in the *Tableau*. Despite all this excellent entertainment, Dido's *Scène* shows that she is listless and needing some other stimulus to her senses. Iopas's song of the abundance of the earth (the part written for that French speciality, the high lyric tenor) is a delicately poised moment, for his beautiful and earnest singing could have become wearisome and the act have sagged – which is precisely what Berlioz makes dramatic capital out of. In his original version of the song he had Dido interrupt before it was finished (see NBE, p. 939). Now we may assume that it is Iopas's top C, just before the end, which enables her tactfully to conclude the performance.

35 *Récitatif et Quintette* [Dido, Aeneas, Anna, Iopas, Narbal] Dido apologizes to Iopas for what she describes as her restlessness. Aeneas is prompted to sit with her and she immediately asks him to continue his story of the misfortunes of the Trojans and, especially, of the fate of Andromache. Aeneas relates that Andromache was captured by Pyrrhus, submitted to his love and is now queen of Epirus. The extraordinary story of Andromache – the epitome of faithful widowhood yet now married to a man who is both son of her husband's killer and killer of her husband's father (see Appendix A: Andromache) – affects Dido deeply, because, through it, she can be absolved

from remorse at the betrayal of her own husband's memory. Aeneas affirms that Andromache loves Pyrrhus. Dido puts her arm round Ascanius. He is 'leaning on his bow like a statue of Cupid' and he gently draws Sychaeus's ring from her finger. None of this escapes the attention of Anna, who approvingly points out what is happening to Narbal and Iopas. Dido abstractedly takes the ring back.
36 *Récitatif et Septuor* [Ascanius, Dido, Anna, Aeneas, Iopas, Narbal, Panthus, with the two Trojan chieftains and Chorus] Aeneas asks them to set aside these sad memories and enjoy instead the beauties of the night. He gets up and moves towards the shore. Dido follows him, leaving her forgotten ring on the couch. All join in a hymn to the night, eventually drifting away into the shadows and leaving Dido and Aeneas together.
37 *Duo* [Dido, Aeneas, Mercury] The two sing tenderly and rapturously of their love, a love so profound that it belongs to all time, and so certain that they can tease each other with it. As they too disappear into the night, the figure of Mercury is there, lit up in a sudden shaft of moonlight which falls close to an unfinished column where Aeneas's armour is hanging. Mercury twice strikes Aeneas's shield with his wand and three times he intones the word 'Italy', stretching his arm towards the sea. He vanishes.

The last three numbers of the act comprise one of the most daring manifestations of creative genius in the history of opera. It may legitimately be expected that an opera will have a 'still centre', a moment of serenity on which the composer lavishes the best of what lyrical gifts he may possess. To do this twice in a row is exceptional – because the result can easily be anticlimax. To do it a third time is unprecedented. Berlioz himself would perhaps have commented that the prescription was demanded of him by the nature and balance of his scenario. The point, however, is that he did it. His solution to the problem of how to close an increasingly ravishing flow of slow music is equally remarkable. The intervention of Mercury is already a brilliant dramatic idea: his music, a set of monstrous, otherworldly gestures, matches it.

The earlier part of this *Tableau* is not really involved with the characters at all and after such an expanse of (in its own terms) 'abstract' music the need to be so becomes paramount. The *Quintette* directs the focus on the purely human again. It is an exquisite amalgam of abandon and regret. It grows imperceptibly out of the recitative (see Ex. 10.13), so that it is only when the ambivalent bass figure in the orchestra emerges that Dido's first melody can be understood as merely introductory. This is symptomatic of the effect of the whole number. Its long lines seem indivisible and unending. On closer inspection it can be seen that Berlioz has structured the Quintet as a metaphor of the situation. As a whole, it is in two sections, AB, an open form, reflecting the emotional release it embodies. The first section contains a varied repeat (another open form); the second is a ternary ABA, a closed form expressing the security Dido believes she now possesses. A codetta absorbs in one gesture the arching melodic style of the complete number. The *Septuor* is much simpler in design, being in two stanzas, the first for the soloists, the second for the chorus with the soloists musing above. It acts as a kind of interlude, the interest certainly lying in the melody and its profoundly original harmony but also in the quality of its accompaniment as pure sound. In this respect Berlioz is conjuring up the chirping of cicadas and the heaving of the sea with that exact attention to onomatopoeia he regarded as axiomatic in the art of composition. Why these sounds should also induce that state of trance-like wonder which melts into the *Duo* can be explained in part by the so-called 'weak' progressions (chord roots moving up a third); but ultimately it is one of those mysteries of music that will never have an answer. Neither will the mystery of love. Berlioz well knows what he is exploring in his love-duet, for he approaches that mystery in a spirit of profound reverence, caressing it, holding it, examining its infinite delights, never presuming to the hubris of understanding, nor to what in this context would be the vulgarity of passion (that, after all, has been discovered earlier). The breathing of his music is gentle, its sound veiled (Berlioz writes in the unusual though not unprecedented tonality of G flat – used earlier in the love-duets of Meyerbeer's *Les Huguenots* and Halévy's *La Reine de Chypre*). And its shaping is again an exact musical metaphor, a rondo – always coming back to the same thing yet always free to make new discoveries. It seems as if it could go on for ever, and we don't want it to stop – which makes the intervention of Mercury all the more shocking.

## Act V

### *Tableau 1*

*The sea shore, covered with Trojan tents. Trojan ships can be seen in the harbour. Night. A young Phrygian sailor sings to himself as he sways at the masthead of a ship. Two sentries mount guard in front of the tents at the back of the stage.*

38 *Chanson d'Hylas* [Hylas, two Sentries] Hylas sings nostalgically of his homeland which, as the sentries comment, he will never see again. He is rocked to sleep by the sea.
39 *Récitatif et chœur* [Panthus, Male Chorus, off-stage Chorus] Panthus convenes the Trojan chieftains to tell them to prepare for departure. Aeneas will break the chain binding him to Dido and respond once again to the summons of the gods, who daily make their anger known through signs: the ghost of Hector, as on the fateful night in Troy, has been seen, followed by a chorus of shades crying 'Italy'. Their voices now sound out audibly. The chieftains resolve to leave that morning, and return to their tents.
40 *Duo* [two Sentries] The sentries continue their watch, grumbling about talk of Italy. They prefer Carthage, where the wine and women are excellent, to the hazards and boredom of the sea. They are interrupted by the appearance of Aeneas and quickly withdraw.
41 *Récitatif mesuré et Air* [Aeneas] Aeneas is in torment at the thought of leaving Dido. He cannot resist seeing her once more and is about to go to her.
42 *Scène* [Aeneas, Ghosts of Cassandra, Coroebus, Hector, Priam, off-stage Male Chorus] The ghosts stop him in his tracks and command him to delay no longer and leave.
43 *Scène et chœur* [Aeneas, Male Chorus] Aeneas rushes to the tents, ordering his men to prepare for departure before sunrise. Turning towards Dido's palace, he delivers a heroic, anguished farewell.
44 *Duo et chœur* [Dido, Aeneas, Male Chorus; Ascanius (silent)] The Trojans are hastily boarding their ships, some of which are already on the move, when Dido herself suddenly appears. She berates Aeneas for his inhumanity and deceit; but nothing she says, nor the leering smiles of his own men, nor even his continuing love for her, can prevent him wrenching himself away. Dido cannot believe it. The rallying sounds of the Trojan March are heard. She curses him and storms out. The stage is filled with Trojans on their way to the ships as Aeneas joins his fleet.

The somewhat disjointed structure of the *Tableau* could be said to reflect Berlioz's initial uncertainty about what it should contain (see p. 60). On the other hand it can be understood as a reflection of the situation he is portraying, with an outcome that in fact is remarkably truthful dramatically. The world of Dido and Aeneas is disintegrating: the consequences must inevitably be messy and fragmentary. In any case the apparent stop-go sequences are subsumed within an overall design of great strength and simplicity – a gradual crescendo and acceleration of tempo across the various sections of the main number, Aeneas's 'aria'. The intensity generated underlines the emotional impact of Aeneas's departure and also serves to return the opera to its central course after the timeless paradise of Act IV.

One of the most telling aspects of Hylas's song is that it allows a last fleeting memory of that paradise. Its nostalgia is thus not only for the homeland that will never be seen again but also for the love that will never be known again. For the rest, Berlioz writes a lullaby – its rhythms floating elusively, its melody flowing dreamily – while adding three little touches which tie it to reality: the ominous breaking of waves, the down-to-earth comments of the sentries and the fact that at the end Hylas stops singing and falls asleep. The reverie is broken by another short number, now fast in tempo and dense in substance. Its musical function is to introduce the idea of urgency and disquiet – which Berlioz promptly deflates in the sentries' duet. Its throw-away style is quite different from anything else in the opera, as is its regular march rhythm (if irregular phrasing) and instrumentation. Berlioz's hand in it can be detected by his relish in the Shakespearean technique involved (see p. 113) and in his display of dramaturgical professionalism – for the jolt of Aeneas's entry is now necessary as well as arresting.

The remainder of the *Tableau* is given to Aeneas. Aeneas is the hub around which the whole opera revolves, yet he has never been allowed the stage to himself for any appreciable time – until, that is, this *Tableau*, when the tension built up by withholding his place in the scheme of things for so long is finally released in an extended aria (here the word is appropriate), where his complex personality, vacillating, tender and heroic, is given free rein. His aria is Italianate: bipartite, with a *cantabile* and an *allegro* preceded by a recitative. In fact it is more elaborate than that, because it is prolonged by two interruptions, the ghosts' scene and the appearance of Dido; only at that point can it be concluded with its *stretta*. These terms can serve to clarify Berlioz's basic design. They cannot however indicate the substance of it. The *Récitatif* teems with memorable phrases, each cancelled by the succeeding one, those concerned with leaving Dido echoed in his soul (wind instruments in the orchestra), those not, accompanied by agitated rhythms in the bass. While revealing that Dido said nothing when he tried to explain himself, the 'recitative' also reveals his agonizing confusion of purpose. In the *Air* he gives up the struggle. The music's aching appoggiaturas and retreat into the warm tonalities of Act IV make it plain why. Deciding to return to her releases, in the *allegro*, rapturous excitement, including a top C; but it also summons up the ghosts. Berlioz here does not recall the orchestral timbres associated with the ghost of Hector in Acts I and II. Characteristically, because the situation is different, he invents new timbres, notably a chord in violin harmonics 'sounding' like hair on end. Aeneas's new-found resolution now summons up the Trojan March, not overt but unmistakable and, as the first reference to its original form since Act I, peculiarly stirring. This leads to his superb apostrophe to Dido and to what seems a clinching conclusion to the scene. The intervention of Dido is as discomforting to the audience as to Aeneas. Berlioz shows remarkable integrity in having her now upbraid him with all the desperate impulses of the rejected lover, for this is an aspect of a love affair most 'Romantics' would prefer to forget. The *Duo* however enables him to write some particularly Berliozian music, including extraordinary 'gulps' when Dido confesses her shame, and to reserve his trump card, the Trojan March now brilliant and assured, for the end.

*Tableau 2*

*A room in Dido's palace. Dawn.*

45 *Scène* [Dido, Anna, Narbal (silent)] Dido, her pride gone, beseeches Anna and Narbal to ask Aeneas for just a few days more.
46 *Scène et chœur* [Iopas, Dido, off-stage Chorus; Anna, Narbal (both silent)] Iopas announces that the Trojans have already put to sea. Dido wildly orders her fleet to pursue them and burn their ships. She stops: it is useless. She should have done so sooner and avenged herself by serving Aeneas his own son's limbs as a banquet. In a terrible spirit of retribution she calls on the gods of the underworld to inflame her with hatred and orders a sacrifice to them, a huge pyre, on which the gifts of Aeneas and those she gave him will all perish in the flames. Anna, Narbal and Iopas do as they are bidden.
47 *Monologue* [Dido] Alone, Dido indulges her grief. She will die. The pyre is for herself. Perhaps Aeneas will weep for her. Aeneas, Aeneas – she wants her love back. The thought of death calms her.
48 *Air* [Dido] She bids farewell to her city, her sister, Africa, her love, her life.

The stage is left to Dido, her grief made all the more poignant for its contrast with the heroic assurance of Aeneas. In the *Duo*, she tries to parley with loss but can hardly articulate her emotions: they are conveyed in the orchestra, two strophes of heart-rending phrases in the cellos. Anna identifies with them but is helpless. In a codetta Dido's pleas gain shape but, as Berlioz's shifting chromaticisms indicate, have nothing to fasten on to. With the news from Iopas her emotions are suddenly let loose. In full command of the stage she begins that descent into the depths which comprises the tragic dénouement of the opera.

In structural terms, Dido has an aria which is a counterpart, a dark counterpart, to Aeneas's in the previous *Tableau*. It is again bipartite, with a preceding recitative that again depicts vacillation. At that point the correspondences diverge, for apart from its continuous, inexorable sequence, the aria's two sections (*Monologue* and *Air*) are slow and even slower, thus creating a large-scale ritardando instead of an accelerando, and a diminuendo instead of a crescendo. The *Scène* of No. 46 is in fact a 'recitative', one that can claim to be the most electrifying in all opera. If the word recitative had hitherto suggested a somewhat inhibited style Berlioz now destroys that idea utterly. As Dido lurches between blind rage, anguish, retribution and steely determination, his music proves her love to have been truly divine, its consequences truly archetypal. At last alone, she permits herself a moment of wild desperation, and then concentrates her thoughts: 'Je vais mourir' ('I will die'). The first words of her *Monologue* are answered in the cavernous tones of a bass clarinet, an instrument which characterizes the whole movement. The immediacy of her anguish is a terrible revelation of how love can sear a soul. By the *Air* Dido is already in a world only she can belong to – pure, eventually slipping away into nothingness.

### *Tableau 3*

*Dido's gardens by the sea. A vast pyre has been raised, with steps at the side. On a platform at the top are a bed, a toga, a helmet, a sword with its belt and a bust of Aeneas.*

49 *Cérémonie funèbre* [Anna, Narbal, High Priest, Male Chorus, the preceding remaining until the end of the opera; Dido (silent)] The priests of Pluto enter and group themselves around two altars, where green flames are burning. Anna and Narbal enter, and finally Dido, wearing a veil embroidered with gold and a crown of leaves. As the priests invoke the gods of darkness, Anna unlooses Dido's hair and takes off the shoe from her left foot [part of funeral ritual,

as Berlioz explains in a footnote]. Anna and Narbal pray that Aeneas meet an ignoble death and his body be left for carrion. The invocation is resumed.
50 *Scène* [Dido] In a trance, Dido asks that the sacrifice be completed. The altars are conducted ceremonially round the pyre by two priests. Dido places her crown of leaves on one of the altars and follows behind. The high priest, with Anna and Narbal to either side, raises the trident of Pluto and points it towards the pyre. Dido rapidly climbs the pyre, seizes Aeneas's toga, takes the veil from her head and throws it and the toga onto the pyre. She looks at Aeneas's armour, prostrates herself on the bed and sobs convulsively. Then she rises, takes his sword and prophesies that her memory will live throughout the ages and that she will be avenged by Hannibal. Suddenly she pulls the sword from its scabbard and stabs herself.
51 *Chœur* [Dido, Anna, High Priest, Male Chorus, Chorus (tutti)] There is general confusion. Anna rushes up to her sister and holds her tightly, trying to staunch the blood. Narbal goes to call for help and returns as a crowd of startled Carthaginians appears. Dido twice rises and moans, only to fall back again. As she rises a third time, she prophesies that Carthage will perish.
52 *Imprécation* [Dido, Chorus (tutti)] A vision forms in her mind of the Capitol in Rome, in front of it legions of soldiers and an emperor surrounded by poets and artists. Her last words are 'Rome . . . immortal'. She falls back, dead. The Carthaginians advance to the front of the stage and hurl out their curse upon the race of Aeneas, while the Trojan March [transmitted, as Berlioz states in a footnote, to the Romans by tradition and now their song of triumph] sounds out against it and eventually absorbs it.

The opera proceeds on its inevitable course. The strange ceremonies are accompanied by a heavy, almost monotonous theme divided between orchestra and chorus (almost monotonous, for Berlioz gives it some unsettling harmonic sideslips). Initially its formality seems unaffected by the events which separate its ritual reappearances – the sharp-edged prayers of Anna and Narbal, which lead to hair-raising modulations, and the disembodied request of Dido, which is shorn of harmony altogether. But in fact this principal theme is being made irrelevant by the real drama and soon is reduced to nothing. Attention is focused on Dido. Berlioz holds the suspense during her painfully real emotions on the pyre and her frightening prophecy to such a degree that her suicide catches everyone unawares. The resulting confusion in the disorientating harmonies of the *Chœur* is as psychologically right as they are technically extraordinary. Whether the *Imprécation* is also psychologically right is open to question. The Trojan March is blatant and short-winded, the curses musically ineffectual. Berlioz's finale leaves a sour taste in the mouth. But maybe he meant it to – his comment on the way history tramples on the supremely human (see also p. 109).

52a *Berlioz's original finale* The finale described above is a radically revised version of his original finale, details of which are given on pp. 63–5.

# 4 *Composition*

**HUGH MACDONALD**

While Berlioz and posterity have both paid full tribute to the part played by the Princess Carolyne Sayn-Wittgenstein in suggesting and urging the composition of *Les Troyens* (Berlioz was probably right when he said that without her it would never have been written), the work sprang from a deep-seated passion for Virgil and a lifelong desire to render musical justice to the 'swan of Mantua', as he did so abundantly to his other crowning source of inspiration, Shakespeare. When, in London in 1848, Berlioz first drafted his *Memoirs*, he recounted his childhood passion for Virgil and the emotional crisis caused by his father's reading of that part of Book 4 of the *Aeneid* where the death of Dido is recounted. 'It was Virgil', he says, 'who first found the way to my heart and opened my budding imagination.' This passage is remarkable for describing in detail, several years before the composition of *Les Troyens*, his mind's eye's vision of Dido's immolation; but there was then no suggestion of fashioning it into operatic drama. He quoted Virgil freely all his life, drawing upon the *Aeneid*, the *Eclogues* and the *Georgics*. Certain lines from the *Aeneid*, such as *Apparent rari nantes* (1.118), *Auri sacra fames* (3.57), *Pendent opera interrupta* (4.88), *Audentes fortuna juvat* (10.283) (here and there a man can be seen swimming, accursed hunger for gold, the unfinished works stand idle, fortune favours the brave) – all of which are echoed in the libretto of *Les Troyens* – were his favourite quotations, recurrently cited in letters and reviews. In Italy in 1831 he was haunted by memories of Virgil. Thus one might say that the composition of the opera occupied him for about two years at his desk, but for over forty years in his mind.

After the composition of *La Fuite en Égypte* late in 1850 there occurs a striking and little-recognised silence in Berlioz's creativity that lasted until the end of 1853, when he decided to enlarge that work (possibly on Brahms's suggestion) into the trilogy *L'Enfance du Christ*. The three-year gap can be explained in terms of his spiritual discouragement, his worries about the worsening health of Harriet, his preoccupation with publishing his existing scores, his frequent concert tours, his obligations as a writer and critic, his ill-fated leadership of the Société Philharmonique, and his revulsion from Parisian musical life. But it is certain that throughout this time the creative wheels were trying to turn against the much stronger braking force that all those factors exerted. The idea of a Virgilian opera seems to have been born in 1851, five years before he ever set pen to paper. On the eve of his second marriage in October 1854 Berlioz completed (as he then supposed) his *Memoirs* and therein acknowledged the idea of a vast opera that had been 'tormenting' him for three years. He does not say what the subject is, but he already envisaged the main outline. 'To me the subject seems magnificent and deeply moving – sure proof that Parisians would think it flat and tedious.'

Two references in *Les Soirées de l'orchestre*, published in 1852, betray the direction of his thoughts. In the 'Ninth Evening', when asked to talk about the Paris Opéra, he quotes Aeneas's reply to Dido when asked to recount the tragic fate of Troy: *si tantus amor casus cognoscere nostros* (if you are so eager to learn of our misfortunes, *Aen*. 2.10); and in the 'Epilogue' music itself is compared to Virgil's Cassandra: 'the inspired virgin fought over by Greeks and Trojans, whose prophetic words go unheeded. She raises her eyes to heaven – only her eyes, for her hands are in chains' (paraphrasing *Aen*. 2.405f).

Although he made no mention of his plans to his regular confidants such as Liszt or Morel, there is a revelatory passage in a letter to Baron von Donop, chamberlain to the Prince of Lippe-Detmold, after Berlioz had visited Brunswick. Out of enthusiasm for *Roméo et Juliette*, the Baron had urged him to write an opera on the same subject. Berlioz refused on the grounds that he would never find adequate singers, that no theatre would do it justice, and that he would never live to see it staged. The Baron may have proposed an opera on *any* subject, for Berlioz wrote to him from Hanover:

> You spoke to me of new works on which I *ought to embark*. Alas, Sir, I think that what energy I have is better expended on making more perfectly known those scores that already exist rather than abandoning them to the hazards of the musical world and giving them sisters whose early steps I could not superintend. (CG IV 1650)

The importance of the Baron's urging is also shown by a later letter from Berlioz, written after he had begun work on *Les Troyens*:

I have finally followed your advice; I am engaged on the composition of a five-act opera, on a subject close to my heart. (CG V 2146)

A prophetic passage in a letter to Hans von Bülow of 1 September 1854 quotes Virgil's description of Dido's death and draws the exclamation:

'What a great composer Virgil is! What a melodist, what a harmonist! *He* could have made the death-bed remark *qualis artifex pereo* [what an artist dies in me] and not that humbug Nero, who was gifted with only one bright idea in his life, the night he had all Rome set on fire. . .' (CG IV 1785)

It was the Princess who finally decided him; her part is described in the *Memoirs* and immortalised in the eventual dedication of the opera to her. Perhaps the subject of a new composition had been discussed during Berlioz's visits to Weimar in November 1852 and May 1854. It certainly was when he went in February 1855, as we know from a postscript scrawled sideways down the first page of a long letter to Fiorentino:

I am urged, spurred on, and positively pestered to write a large-scale operatic work. I must consult you about this; we ought to resume the conversation we began in the Rue St-Georges about the material obstacles involved, caused by the attitudes and habits of the Paris Opéra. (CG IV 1903)

Berlioz still hesitated and his resistance remained resolute. 1855 was another busy year with tours to Brussels and London, the first performance of the *Te Deum*, the rewriting of the *Traité d'instrumentation*, his work for the Paris Universal Exhibition and many scores to see through the press. Yet we may be certain that his copy of the *Aeneid* remained close at hand. And not only the *Aeneid*: the pages of *The Merchant of Venice* were also open. In a notice of Ortolan's opéra-comique *Lisette* he wrote, with unabashed irrelevance:

It was on such a night that young Cressida left the Greek tents to meet her lover Troilus beneath the walls of Troy. And it was on such a night that young Jessica slandered her lover and he forgave her.[1]

The turning-point was another visit to Weimar which took place in February 1856. The subject of a new composition was again brought up; Berlioz records the Princess's words as follows:

You must write this opera, this lyric poem or whatever you like to call it. You must tackle it and you must finish it. . .If you shrink from the difficulties this work may and must bring you, if you are so feeble as to be afraid to face everything for Dido and Cassandra, then never come back here – I refuse to see you again.[2]

Berlioz's decision was immediate, for Cornelius recorded in his diary: 'This summer Berlioz is going to begin a new opera, which I shall translate.'[3]

On his return to Paris he had two more pressing tasks: the orchestration of four songs of *Les Nuits d'été* and a general revision of his printed scores and parts. He could then write to Liszt on 12 April:

I have begun to rough out an outline of the great dramatic machine in which the Princess kindly takes such interest. It is beginning to take shape, but it is vast and consequently dangerous. I need great tranquillity of mind, and that is precisely what I lack. Something will come of it perhaps. Meanwhile I ruminate; I am gathering myself like a cat crouching for a spring. Above all I am trying to resign myself to the misery this work is bound to cause me. (CG V 2115)

The versification of the poem began on 5 May. To his uncle Félix Marmion, a Napoleonic veteran, Berlioz could proudly say:

I had been ruminating the plan for two years. It was an auspicious date to choose to set to work, the illustrious date 5 May, an epic date if ever there was one [the anniversary of Napoleon's death]. Now I will need at least 15 months for the labour of composing. At the Opéra they know nothing of my project, and they'll know nothing until it's finished; and if they agree to stage this great lyric machine it will be on my own terms which will safeguard me from the wicked intrigues that go on in that Capharnaum of art. (CG V 2144)

It was rightly the Princess who was to be kept most closely informed of the progress of the opera, and Berlioz's letters to her, published in 1903, are the principal source of information about the composition of it. His first report, later than the letter to Liszt, was on 17 May. The libretto of Act I had taken ten days to write, from 5 to 15 May:

I cannot describe to you the moods of discouragement, joy, disgust, pleasure and fury I have passed through during those ten days. I have twenty times been on the point of throwing the whole thing into the fire and devoting myself for ever to the contemplative life. Now I am certain that I will find the courage to carry through to the end; the work has seized me.

For the music I will need at least a year and a half, I guess (Americanism), to construct it. It will be a great construction; may it be built of baked bricks and not of soft bricks, as the palaces of Nineveh were. Without the baking, bricks soon turn to mud and dust. . .

Adieu, Princess, you too shall one day be answerable to the shade of Virgil for the outrages I am committing against his fine verse. . .especially if my palace is made of soft bricks and if my hanging gardens are planted only with wild willows and fruit trees. (CG V 2126)

He was determined to keep his new preoccupation out of the newspapers. Yet his close friends were informed. To Toussaint Bennet and his son Théodore Ritter Berlioz confessed:

Between you and me, now that I have written two acts of my poem, the music torments me, it wants to come and makes me impatient. . .but I resist. I must finish the poem. Even so I jot down notes. (CG V 2132)

During the writing of the third act his power to resist deserted him, for he announced the completion of this part of the poem at the same time as that of the music of the love duet in Act IV (No. 37), to which he had jumped ahead under the inspiration of lines from *The Merchant of Venice.* He told his sister Adèle:

The music settled on this scene like a bird on ripe fruit. . .This preoccupation intoxicates me, as the composition of *Roméo et Juliette* once intoxicated me. I am swimming powerfully on this lake of classical poetry. . .I feel I knew Virgil and Shakespeare. I feel I can see them. . .[4]

A fortnight later he told the Princess:

I want to have the libretto quite finished before starting on the score. Last week, however, I could not help writing Shakespeare's duet:

In such a night as this
When the sweet wind did gently kiss the trees.

And the music of this litany of love is done. But I will need another fortnight to shape, fashion, polish, correct, twist and redress the verses as they stand. (CG V 2145)

The duet is unique in Berlioz's output for the number of sketches which have survived.[5] These reveal that inspiration, for all its urgency, did not lead Berlioz to the finished duet in an instant. There was much reworking of all sections of the music and of the words, and was far from its definitive state when Berlioz claimed that the 'litany of love is done'. The orchestration of the duet was left until the following December, after the composition of Act I (CG V 2195); and an important revision of bars 82–94 (the strophes where Dido sings about Aeneas, and Aeneas about Dido) was carried out much later, probably in February 1859 when he reported 'several important' corrections in Act IV (CG V 2351).[6] Of this scene Berlioz later admitted:

When I read my score some days I am enchanted, others I am disgusted. . . Yet I assure you I cannot read Dido's garden scene with dry eyes. (CG V 2211)

On 26 June the poem was finished, and three days later he told Liszt, hopefully, that he did not think he would be making any more changes (CG V 2149). In July little progress was made save for arriving at a definitive title for the work, *Les Troyens*. Berlioz mentioned other possible suggestions, but none had found satisfaction; they were: *Énée*, *L'Énéide*, *Didon*, *Troie et Carthage* and *Italie*!

Would you believe it, I have fallen in love, hopelessly in love, with my Carthaginian queen! I love this beautiful Dido to distraction! You will find [Berlioz had sent the Princess a copy of the libretto] a number of Shakespearean borrowings in the middle of the Virgilian poetry.

(CG V 2150)

There was probably no more than the single direct quotation from Shakespeare to be found, but the libretto differed in many important respects from that finally set to music.

The Princess praised the libretto and appears to have made no radical suggestions for its improvement.[7] From Baden-Baden, where Berlioz went annually to direct concerts, he replied on 12 August:

It is beautiful because it is Virgil; it is thrilling because it is Shakespeare; that I know for certain. I am no more than a plunderer; I have been foraging in the garden of two geniuses, there I have reaped a garland of flowers to make a couch for music. God grant that it does not perish asphyxiated by the perfume.

Liszt is right about the word *Italie*, which sounds so poorly beside *Italiam* with its accent on the second syllable. But I am writing in French. . .I had even used the two Latin words *Votum* and *Peplum* and I have been advised to replace them with their French equivalents. (CG V 2163)

After discussing certain scenes in detail, Berlioz then declared his intention to embark on the music, and his letter develops into a statement of aesthetic aims and problems that is one of the most pertinent and revealing of all his writings on his own art, and therefore merits quotation at length:

May Virgil's gods come to my aid; otherwise I am lost. The hardest task is to find the musical *form*, this form without which music does not exist, or is only the craven servant of speech. That is Wagner's crime; he would like to dethrone music and reduce it to 'expressive accents', exaggerating the system of Gluck, who, fortunately, did not succeed in carrying out his ungodly theory. I am in favour of the kind of music you call *free*. Yes, free and proud and sovereign and triumphant, I want it to grasp and assimilate everything, and have no Alps nor Pyrenees to block its way; but to make conquests, music must fight in person, and not merely by its lieutenants; I should like music if possible to have fine verses ranged in battle order, but it must itself lead the attack like Napoleon, it must march in the front rank of the phalanx like Alexander. Music is so powerful that it can sometimes conquer on its own, and has a thousand times claimed the right to say, like Medea, 'Moi, c'est assez' [Corneille's *Médée*]. To want to tie it down to the old kind of recitation of the ancient *choros* is the most incredible, and, mercifully, the most fruitless folly ever recorded in the history of art.

How to find the means to be *expressive* and *truthful* without being any the less musician, and how to give the music new means of action, is the problem. . .

Another pitfall in my way is that the feelings I have to express move me too strongly. That is no good. One must try to do fiery things coolly.

(CG V 2163)

The main task of composing the score began at the end of August 1856; it was to be his chief preoccupation for the next twenty months, until April 1858, when he dated the final page. Each act was taken in its normal sequence with the exception of Act IV, whose closing scene was already done; Act IV was composed between Acts I and II.

Act I, the longest of the five, was composed between August 1856 and February 1857 in order of sequence with the exception of the Andromache scene (No. 6). Nos. 1 and 2 were written at Plombières, where Berlioz liked to go after Baden-Baden. In all probability he still planned to compose an overture once the rest of the opera was finished. Later he came to see the force of dispensing with it. His reason is given in a letter to Liszt of 19 July 1862:

During the crowd scenes at the beginning, the Trojan mob is accompanied solely by the wind; the strings remain idle and do not make an entry until the moment when Cassandra first speaks. It is a special effect which would have been ruined by an overture.[8]

One detail in the opening scene was the Princess's idea. Berlioz had the Trojan people disporting themselves near the spot where Achilles had pitched his tent. The Princess, misreading 'tombe' for 'tente', gave him the idea of having the burial mound in the same place (No. 1, bar 190) (CG V 2163). Two passages were later shortened[9] and a canonic passage for sopranos and tenors (No. 1, bars 84–9) is a borrowing from *Erigone*, an unfinished fragment from the late 1830s.[10]

No. 2, the scene for Cassandra alone, was finished on Berlioz's return to Paris on September 10. This, with the duet with Coroebus which follows, was the only part of the first two acts that Berlioz was ever to hear performed. Late in October he wrote:

I am trembling from head to foot with impatience, pain, enthusiasm, over-abundance of life. . .I cannot write my score fast enough, I need a calamitously long time for it. I am worried about its future. (CG V 2181)

He completed Nos. 3 and 4, after which came two ballets in the original plan. No. 5, the *Combat de ceste*, may have been composed at this time or slightly delayed; No. 6, Andromache's scene, which replaced the second ballet, was held over for a few months. So he pressed forward to the Sinon scene, No. 6a, and Aeneas's narration, No. 7, and by 14 November was on the ensemble, No. 8. In his letter to the Princess of that day (CG V 2183) he reported that each number took two days to compose, sometimes one, with three weeks to 'ponder it, polish it, and score it':

> I have not left off my Phrygian task for a single day, despite the disgust my illness causes me. At such times I find everything I have done cold, flat, dull and foolish; I have the urge to burn it all. . .The human mechanism is indeed bizarre and incomprehensible. Now that I feel better I look at my score again and come to the conclusion that it is no longer quite as stupid as I thought.

The scene featuring the Greek spy Sinon, based on a lengthy episode in Virgil, was an important element in explaining how the Trojans' initial distrust of the horse turned to the belief that by bringing it within the city their victory over the Greeks would be complete. It remained in place for nearly five years, being still included in the proofs of the vocal score in 1861. A letter of 6 July 1861[11] mentions 'an important change' in Act I, made in order to accede to the wishes of Royer, director of the Opéra. At that time *Les Troyens* enjoyed some prospect of production there, so that compliance on Berlioz's part in reducing the scale of the opera was essential. Yet the full score of the scene was destroyed and it was never reinstated. Removing it required some repairs in other parts of Act I, notably in the opening chorus and in No. 9.

Some months before composing No. 7, the narration of Laocoön's death, Berlioz wrote: 'Laocoön's serpents will have a *barcarolle*' (CG V 2126), in ironic reference to a favourite feature of opéra-comique. The first sketches were in fact in 5/4 time. In the event he took some pride in the scene:

> The account of Laocoön's catastrophe, and especially the ensemble that follows it are, it seems to me, two scenes of horrific grandeur that would stir you deeply. (CG V 2380)

The linking scene, No. 9, was subject to the most extensive revision as a result of the removal of the Sinon scene in 1861. No. 10, Cassandra's *Air*, draws on music written twenty-six years earlier for Berlioz's successful Prix de Rome cantata of 1830, *Sardanapale*. Bars 53–60 exist in their original form as follows:

Ex. 4.1

The text at this point, 'Et voir s'évanouir/Du bonheur le plus pur la séduisante image!', is strikingly close to that of the earlier work.

No. 11, the finale, followed at the very end of 1856, held up by Berlioz's desire to orchestrate the Act IV love-duet composed the previous June. The finale took at least a month. Its genesis was accidentally affected by an enquiry from George Hainl concerning Spontini's *Olimpie*: Hainl was planning to include the triumphal march from *Olimpie* in a concert in Lyons, with extra off-stage brass added. Berlioz protested at Hainl's lack of respect for the composer's original, and sent for the score, causing him to compare Spontini's march with his own. It contained 347 bars, he discovered, compared with 244 in his own (CG V 2201–3). Whether it was Hainl who thus implanted the idea for Berlioz's triple-layer off-stage bands is hard to determine, though it is unlikely that Berlioz, fond of off-stage effects in all his music, would have planned this grand finale without any. As for modelling a triumphal march on that from *Olimpie*, Berlioz had many years before suggested that Wagner had done so in *Rienzi*.[12]

Cassandra's lines, 'Arrêtez! arrêtez!', from bars 180 to 188 (and possibly further) were superimposed on the march, as it moves into the distance, three months later (CG V 2219). An outline of a march in A minor, possibly intended as the Trojan March, is found among the sketches of Act I.

There remained Andromache's scene, No. 6, in order to complete Act I. Berlioz had deferred working on it:

> Its importance terrified me. . .but now it's done, and of the entire act I believe it is the most successful piece. I have wept over it like eighteen calves.
> (CG V 2207)

Berlioz's letter to the Princess of 14 November 1856 (CG V 2183) described the scene in detail, since it was missing from the libretto she had originally been sent:

> I decided that one of the most touching figures in the story ought to make an appearance at the ceremony. So after the various groups have laid their offer-

ings on the rustic altar and at the moment when the festal games are at their height, the musical style changes suddenly, and to a tearful, woebegone, heart-breaking (if that's possible) air in dumb-show, Andromache advances leading Astyanax, who carries a basket of flowers, by the hand. They are in white (the ancients' symbol of mourning).

With Act I finished by 5 February 1857 Berlioz proceeded not to Act II but to Act IV, lured by the fact that the love-duet, No. 37, was already done. He had also written the close of the act, with the ghosts of Cassandra and Hector rising out of the ground. The rising D major scale in bar 136 is a remnant of that version, which used the canonic motive associated with Cassandra from the beginning of Act I No. 2. Some unease with this ending was expressed by Legouvé (CG V 2207), so Berlioz replaced it with the appearance of Mercury, calling 'Italie!' to the departing figures of Dido and Aeneas. Mercury could have been suggested by Virgil, but it is a curious fact that Berlioz introduced him within a week of writing a mocking notice in the *Journal des Débats* on Ambroise Thomas's opéra-comique *Psyché*, in which the god Mercury is a principal character. 'Des dieux je suis le messager, je suis Mercure!' he sings.

What is the composer supposed to do with this declaration of name and profession, without interest, without passion, without anything that might inspire the musician? So you're the messenger of the gods, are you? We know perfectly well, since your name is Mercury and you have wings on your temples and on your heels. Get on and do what the gods told you to do and leave us in peace.[13]

Mercury's further degradation, as a bus conductor in Offenbach's *Orphée aux enfers*, was nearly two years in the future.

Working backwards, he wrote the Septet, No. 36, in early February 1857. At this time it was a sextet, with Dido silent.

There seems to me something new in the expression of joy at *seeing the night*, *hearing the silence*, and at lending sublime inflexions to the somnolent sea. Furthermore this ensemble joins on to the duet in a totally unexpected way. This was the working of chance, as I had given it no thought when I was writing each one in isolation. (CG V 2209)

The Septet contains a clear allusion to the closing scene of Gounod's *Sapho*, in which Sapho's moving farewell to the world, 'O ma lyre immortelle' – itself an anticipation of Dido's farewell – is punctuated by the sound of breaking waves. Berlioz had warmly praised this scene in 1851.

Thereafter Berlioz seems to have worked through the rest of Act IV (2nd *Tableau*) in sequence, although no mention is made of the Anna–Narbal scene (Nos. 30 and 31) in his correspondence and it may possibly have been a later addition. By 25 February he was starting on the ballets (No. 33); these too may have been composed later, since the autograph score is clearly different from the rest of the act. Yet his letter sets out his plans quite clearly:

I want to have a *pas d'almées* with the music and dancing exactly like the Bayadères' ballet which I saw here sixteen or seventeen years ago. My colleague Casimirski, on the *Débats*, is going to give me some verses by Hafiz, the Persian poet, which I will have sung in Persian by the singing almas, as the Indian women used to. There is no anachronism, I have gone into it; Dido could easily have had Egyptian dancers at her court who had earlier come from India. (CG V 2211)

In the separate offprints of the ballets published by Choudens in 1863, the first of the three ballets was headed 'Pas d'Almées'. The words chanted in the third ballet, *Pas d'esclaves nubiennes*, belong to a fabricated language, not Persian, still less by Hafiz.

By 12 March he had completed Iopas's song (No. 34) and the Quintet (No. 35), although at that time the song had a different ending, with Dido interrupting Iopas in mid-song, and the Quintet was a quartet, Aeneas being silent throughout. The setting, as specified in the stage-directions, was based on the painting *Énée racontant à Didon les malheurs de la ville de Troie* by Pierre-Narcisse Guérin (1774–1833), which hangs now, as it did in Berlioz's time, in the Louvre (see Plate 6). Berlioz had probably met Guérin in Rome and may have seen him at work on another Virgilian canvas, *La Mort de Priam*, left unfinished at the artist's death. This now hangs in the Musée d'Angers.

The *Chasse royale et orage*, the first *Tableau* of Act IV, then followed. It occupied him for four weeks, concluding on 7 April. Despite its original and daring blend of mimed stage action and ballet, with complex orchestration, Berlioz commented remarkably little on it. The saxhorns used for the finale of Act I were drawn in again, although the piece was severely reorchestrated in 1863 when conditions at the Théâtre-Lyrique forced certain economies on the composer. The original scoring was not published until 1969. The stage-directions were also modified in the 1863 version. The fact that his main preoccupation in the preceding weeks had been Weber's *Oberon*, revived at the Théâtre-Lyrique and reviewed by Berlioz in the *Débats* on 6 March, is perhaps reflected in a certain similarity between the storm music and ensuing calm in the Air and Chorus in Act II ('spirits of air and earth and sea') of that opera and the close of Berlioz's *Intermède symphonique.*

6 Pierre-Narcisse Guérin: ‘Énée racontant à Didon les malheurs de la ville de Troie’. The painting which gave Berlioz the idea for the Quintet (No. 35) in Act IV

In April 1857 he resumed the normal sequence, returning to Act II. By the 25th the first *Tableau* was done, with the scene for Hector's ghost closely based on the *Aeneid* text. 'This recitative for Hector', he wrote over a year later,

> who is brought to life for a moment by the will of the gods and who gradually returns to a state of death as he accomplishes his mission to Aeneas is, I believe, a musical idea of strange and lugubrious solemnity. I mention it to you because it's precisely such ideas as this which the public takes no notice of. (CG V 2332)

In the following scene, No. 13, Berlioz had added an idea to his original libretto draft which was then omitted when the music was composed. We learn of it from a letter of 3 September 1856 (CG V 2168):

> I could not resist an episode in Virgil about Coroebus and his men exchanging shields with the Greeks:
>
> Mutemus clipeos Danaumque insignia nobis
> Aptemus. Dolus an virtus, quis in hoste requirat?
> [Let us exchange shields and fit the badge of the Greeks to ourselves.
> Trickery or valour, who would ask in the case of an enemy?
> (*Aen.* 2.389f)]

Berlioz's version was:

> *Chorèbe*:
> Quarante Grecs surpris par nous
> Au seuil de ton palais viennent de tomber tous;
> Leurs cadavres sanglants en encombrent la porte.
> Prenons leurs boucliers!
>
> *Le Chœur*:
> De nos vils ennemis,
> Oui! revêtons les insignes. Qu'importe!
> Ruse ou valeur, contre eux tout est permis.
> Prêts à mourir, tentons de nous défendre,
> Le salut des vaincus est de n'en plus attendre.

The last two lines of this survived when the exchange idea was later abandoned. It was perhaps one of the things Pauline Viardot took exception to, since he mentions corrections in Act II in his letter to her of 25 September 1859 (CG V 2404).

The second *Tableau* of Act II, in contrast, took two months. By 26 June Berlioz had almost completed it, observing that it was perhaps the hardest part of his task:

The scene for Cassandra and the Trojan women, especially, presented some considerable problems. But I hope I have achieved my aim and properly expressed that ever-growing fervour, that love of death that the inspired virgin instils in the Trojan women, finally wringing a cry of horrified admiration from the Greek soldiers. (CG V 2235)

The entire *Tableau* exists in sketch form, which helps us to comprehend Berlioz's difficulties and his solutions. He was proud of the modal scale on which No. 14 is based (Hypophrygian, G to G in A flat major) and quoted it in a letter to the Princess of 20 June 1859 as being 'une chose neuve':

The sense of desolation that arises from the continual predominance of the note G and its relationship with D flat is something of curious interest. I feel it evokes the despairing cries of Virgil's *feminae ululantes.* (CG V 2380)

He was proud, too, of the end of the Act:

A few days ago, as I was sleeping beneath a beech tree in a field (like Virgil's shepherd) I had a brilliant idea for the staging and the heightened intensity of my finale with Cassandra and the Trojan women. I had a few lines of verse to write, changing barely anything in the music. I cannot help telling you that it has a radiant, classical beauty. (CG V 2238)

Owing to a misunderstanding concerning Liszt, there was a gap in Berlioz's correspondence with the Princess between March and November 1857, so that information on the composition of Acts II and III is less full than for the others. Berlioz pressed directly on into Act III, completing the Carthaginian *Chant national*, No. 18, even before Act II was complete. Berlioz described it as Carthage's 'God Save the Queen' (CG V 2235). Its similarity to the British National Anthem was observed by d'Ortigue in his notice of the opera in 1863.[14] Berlioz may have recalled that in 1847, in London, he had been urged by Jullien to make an arrangement of the National Anthem with a view to recreating the furore caused by the *Marche hongroise* in Budapest the year before (CG III 1134), a plan of which no more was ever heard.

The composition of the opening chorus of the act is vividly evoked in a letter of 4 August 1857 from Plombières:

You cannot imagine the beauty of the woods here at sunrise or by moonlight. Three days ago I went very early in the morning by myself to the Stanislas spring. I took my *Troyens* manuscript, manuscript paper and a pencil; there I had put out for me a table in the shade, with a bowl of milk, some Kirsch and some sugar; and there I worked quietly in beautiful surroundings until nine o'clock. I wrote a chorus whose words seemed appropriate:

Vit-on jamais un jour pareil? (CG V 2238)

The full score, not otherwise dated except at the end of the opera, is dated 23 August 1857 on the first page of this chorus.

On his return to Paris he complained that he lost one day in every three from interruptions and distractions and that he was not well enough to make use of more than half of what was left. He expected (accurately, as it turned out) to finish the opera the following March or April (CG V 2245). Illness cost him many lost days that autumn, yet his ardour for the work increased. Repeated visits to friends in St-Germain-en-Laye, west of Paris, provided ideal surroundings:

> I have been given a room facing the sun, opening on to a garden looking over the Marly valley, the aqueduct, woods, vineyards and the Seine; the house is isolated; peace and quiet all around; and I work on my score with inexpressible joy, without a thought for the agony it is bound to bring me later on. (CG V 2245)

By the end of October he had reached No. 25, up to the point where the Trojans arrive. As in Act IV, it is not clear whether the 'ballets' (Nos. 20–2) were composed within sequence or left until December 1859. The brief chorus that greets the labourers, 'Vivent les laboureurs', appears to be the remnant of a longer scene planned in the original libretto (CG V 2168). The duet for Dido and Anna, No. 24, originally contained a passage describing Dido's unawakened passion:

> When you suppose that Dido was speaking of Aeneas, before his arrival, I cannot explain your misapprehension. I was almost annoyed that you should think me capable of such a monstrous absurdity. Yes, of course, the queen 'would need lynx's eyes' to see the Trojan chief on his ship during a stormy night, but there is no question of that. That was not in my mind at all. I was simply imagining a mirage of love, in order to avoid the eternal classical dream sequence. Dido suffers from insomnia like that so beautifully described by Bernardin [de St Pierre] in *Paul et Virginie*; she goes up to the topmost tower of her palace to dream, facing straight into the raging storm. Then her volcanic passion induces a trembling heart and she *thinks* she sees afar off a stranger of noble stature; it is a hallucination. She has not seen anything in fact and she knows she has seen nothing. (CG V 2163)

The letter quotes what were then Dido's words to Anna:

> Perdue en mes pensées, du sommet de la tour
> Je croyais voir au loin, etc.
>
> Mon être tout entier
> Sur des ailes de flamme
> Semblait voler à lui.
>
> Jusqu'au lever du jour
> En proie à cette illusion

J'ai versé de brillantes larmes,
Sans pouvoir me soustraire aux charmes
De la cruelle vision.

Berlioz underlined the words *Je croyais*, *Semblait*, *illusion* and *vision* to drive home his point, but the seeds of doubt were sown and the idea of Dido's vision disappeared from the libretto at some subsequent date. No sketches of this scene have survived.

No. 25 lost a passage of seventeen bars in a later revision. No. 27 was to have been revised:

> I am going to rewrite Ascanius's scene; he ought not to say: 'ô reine sur nos pas une sanglante trace'. That is not a child's reply. He will join in again with 'Je suis son fils!', his childish pride being unable to contain itself when Panthus has said 'Notre chef est Énée!' (CG V 2163)

This seemingly admirable revision was never carried out, perhaps for fear of reducing Ascanius's part too severely, for we find in the final version the full six lines given to Ascanius, and Panthus left silent.

The finale, composed in November, gave Berlioz much satisfaction (CG V 2280). The middle section, Aeneas's farewell to his son, draws on a melodic outline from the 1830 cantata *Sardanapale*:

Ex. 4.2

In a letter of 3 March 1858 (CG V 2281) Berlioz quoted the text of this section with the remark: 'Where is there a tenor who could hold his shield heroically, embrace Ascanius, and sing with any nobility the following lines:

D'autres t'enseigneront, enfant [etc]'

Resuming communication with the Princess on 30 November 1857 (CG V 2264), he reported that he had only the final act to compose. Act V was begun in mid-December. The opening part of the act underwent changes and modifications more drastic than any other part of the opera. It originally opened, apparently, with Aeneas's monologue (No. 41) leading to the appearance of the ghosts and the departure of the Trojan fleet – a short first scene. In September 1856 Berlioz inserted at the beginning of the act two 'short, but useful and curious' scenes, the first of which had some connection with the close of Act IV and may therefore have involved the ghosts, or perhaps Mercury (CG V 2168); the second was the scene for two sentinels. His purpose in placing two common soldiers in direct contrast to the heroic aspirations of Aeneas is explained in two letters of the time (CG V 2165, 2168), with the information that it was to be a march in triple time and that it was 'half done', a reference perhaps to the verbal text since the composition of Act V was otherwise all done sixteen months later.

A letter of March 1857 (CG V 2219) shows that both these scenes had been scrapped, the first because of the revision of the close of Act IV to introduce Mercury, the second (the sentinels' scene) without comment. Aeneas's monologue was now preceded by a new idea: the entry of Panthus and the Trojan chiefs (No. 39) reporting the sighting of the ghosts, which are in fact heard there and then. When he began to compose the music of Act V in December 1857, it was this scene and Aeneas's monologue which preoccupied him first:

> I have been absorbed by Aeneas's final monologue. . .At such times I am like those bulldogs which would rather be torn in pieces than give up what they've got between their teeth. (CG V 2269)

On 20 January 1858 he told von Bülow: 'Aeneas has left; Dido still does not know.' (CG V 2273). On 9 February he had reached Dido's farewell 'Je vais mourir' (No. 47) (CG V 2277), and in the same letter Berlioz told his sailor son that he had written a song for the young Hylas with which to begin the act, obviously a sudden inspiration since he had not mentioned it in his previous letter to him two weeks earlier. It is clear that Hylas's song, No. 38, was to perform the function originally reserved for the sentinels' scene: to provide a telling contrast with the epic and passionate style of the rest. 'I thought of you, dear Louis, as I wrote it.' It originally closed with an eight-bar modulation from G minor to A minor, which suggests that the following scene was in A minor, not the present G minor. This is supported by a letter to Pauline Viardot of late 1859: '[You] were wrong not to criticize the modulation which closes the third verse of the sailor's song; it makes a poor join with the following chorus, which ought to be in G minor and not in A minor.'[15]

Two additions were to be made before the first *Tableau* of Act V was complete, both inserted some time after the completion of the opera in April 1858. One was the sentinels' scene, No. 40, abandoned as an idea in March 1857 but taken up again, probably as late as the summer of 1859, since it is a late insertion in the autograph libretto presented to Rosine Stoltz on 12 August 1859. The text was probably resuscitated from the original libretto, while the music was newly composed as a march in 4/4. From both the musical and the documentary point of view (the evidence of the autograph score) the scene is clearly a late addition to the link between Nos. 39 and 41.

The other extra scene was the duet for Dido and Aeneas, No. 44, which can similarly be seen to have been inserted in the middle of No. 43, the last thirty-three bars of which thus became the close of No. 44. It is absent from the libretto of August 1859 but present in the proofs of the vocal score dating from spring 1861. No correspondence survives to shed any light on these afterthoughts. It is remarkable that this first *Tableau*, originally drafted as containing three numbers only, Nos. 41–3, ended up with seven.

Of the second *Tableau*, in Dido's apartments, Berlioz expressed great apprehension before composing the music:

How shall I manage to express this anguish or set these cries of agony? The task frightens me. How shall I succeed? (CG V 2273)

But when it was done his satisfaction was real:

Of all the passionately sad music that I have ever written, I know of none to compare with Dido's in this passage and the aria which follows. (*Memoirs*, Postface)

It includes another echo of the 1830 *Sardanapale*:

Ex. 4.3

The final scene of the opera remained to the end an intractable problem. He approached it with considerable unease:

I am especially worried by the phrasing of this passage sung by Anna and Narbal during the religious ceremony of Pluto's priests: 'S'il faut enfin qu'Énée aborde en Italie [etc]'. Is it a violent imprecation? Should it be dumb, concentrated fury? If poor Rachel were not dead, I would have asked her.[16] (CG V 2273)

But throughout February and March 1858 his absorption in the work caused him to appreciate the greatness of what he had achieved:

It matters little what happens to the work, whether it is ever performed or not. My musical and Virgilian passions will have been gratified, and I shall have at least shown what I think can be done on a classical subject on a large scale. (CG V 2280)

To his sister Adèle:

I assure you that the music of *Les Troyens* is noble and grand; furthermore it has a poignant veracity, and there are a number of ideas in it which would make the ears and perhaps the hair of all the musicians in Europe stand on end, if I am not much mistaken. I feel that if Gluck were to return to earth he would say to me if he heard it: 'Truly, this is my son.' That's not modest, is it? But at least I have the modesty to admit that lack of modesty is my failing. (CG V 2283)

On 28 March (in a letter which in the event was not posted) he told the Emperor that the opera was finished (CG V 2285); on 7 April he told Adèle: 'I have just written the last bar of the score' (CG V 2286). The last bar is in fact dated 12 April 1858, with the inscription: 'Quidquid erit, superanda omnis fortuna ferendo est' (Whatever will be, every turn of fortune must be overcome by bearing it).

But he had dated and inscribed a version of the ending which was not his first idea, nor would it be his last. His first plan had been a prophecy on the lips of the dying Dido of French dominion in North Africa:

– an allusion that now seems pure childish chauvinism to me. It would be much more dignified and impressive to stick to the idea suggested by Virgil himself. So I have given the queen the following lines; this seems more logical too. (CG V 2195)

He then quotes his new version, in which Hannibal's name is invoked. At a reading of the poem in March 1857 the idea about modern Algeria was finally scotched and the prophecy of Hannibal endorsed. This was no doubt the 'new, grander' ending referred to in a letter to the Princess of November 1857 (CG V 2264), perhaps the same as that described to von Bülow in February 1858 and set between 26 February and 12 April:

I have added a close to the drama, much more grandiose and conclusive than that with which I had previously been content. The spectator will thus see Aeneas's task accomplished, for Clio cries out in the last scene, with the Roman Capitol glowing in the distance:

Fuit Troja!. . .Stat Roma! (CG V 2273)

The setting of this finale survives. The action is as follows. As Dido lies dying in her sister's arms, a rainbow is seen above the funeral pyre, and a spectrum of seven colours falls on Dido's body. Iris appears in the air and passes over the pyre scattering poppies over the dying queen, while the high priest of Pluto announces that the gods have taken pity and sent Iris to conclude Dido's agony. The rainbow disappears with the goddess; the spectrum remains. Then the high priest advances and intones a funeral chant, repeated by the Carthaginians. The spectrum disappears. Dido dies. The Carthaginian flag is laid over Dido's body. All stand, move forward and, raising their right arms, pronounce a curse on the race of Aeneas (for the most part the same as the imprecation in the final version, but set to music *allegro con fuoco* in D major).

This is followed by a lengthy epilogue. A curtain falls representing Time followed by the procession of the Hours, of which twelve are in white and pink tunics and twelve in black tunics with gold stars. 'A mysterious murmuring can be heard in the orchestra interspersed with solemn sounds.' This 'mysterious murmuring' is a long passage in which a five-bar modulation is repeated four times over, using the progression:

Ex. 4.4

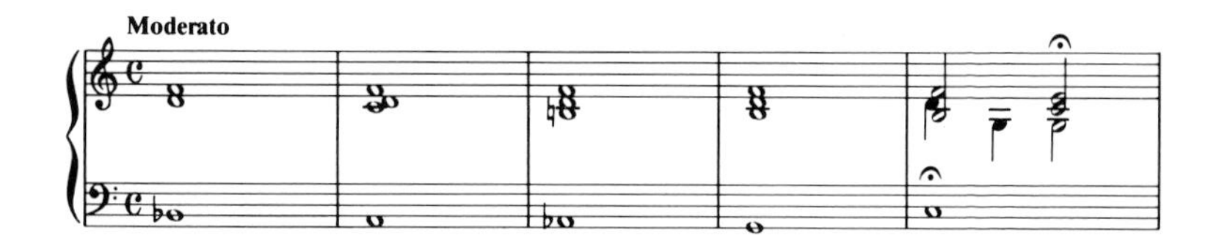


It moves step by step from B flat to F sharp where the modulation is varied moving through E and G minor to B flat major. The whole is forty-two bars, common time, marked *moderato*, and might therefore seem, at the end of a five-act opera, rather more than a mere symbol of the passing of time.

Finally the curtain rises again to reveal the Capitol in Rome 'in all its glory'. The stage is empty but for Clio (the muse of History) on one side with a *Renommée* (allegorical figure of Fame). The Trojan March is heard reappearing in the triumphal mode (carried on by tradition and now the triumphal hymn of the Romans). A procession passes before the Capitol: first a warrior in dazzling armour at the head of the Roman legions. Clio cries out: 'Scipioni Africano gloria!' ('Glory to Scipio Africanus!'). Secondly another warrior crowned with laurel marching at the head of other legions: 'Julio Caesari gloria!' ('Glory to Julius Caesar!'). Thirdly an Emperor with a train of poets and artists: 'Imperatori Augusto et divo Virgilio gloria! gloria! Fuit Troja. . .Stat Roma!' ('Glory to the Emperor

Augustus and to the divine Virgil! Glory! Troy is past! Rome abides!'), answered by distant echoes of 'Stat Roma!. . .' The final strains of the Trojan March resound across the theatre.

This is an uncompromisingly idealistic plan, whose aim was lofty enough: to transmute the ultimate purpose of the *Aeneid* into operatic form. Its grandeur is undoubtedly worthy of the poet to whom the opera was dedicated; but the material difficulty of making Clio and Iris meaningful characters to an audience who knew their classical literature less well than Berlioz and the daunting duration of the opera caused him to revise with a compromise ending that retains some characteristics of the larger scheme.

The finale remained for some time untouched. On 24 January 1860, however, he suddenly scrapped it. To Pauline Viardot he wrote:

> I had to attack the finale, which you were so cool about, with fire and hatchet. I think it will work better now. What a lot I owe you for having drawn my attention to so many faults! But it will be right in the end, we shall see![17]

The new ending retains the grandiose conception while considerably simplifying the *mise-en-scène* (although the legions are still supposed to be seen *above* the funeral pyre). Thus Iris, Clio, Scipio and Caesar do not appear, but over Dido's dying body a vision of the Capitol in Rome is to be seen, with the legions and 'an emperor' with his train of poets and artists filing past to the sounds of the Trojan March, now the Romans' adopted national anthem. At the same time the Carthaginian people 'hurl an imprecation, the first Punic war cry, contrasting in its fury with the solemnity of the triumphal march'.

Other revisions made after April 1858 were these: in February 1859 he reported 'several important corrections' in Act IV (CG V 2351) and in September of that year he mentioned four or five corrections in Act II, shortly after a visit to Pauline Viardot at Courtavanel (CG V 2402). He clearly invited the singer's criticisms of the opera and acted on them in many cases. In December 1859 he wrote some ballet music, probably that for Act III, followed by the new finale in February 1860. The duet in Act V (No. 44) may have been composed at the same time. As explained above, in the summer of 1861, while preparing the vocal score for printing, he discarded the Sinon scene in Act I. When a performance of part of the opera became a reality in 1863, he wrote the music necessitated by dividing the opera into two parts and by the reallocation of acts, including the separation of No. 3 (Cassandra and Coroebus) from No. 4 (*Marche et hymne*), and the composition of the Prologue to *Les Troyens à Carthage*, largely put together from existing material. Carvalho's production of *Les Troyens à Carthage* introduced a good number of cuts; yet one new passage was composed, apparently to aid the *mise-en-scène*: bars 52–62 of the Septet (No. 36), allowing everyone except Dido and Aeneas to leave the stage. Berlioz's last musical composition was the concert arrangement of the *Trojan March*, which occupied him in the early part of 1864. For the remaining five years of his life he wrote no more music at all.

# 5 *Berlioz the poet?*

A. R. W. JAMES

'None of these dreary old contrivances. We're not putting on l'abbé Delille, but Virgil, and Virgil *Shakespeareanized*.'[1]

Berlioz wrote the libretto for *Les Troyens* almost entirely before composing the music. He speaks somewhat deprecatingly of it as 'poésie d'amateur', yet he invests considerable energy in composing, polishing and revising it and he gives semi-public readings which recall those which French poets had been accustomed to give in the 1820s. For him it clearly was an unusually challenging task, a *poème d'Opéra* for which, because of his love for Virgil, no foreign hand would suffice. In the letter to Carvalho quoted above, three kinds of poetic language are present by implication; one is repudiated, the other two are embraced. In order to examine the poetry Berlioz actually wrote for his opera, I shall begin by elucidating the first part of the above remark; this will supply us with a poetic context and some indications about Berlioz's view of nineteenth-century poetry in French. Focusing then on his libretto, we shall be able to ask how far that context and those views affect his practice.

Now almost forgotten, l'abbé Delille (1738–1813) was once dubbed 'the French Virgil'. Not only did he translate the *Georgics* (1767) and the *Aeneid* (1804), but he also gave to France its own 'Eclogues' in the form of his poem *Les Jardins* (1782). Throughout the first half of the nineteenth century his poetry was studied in schools as a model. Larousse, in 1876, still calls him 'one of our most celebrated French poets'. When Berlioz wrote the above words, therefore, the reference would have been as familiar to his contemporaries as Virgil or Shakespeare. But why the pejorative note?

Delille's reputation as a poet had been subjected to severe attacks during the 1820s, when Hugo, Vigny, Sainte-Beuve and others were attempting to free poetic language from some of the rhetorical constraints imposed by the prevailing eighteenth-century mode. The chief grounds for criticism were his use of circumlocution rather than plain words and the frequency of vague, stock epithets. Only the abbé Delille, says Sainte-Beuve,[2] exaggerating somewhat, could have written:

> . . .Tombez, *altières* colonnades,
> Croulez, *fiers* chapiteaux, *orgueilleuses* arcades

> . . .Fall, ye lofty colonnades,
> Crumble, proud capitals and haughty arches

in the belief that he was depicting anything visually. And Hugo, in a passage in the preface to *Cromwell* (1827), with which Berlioz was almost certainly familiar, inveighs against the influence of Delille on the language of tragedy: in Delille's work, the grotesque, the commonplace, the vulgar are allowed as subject-matter, provided they are 'ennobled', that is to say dressed up through the art of circumlocution in such a way that the immediacy of their impact is lost. In French tragedy before 1830, it was inconceivable to call a spade a spade; the prevailing *bienséances* required that language used on the stage be noble; certain kinds of common word either had 'poetic' equivalents (like *trépas* for *death*) or had to be expanded with the aid of an 'elegant' circumlocution. Hugo sums up, metaphorically, the nature of the tragic muse under Delille's influence as follows:

> Cette muse, on le conçoit, est d'une bégueulerie rare. Accoutumée qu'elle est aux caresses de la périphrase, le mot propre, qui la rudoierait quelquefois, lui fait horreur.[3]

> Understandably enough, this muse is singularly prudish. Accustomed as she is to the gentle touch of circumlocution, she recoils in fright from plain words which might ruffle her sensibility.

This is why Vigny's translation of *Othello*, staged in 1829, caused an uproar by translating the 'low' word *handkerchief* directly as *mouchoir*. Many of the changes wrought in the language of both poetry and drama during the Restoration in France – changes which were seminal for the whole of nineteenth-century poetry – can be seen as a repudiation of the poetic mode represented by Delille. Since Berlioz also rejects this poetic mode, we may preface our study by enquiring how far Berlioz sympathized with attempts to change the nature of poetic language.

In the early part of the year 1830 he went, probably several times, to performances of Hugo's play *Hernani*.[4] This drama, and the 'battle' which greeted each of its thirty-nine performances, represented a key moment in the struggle for changes in the hidebound conventions which regulated what could and could not be said on stage, and in what verse-form. The traditional twelve-syllable line of French tragedy, the Alexandrine, is used in *Hernani*, but often in an unconventional way. In classical verse, either the line was a syntactic unit (e.g. 'Oui, je viens dans son temple adorer l'Eternel' ('Yes, I come to worship the Lord in his temple'), first line of Racine's *Athalie*, 1691), or, if the sense overflowed, convention required that it be completed at the *end* of a succeeding line (e.g. 'Je viens, selon l'usage antique et solennel, / Célébrer avec vous la fameuse journée / Où sur le mont Sina la loi nous fut donnée.' ('I come, according to the ancient and solemn custom / To celebrate with you the day of days / When the law was given us on Mount Sinai.'), ibid.). *Hernani* begins by deliberately flouting this convention:

> Serait-ce déjà lui? C'est bien à l'escalier
> Dérobé. Vite, ouvrons! Bonjour beau cavalier,
>
> Could it already be he? It is indeed at the hidden
> Staircase. Quick, let's open. Good day, handsome rider!

thus committing the 'crime' of separating, at the line-end, a noun from its adjective. Such *enjambements* and the relatively straightforward speech ('Quelle heure est-il?. . .Minuit bientôt' ('What time is it?. . .Near midnight')), instead, says Théophile Gautier,[5] of '– l'heure / Atteindra bientôt sa dernière demeure' (– 'Time's hand approaches near the radir of its arc') were allowed by the censor – not without a fight – on the medicinal ground that 'It would be good for people to see to what state of wild extravagance the human mind, unfettered by rules and propriety, could attain.'[6] Berlioz's reaction to *Hernani* is conveyed in a letter to his sisters in April 1830. Although there are in it 'des choses et surtout des pensées sublimes', the versification leaves him cold:

> . . . mais quant aux vers, comme je les déteste au théâtre, ces enjambements de l'un à l'autre, ces hémistiches rompus qui font donner au diable tous les classiques me sont entièrement indifférents, parce que, quand on parle, cela ressemble exactement à de la prose; à cet égard même je les aimerais mieux; toutefois, je trouve que, puisque *Hernani* a été écrit en vers et que Hugo sait bien les faire quand il veut, il était plus simple de faire des vers suivant les règles du goût de la masse. . . (CG I 159)

> . . . but as for the lines of verse, since I detest them in the theatre – these *enjambements* from one line to another, these broken hemistichs which so outrage the classicists – I'm completely indifferent to them because, when spoken, they're just like prose; from that point of view I might even prefer them; yet, since *Hernani* has been written in verse, and since Hugo is quite capable of writing it when he wants, I think it would have been simpler to write verse according to the rules of majority taste. . .

This appreciation is mixed. The prosaic quality clearly precludes the most flagrant kinds of circumlocution but, equally clearly, Hugo has not succeeded, for Berlioz, in his aim of writing 'verse which would be as fine as prose'.[7] But would *Hernani* be *Hernani* if written in classical Alexandrines? The answer must be no, unless we take the play to be identical with a synopsis of its plot. Berlioz appears to have grasped the dramatic structure and felt the 'sublimity' of thought and situation; he approves of rebelling against the 'unities' of time and place, but not of the attempted renewal of poetic language.

He is, however, sympathetic to contemporary lyric poetry. As is well known, he set three of Hugo's *Orientales* to music ('La Captive', 'Chanson de pirates' and 'Sara la baigneuse'), as well as the 'Romance' (now lost) from *Marie Tudor*; he set six poems by Gautier (in *Les Nuits d'été*); in 1836, he directed rehearsals for *La Esmeralda*, an opera based on the novel *Notre-Dame de Paris* with a libretto by Hugo himself, written at the instigation of the composer Louise Bertin; he wrote warmly to Hugo about his poetic work *Les Rayons et les ombres* (1840), quoted him from memory in a letter to Princess Sayn-Wittgenstein (1859)[8] and cited him, while sketching out the plan for *Les Troyens* in 1855, as the only French name in a list of poets who had influenced him.[9]

Taken together, these factors indicate considerable sympathy with contemporary poetic ideals, but with a touch of conservatism, and it is precisely this mixture which we find in his libretto. *Les Troyens* reads as more 'poetic' than Scribe, that omnipresent composer of nineteenth-century librettos, but the poetry tends to have a very Empire or early Restoration flavour. There may be no circumlocutions *à la* Delille, but there are a great many stock epithets in the eighteenth-century mode. Conventional pairings of noun and adjective such as the following – *trépas glorieux*, *hymen odieux*, *cœur agité*, *main débile*, *noble fête*, *fête importune*, *affreux destin*, *destin impérieux*, *glaive terrible*, *héros invincible* (glorious death, hateful marriage, trembling heart, feeble hand, noble celebration, importunate feast, awful destiny, imperious destiny, fearful sword, invincible hero) – are sprinkled throughout the poem and serve to give it a strong neo-classical ring. Another device which has the same effect is inversion of word-order. Frequent in seventeenth-century verse and still in Scribe's librettos, it had become rare in Hugo, Gautier and Baudelaire. Berlioz makes abundant use of it, for instance:

> J'ai fui de son regard la terrible éloquence (No. 41)[10]
>
> I have fled the fearful eloquence of her gaze

which though neo-classical, is a forceful Alexandrine. The following example, given to Dido, is less felicitous. Aeneas is leaving. She sings:

> . . .Sans qu'à l'aspect d'une telle misère
> La pitié d'une larme humecte sa paupière (No. 44)
>
> Without, at the sight of such misfortune,
> Pity, by a tear, moistening his eyelid.

Classical in a different sense, and more memorable, are those striking, well-framed Alexandrines which sum up a thought, as when Cassandra scathingly and poignantly rails against the gods:

> O digne emploi de la toute puissance,
> Le conduire [ce peuple] à l'abîme en lui fermant les yeux!. . .
> (No. 11)
>
> A worthy use for your omnipotence!
> To lead the people to the abyss whilst closing their eyes!

or when Aeneas in defeat frames the following maxim:

> Le salut des vaincus est de n'en plus attendre[11] (No. 13)
>
> Salvation for the conquered is to expect no salvation.

Powerful though some of these lines may be, nothing marks them out in their feeling, their form, or their vocabulary as belonging to poetry written in the second half of the nineteenth century.

Paradoxically enough, in view of his reaction to *Hernani*, it is in the movement of verse and the control of syntax, that Berlioz is most modern. The libretto, of course, allowed more freedom in variation of the length of lines than did most contemporary forms of poetry or drama. In opera librettos there was no obligation to write series of Alexandrines, or absolutely regular strophic forms.[12] Berlioz uses 'even' lines mainly of six, eight, ten and twelve syllables. Within them, however, he is far superior to Scribe in his control of movement and syntax. Take, for instance, Aeneas's account of Laocoön:

> 1 Laocoon, voyant quelque trame perfide
> Dans l'ouvrage des Grecs, a d'un bras intrépide
> Lancé son javelot sur ce bois, excitant
> Le peuple indécis et flottant
> 5 À le brûler. Alors gonflés de rage,
> Deux serpents monstrueux s'avancent vers la plage,
> S'élancent sur le prêtre, en leurs terribles nœuds
> L'enlacent, le brûlant de leur haleine ardente,
> Et la couvrant d'une bâve sanglante,
> 10 Le dévorant à nos yeux! (No. 7)

Seeing some perfidious plot
In the Greeks' handiwork, brave-armed Laocoön
Threw his javelin into the wooden horse, encouraging
The undecided and hesitant people
To burn it. Then, swollen with rage,
Two monstrous serpents made for the shore,
Leapt upon the priest, and in their fearful coils
Entwined him, scorching him with their fiery breath,
And, covering him with a bloody foam,
Devoured him before our eyes.

This is, to begin with, much more concise than Virgil or than Delille's translation, even if it shares, with Delille, adjectives like *monstrueux* and the phrase *nœuds terribles* (*spirisque ligant ingentibus*). Leaving aside, however, the neo-classical epithets, the movement of the verse, with an *enjambement* such as that in lines 3–5 or 7–8 above and with the main verb held in suspense for the last line, is, *mutatis mutandis*, reminiscent of Chénier or Hugo. It is certainly very different, in this respect, from the classical passage whose theme is most similar, the *récit de Théramène* in Racine's *Phèdre* (V. vi). The passage can thus be taken as representative of the mixture of conservatism and modernity mentioned earlier.

The celebrated love-duet ('Nuit d'ivresse') is of course one of Berlioz's cribs ('larcins' – his own word: CG V 2163) from Shakespeare, recalling expressly the 'In such a night as this. . .' of the last scene of *The Merchant of Venice*. It is exceptional in two respects. First, it is the only number whose music Berlioz composed before he had finished the rest of the libretto. Secondly, it is more regular in both strophic form and rhyme-scheme than any other part of the libretto (apart perhaps from Hylas's song) and in this sense becomes almost like a separable lyric poem. From Shakespeare it retains the allusions to Troilus and Cressida, the presence of Dido (transformed here from a mere allusion into a protagonist), the shorter line at the end of each strophe and the way the lovers, in conclusion, use the third person to refer to each other, thus translating their love into the realms of story. Berlioz also borrows from Shakespeare the final note of forgiveness ('and he forgave it her' – 'obtint de lui sans peine / Le plus tendre pardon'), which in the Trojan context carries a fair weight of irony. Berlioz here uses the verse structure neatly, two Alexandrines being followed by a six-syllable line which completes the sense by providing either an adverbial clause

Enée

Mais bannissons ces tristes souvenirs .....
Nuit splendide et charmante! (Il se lève)
Venez, chère Didon, respirer les soupirs
De cette brise caressante.
(Didon se lève à son tour.)

Sextuor avec chœur.

Enée, Ascagne, Anna, Iopas, Narbal, Panthée et le chœur.

Ensemble

Tout n'est que paix et charme autour de nous!
La nuit étend son voile et la mer endormie
Murmure en sommeillant les accords les plus doux....

(Pendant cet ensemble tous les personnages, excepté Enée et Didon, se retirent lentement vers le fond du théâtre, et finissent par disparaître.)

Scène 4me

Didon, Enée seuls. (Clair de lune)

Duo

Ensemble

Ô nuit d'ivresse et d'extase infinie!
Blonde Phœbé, grands astres de sa cour,
Versez sur nous votre lueur bénie
Fleurs des cieux souriez à l'immortel amour!

Didon

Par une telle nuit, le front ceint de cytise,
La déesse Vénus suivit le bel Anchise
Aux bosquets de l'Ida.

Enée

Par une telle nuit, fou d'amour et de joie,

7 A page from Berlioz's autograph libretto, dedicated to Rosine Stoltz and dated 12 August 1859. It was written out when the Septuor (No. 36) was still a Sextuor, Berlioz not yet having added the part for Dido. The beginning of the love-duet (No. 37) is also shown.

Par une telle nuit, le front ceint de cytise,
La déesse Venus suivit le bel Anchise
Aux bosquets de l'Ida. (No. 37)

In such a night, laburnum-crowned,
Did your mother Venus follow handsome Anchises
To the groves of Ida.

or a necessary direct object

Par une telle nuit, fou d'amour et de joie,
Troïlus vint attendre aux pieds des murs de Troie
La belle Cressida.

In such a night, enraptured with love and joy,
Did Troilus await, beneath the walls of Troy,
The beautiful Cressida.

The repetitions, the refrain and the rhyming couplets followed by a final line which rhymes between stanzas (Ida/Cressida; Endymion/Didon/pardon) give the whole duet a strong feeling of cohesion. The form thus conveys the union of the lovers with each other, with the lovers of history and legend and with the moonlit night. There are some weaknesses, such as 'la *pudique* Diane' or the conversion of Shakespeare's very direct 'The moon shines bright' into a piece of neo-classical mythologising: 'Blonde Phœbè. . .', but there is no doubt that Berlioz is writing here not just verse, but poetry.

Even here though, if one were asked to read the piece unseen and to date it, the most likely response would be 'between 1800 and 1830'. Not just because there are classical allusions – they are unsurprising in the context and frequent enough in Hugo, Gautier and even Baudelaire – but because of the stock mythologising ('Blonde Phœbè. . .'), the *expected* epithets ('voile *diaphane*') and above all the absence of any strikingly direct concrete description or original imagery. These were, with changes in verse-form, the chief gains of nineteenth-century poetry before 1860. In *Les Troyens* it is rare (and of course surprising in view of Berlioz's love of Shakespeare) to come across a memorable image. One such occurs when the Greek chief stumbles upon Cassandra and the women who have rallied round her. In strong contrast to the preceding, rather colourless neo-classical lines, it leaves us with a startling image (unheard, incidentally, in performance) of Cassandra at the moment of death:

Bacchante à l'œil d'azur s'enivrant d'harmonie! (No. 16)

Bacchic priestess, azure-eyed, drinking the wine of music!

There is here an unexpected vividness both in the context and the combination of words chosen: *harmonie*, instead of a beverage and *d'azur*, with connotations of sky and immensity, suggesting a realm beyond the immediate, ugly situation. In their rarity, in the need we feel to disentangle them from the less impressive 'poetic' language which surrounds them, such lines or passages confirm the point suggested earlier; *Les Troyens* may not be 'l'abbé Delille', but the libretto does display a marked linguistic conservatism.[13]

The question of what kind of poetry was suitable for opera – or indeed whether the language used should be poetry at all – had been debated since the eighteenth century. Around 1830, when the languages of painting, literature and music were undergoing renewal, the art of the librettist remained untouched.[14] With the single exception of Emile Deschamps,[15] no attempt was made to renew *la poésie d'Opéra* which was to remain in reality rather an art of verse than an art of poetry. Castil-Blaze, in 1856, lambasts the 'puddingy mixtures' which continue to be served up to the Parisian public[16] and considers the Italians far superior. It can be seen, therefore, that in *Les Troyens* Berlioz has written a 'poème d'Opéra' of a distinctly rare kind. It owes its conception to Virgil and its dramatic form to Shakespeare, perhaps partly as reflected in romantic drama. As a poetic achievement in its own right, however, it is a kind of hybrid, belonging in large part to the century before and as such, perhaps, reflecting Berlioz's profound attachment to the operas of Gluck. It would indeed have been extraordinary had Berlioz succeeded not only in composing a musical transmutation of the *Aeneid* in a 'Shakespearean' dramatic form, but also in giving to French poetry some new fusion of Latin and Shakespearean density and metaphorical life. If, as is sometimes said, the words are the handmaid to the music, they must not indeed be tawdry and cheap, as they frequently were and here are not, but neither must their power and sophistication rival that of their mistress. The listener who is alert to the music need not regret that the poetry, almost everywhere, falls far short of the same heights.

# 6 *Berlioz and Virgil*[1]

**DAVID CAIRNS**

Despite illness and the distractions of journalism, Berlioz wrote the huge, richly wrought opera, words and music, in slightly less than two years. Such rapidity of creation was the fruit of a lifelong germination. He himself acknowledged it in a letter to the Princess Carolyne Sayn-Wittgenstein:

> As for the principal object of the work, the musical rendering of the characters and the expression of their feelings and passions, it was always the easiest part of my task. I have spent my life with this race of demi-gods; I know them so well that I feel as if they must have known me. And this recalls to me a boyhood experience which will show you how fascinated I was from the first by those splendid creatures of the ancient world. It was during the period in my classical education when I was construing, under my father's direction, the marvellous twelfth book of the *Aeneid*. My mind was possessed by the glory of its characters – Lavinia, Turnus, Aeneas, Mezentius, Lausus, Pallas, Evander, Amata, Latinus, Camilla and the rest. I was like a sleepwalker 'lost in my starry meditations' (to borrow Victor Hugo's phrase). One Sunday I was taken to Vespers. The sad persistent chant of the psalm *In exitu Israel* had the magnetic effect on me that it still has today, and plunged me deep in the most real and vivid day-dreams of the past. I was with my Virgilian heroes again: I could hear the clash of their arms, I could see Camilla the beautiful Amazon running; I watched the maiden Lavinia, flushed with weeping, and the ill-fated Turnus, his father Daunus, his sister Juturna, I heard the great palaces of Laurentium ring with lamentation – and I was seized by an overwhelming sadness. I left the church, sobbing uncontrollably, and cried for the rest of the day, powerless to contain my epic grief. No one could ever get me to tell the reason, my parents never knew nor had any inkling what sorrows had taken possession of my childish heart that day. Is that not a strange and marvellous manifestation of the power of genius? A poet dead thousands of years shakes an artless, ignorant boy to the depths of his soul with a tale handed down across the centuries, and with scenes whose radiance devouring time has been powerless to dim.

Berlioz inscribed *Les Troyens* 'to the divine Virgil', *Divo Virgilio.* A special sense of affinity bound him to Virgil, an affinity only strengthened by the supreme artistic experience of transmuting his poem into music. Near the end of his life he wrote: 'I must be reconciled . . . to not having known Virgil – I should have loved him.' Not even Shakespeare occupied a more personal place in his Pantheon. Shakespeare, to Berlioz, was a kind of humanistic God the Father; artistically, he was the most far-reaching influence of all (an influence vitally felt in *Les Troyens* itself, the libretto articulating the poem by methods learned from the history plays: open form and bold juxtaposition of genres, lofty soliloquy and vernacular conversation, private emotion expressed in a framework of public action). But with Virgil it was something more intimate, a companionship, a sense of identification. While composing *Les Troyens*, he felt that Virgil was alive again in him:

> The countryside [at Saint-Germain] seems to make my Virgilian passion more intense than ever. I feel as if I knew Virgil, as if he knew how much I love him . . . Yesterday I finished an aria for Dido which is simply a paraphrase of the famous line: *haud ignara mali miseris succurrere disco* [my own troubles teach me to help the unfortunate (1.630)]. When I had sung it through once I was naïve enough to say, out loud: 'That's it, isn't it, dear Master? *sunt lacrymae rerum*? (1.463)' just as though Virgil himself had been there. (CG V 2245)

Studying the opera and the poem together, we cannot but become increasingly aware of deep correspondences between the two artists.

*Les Troyens* is Virgilian in countless ways. There is the blend of romantic rhetoric and classical restraint, of monumentality and pictorial vividness; the fondness for mixing genres and in particular for using the lyrical to diversify the tragic and at the same time to bring it into sharper focus; the systematic alternation of scenes or passages of violence and calm as a structural rhythm in the composition of the work; the combination of an aristocratic aloofness with an awareness of the sufferings of ordinary humanity; the sense of fatality, of obscure inimical powers that lie in wait for man, and of the madness that can strike a people and drive it blindly to its own destruction. (The two men have also in common their fear of the collapse of civilization as they knew it, and the doubts that assailed them at the end about the value of their work.) As with the *Aeneid* in Virgil's life, *Les Troyens* grew from seeds planted in youth. As Virgil went back to Homer in order fully to realize himself, so Berlioz turned to Virgil. The opera's outward structure, too, shows Berlioz's fidelity to his model (he has shared the criticism sometimes levelled at Virgil that the character and fate of Dido are treated with such power that they dominate the epic and deflect it from its course).

*Les Troyens* follows the *Aeneid* in making the tragic death of an individual the last action that the audience sees enacted on the stage. And just as the *Aeneid* is an epic constructed of two personal tragedies (Dido's and Turnus's), so is *Les Troyens*. Even in consisting of two distinct though interlocking halves the opera reflects the shape of the poem, which is divided into the wanderings of Aeneas, including his narrative of the sack of Troy, and the struggle to found a new Troy in Italy. And though the action of the opera does not take the Trojans as far as Italy, the poem's central idea of the founding of Rome runs through it; Italy is the *Leitmotiv* of the drama.

Virgil is the constant guiding spirit of the libretto. It is not only that a great deal of it is direct translation or paraphrase of the Latin of the books from which the main action is taken – Books 1, 2 and 4. The whole poem is pressed into use. Even the stage direction at the beginning of the opera, 'three shepherds playing the double flute' – represented in the orchestra by oboes – is derived from the *Aeneid*, echoing a passage in Book 9 where the Rutulian warrior Numanus taunts Ascanius with 'Go and dance to the double-mouthed pipe on Mount Dindyma, that's all you're good for (9.617ff).' Where Berlioz adds to the poem for dramatic purposes, he nearly always goes to Virgil for his material or his inspiration, working in ideas taken from anywhere and everywhere in the epic. Thus the scene in Act I where Hector's widow Andromache and her son Astyanax, dressed in the ritual white of mourning, lay flowers at the altar and receive Priam's blessing, springs from two different sources, one in Book 2, where Aeneas, climbing up to the palace roof by way of a secret postern gate during the sack of the city, remembers that through this gate Andromache used to bring her child to see his grandfather Priam, the other in Book 3 where Aeneas meets Andromache in the Epiran city of Buthrotum, performing the rites of the dead at an altar dedicated to the ashes of Hector (2.453ff and 3.301ff). Virgil, in fact, has inspired both the visual content and the tragic irony of the scene.

The episode in Book 5 where the disgruntled Trojan women gaze out to sea and groan at the thought of the endless voyaging that lies before them (5.615ff) is transmuted into the scene in Act V for the two sentries who march up and down by the Trojan ships, grumbling at the prospect of leaving Carthage, where they are comfortably billeted, and entrusting themselves to the sea's tedium and the rough mercies of the storm. Cassandra, urging Coroebus to fly from the wrath to come, is answered with sentiments similar to those of Aeneas's reply to Anchises in the burning house: *Mene efferre pedem, genitor, te posse relicto / sperasti?* (Father, did you really expect me to run away and leave you behind?, 2.657ff). Aeneas's words to his son, spoken before he goes off to fight the Numidians, paraphrase the hero's words in Book 12 on the eve of the final battle against Turnus and the Rutulians (12.435ff and 3.342f). The invasion by Iarbas and his Numidian hordes, an interpolation made in order to provide a climax for the third act and give dramatic emphasis to Aeneas's arrival in Carthage, is a development of an idea in the *Aeneid* put forward by Dido's sister Anna when she argues that Dido ought to marry Aeneas and share her kingdom with him: Carthage is surrounded by wild tribesmen, among them the Numidians and their chief Iarbas, who is all the more dangerous since Dido humiliatingly rejected his offer of a dynastic marriage (4.36ff, 196ff and 326).[2]

The process by which Berlioz fashioned his libretto is most clearly illustrated in Acts I and II. The opera follows the main events of the sack of Troy. But new material is added by the development of hints in the poem, and a good deal else has necessarily been subjected to compression or expansion. Thus the one-and-a-half lines in which Virgil tells of the cold fear that creeps over the Trojans at the news of Laocoön's death (2.228f) are built into a full-scale ensemble (No. 8) which shows the city poised at the fatal moment of decision. In Act II Aeneas is made to succeed in his desperate attempt to relieve the citadel (in the poem he merely conceives the wild idea of doing so, 2.315f); and he escapes with the royal insignia of Troy. The motive for this change may partly have been tidiness and coherence: Ascanius later presents a rich selection of Trojan relics to Queen Dido (a scene which is a conflation of two separate passages in Book 1, 1.520, 524f and 647ff). But the main reason, as with the finale of Act III, is one of dramatic emphasis, to clinch the act with a decisive forward-looking event. In this case the action is not shown. We hear of it, from Cassandra, in the course of a scene which does not figure in the *Aeneid* except by implication, in the cries of the wailing women in Priam's palace (*plangoribus aedes / femineis ululant*, 2.487f), in the glimpse of Helen cowering by the entrance to the temple of Vesta (2.567f), and in the brief description of Cassandra being dragged from Pallas's sanctuary (2.403ff).

The development of Cassandra into the protagonist of Acts I and II is the biggest single change that Berlioz made. But here too he went to Virgil, deriving the character from a few lines in the *Aeneid*, just as Virgil derived Aeneas from a brief sketch in Homer's *Iliad*.

Cassandra fills the role taken in Book 2 by Aeneas, who in the poem recalls Troy's downfall several years after the event. In the opera the tale comes to us through the eyes of the prophetess cursed with second sight. We see the catastrophe twice over: as it gradually forms in her mind (from the vague fears of 'Malheureux roi' to the fierce clarity of her vision in the following scene), and when it comes. This double process has the dramatic effect of heightening the sense of tragedy and doom. The vehemence and certainty of her unheeded prophecies throws the blindness of her fellow-countrymen into more merciless relief – that of Coroebus in particular; the young warrior is mentioned briefly by Virgil as being 'on fire with desperate love for Cassandra', to whom he is betrothed (2.343ff), and as refusing to listen to her warnings; in the opera, Berlioz's lyrical development of these hints sharpens the cruel irony of Cassandra's personal tragedy, by holding out the possibility of a happiness that will never be fulfilled. The text of Cassandra's scenes inevitably contains few direct Virgilian echoes; the prophecy to the Trojan women about the founding of a new Troy in Italy, based on Anchises' words in Book 3 (3.183ff), is a rare exception. Yet the whole character and her heroic, despairing utterances are in a sense simply a personification of Aeneas's tragic cry:

> o patria o divum domus Ilium et incluta bello
> maenia Dardanidum! (2.241f)
>
> O my country! O Ilium, home of the gods and fortress
> of the descendants of Dardanus, renowned in war!

uttered at the moment when he describes the entry of the wooden horse into Troy while Cassandra vainly prophesies. Cassandra is the first of the two tragic pillars which support the edifice of *Les Troyens*; across her fate, and Dido's, the epic of Roman destiny marches to its fulfilment. Berlioz had no choice but to kill her off in heroic circumstances at the end of his Act II. The scene is not in Virgil; but its conception does not dishonour him.

In adapting the *Aeneid* to the totally different medium of opera, Berlioz also made some changes in the order of events as recounted by Virgil. The conversation (already referred to) between Anna and her sister Dido (4.9ff), with its tender urgings on one side and its barely suppressed emotion on the other, prompted the very similar duet in Act III, 'Reine d'un jeune empire'. But whereas in the *Aeneid* the conversation occurs after the Trojans' arrival in Carthage and is very much concerned with them, Berlioz places it just before, as a means of projecting the state of Dido's heart at the moment of Aeneas's intervention in her life – her restlessness, her half-conscious yearning for love, her ripeness to yield. His dramatic judgement is correct. By doing so he is able partly to compensate for the fact that he has had to unfold the events of the plot in straightforward chronological sequence and therefore to start the Carthaginian part of his story cold, where Virgil, by recounting the sack of Troy and its aftermath in flashback, through the mouth of Aeneas, with the fascinated Dido devouring his words, can accumulate tension over two or three thousand lines of verse and so prepare gradually for the explosion of passion which comes at the beginning of Book 4. The opera also redistributes and telescopes the sequence of events between Aeneas's decision to leave Dido and her death – a sequence which in the poem occupies four or five hundred lines, or well over half Book 4. A chart of the various sources, line by line, of Dido's soliloquies in Act V – 'Dieux immortels, il part', 'Je vais mourir', 'Adieu, fière cité' and the final invocation from the pyre – would show the text as woven of threads freely drawn from many different points in the last 250 lines of the book. The result is clear, logical and compelling, and does no violence to Virgil's psychology.

The third and final category of change concerns the new emphasis that Berlioz gives to certain events or ideas in the poem, his intention normally being to make explicit and theatrically telling what in the poem can afford to take its time and grow by degrees in the reader's mind. To take one of the most obvious instances: the theme of *fatum*, destiny, which is fundamental to the *Aeneid*, has had necessarily to be much more simply and directly set forth (a process in which the traditional importance of the chorus in French opera plays a vital part). This need applies also to the specifically Italian direction of the destiny of the Trojan survivors; not being native and instantly intelligible to Berlioz's audience as it was to Virgil's, it had to be made plain. In the *Aeneid* there is some doubt about the true identity of the mysterious object of Aeneas's wanderings. The ghost of his wife Creusa tells him, on Troy's last night, that his goal is Hesperia, or Italy; but after that, uncertainty descends and it is only subsequently, several false scents later, that it is defined as the destined country of Troy reborn. An opera composer cannot afford such inconsistency (if indeed it is not deliberate and subtle poetic realism on Virgil's part) and, as we see, Berlioz is at pains to state the theme clearly and reemphasize it at regular intervals, so that we shall be in no serious danger of not recognizing it as the majestic impulse of the epic, before which everything must ultimately give way. Contrary to Virgil, he makes Hector's ghost specify the object of Aeneas's wanderings. Later, he ends his picture of the sack of Troy with the Trojan women's defiant repeated cry of 'Italie'. Similarly, when the Trojans land at Carthage, their spokesman Panthus is more emphatic about the god-fated and only temporarily frustrated aim of their voyage than is Ilioneus in the equivalent passage in the *Aeneid* (1.530ff). In the opera, at the peak of the lovers' ecstasy, Mercury appears in the moonlit garden and, striking Aeneas's shield, intones three times 'Italie'. Mercury's larger role in the *Aeneid*, as explicit messenger of the gods (4.265ff), is not sacrificed but is filled, with the greater directness appropriate to drama, by the spirits of the illustrious Trojan dead, who rise up in turn to whet Aeneas's almost blunted purpose. Again, Berlioz sees to it that Aeneas is fully awake and conscious when Hector's ghost delivers his message; in the *Aeneid* the apparition comes to Aeneas in a dream, through the veil of sleep (2.268ff). All this makes for a necessary gain in clarity and conciseness, inevitably at a slight cost in poetic suggestiveness and truth to life.

In the same way, Aeneas's heroic role and his consciousness of his destiny as a hero have to be spelled out; the point must be established quickly – it cannot be left to the cumulative effect of epic verse. In *Les Troyens* the last words uttered by Hector's ghost before the vision fades tell of the death that Aeneas will meet in Italy; the final line, 'Où la mort des héros t'attend', is not in Virgil. Later Panthus, in his speech to Dido in Act III, refers to it as an accepted fact. Aeneas himself, in his monologue in Act V, says that he could not sway the outraged Dido even by reminding her of 'la triomphale mort par les destins promise' – the end awaiting him on Ausonian fields that is to crown his glory; and almost his last words to her, when she confronts him by the ships, speak of the death to which he is going.

It is sometimes objected that Virgil, concerned with the overriding theme of the epic of Rome, failed to make Aeneas sufficiently sympathetic. This is usually said by people who have fallen in love with his glorious Dido and who consequently regard any man capable of abandoning her as an unspeakable cad. Such indignant charges do more credit to the critics' chivalry than to their careful reading of the poem. Berlioz might appear to belong to their number, from the references in his *Memoirs* to the 'hypocrite', the 'perfidious' Aeneas. But the composer of *Les Troyens* understood the depth of passion hinted at in Virgil's resonant understatements and justly praised silences;

and he was quite right, on Virgilian as well as on operatic terms, to make Aeneas's love for Dido whole-hearted and avowed and to dramatize the resultant conflict in the hero's mind. The famous duet in Dido's garden is not only obligatory for the composer of grand opera but also artistically essential to the drama as a whole. The words, adapted from the scene between Lorenzo and Jessica in the moonlit garden at Belmont in the fifth act of *The Merchant of Venice* (whose allusions to Dido and Troilus suggested the idea), represent the one major textual innovation that is not Virgilian in origin. Its setting gave Berlioz the opportunity to lavish all his lyrical and orchestral art on a poignant evocation of the warmth and vast splendours of the starlit Mediterranean night. In the *Aeneid* the season of the Trojans' sojourn in Carthage is winter (4.193). In *Les Troyens* it is, unequivocally, summertime; the great feasts with their bards and heroic tales and jewel-encrusted goblets take place out of doors under the open sky. Berlioz has also transferred the setting of the hunt and storm from open mountainous country to virgin forest, and has peopled his scene with the woodland satyrs, naiads and glinting streams and waterfalls which help to make it the neo-classical masterpiece it is, a movement that has been compared to some great Claude or Poussin, and that combines attributes of both painters, Poussin's grandeur and universality and dynamic form, Claude's numinous clarity and sense of the golden, fateful moment.

An example of all three types of change – the interpolating of new material derived from Virgil himself, the re-ordering of the sequence of Virgil's narrative, and the making explicit what in the poem is implied – is the Quintet in Act IV, 'Tout conspire à vaincre mes remords'. Here we see Berlioz's dramatic imagination at work on the *Aeneid*, distilling from it a moment which, as such, is not found in the poem, but which is necessary to the scheme of a dramatic work based on it – in this case, the moment of Dido's change of heart, from lingering attachment to the memory of her dead husband Sychaeus to unreserved commitment to her new love. In the first place, the picture of Dido feasting Aeneas and begging him to repeat the tale of Troy's woes is moved on in time so as to follow the acknowledgment and consummation of their mutual passion; in Virgil it belongs to the preceding stage of their relationship (a part of the poem not included in the opera, except by implication). Then, Virgil's divine intervention (Venus and Juno in league) is discarded. In the *Aeneid* Cupid, in the likeness of Ascanius, fans the flame and 'gradually dispels from Dido's mind all thought of Sychaeus', while she, unaware of his true identity, 'fondles him and holds him close' (1.719ff). Berlioz retains the visual setting but replaces the supernatural with a dramatic idea developed from a reference, in Book 3, to Hector's widow Andromache having married Pyrrhus (3.296 and 319). In the opera it is the discovery that Andromache is now the wife of the man whose father slew Hector that acts as a catalyst on Dido, severing the threads that bound her to her old life (and at the same time setting up in the spectator's mind a sudden resonance with the almost forgotten moment, three acts ago, when the desolate figure in white walked silently through rejoicing crowds by the walls of Troy). Finally, an echo of Cupid substituted for Ascanius survives in the stage direction which shows the boy 'leaning on his bow, like a statue of Eros', and in the smiling comment of the royal entourage that he resembles Cupid as he slips Sychaeus's ring from the heedless Dido's finger. This last action, taken from the Guérin painting *Enée racontant à Didon les malheurs de Troie*, is one of the very rare non-Virgilian ideas in the libretto.

Most of this examination has shown only the skill with which Berlioz reshaped the *Aeneid* into a fresh mould – a mould for the music that was waiting to pour out of him. It is the music that makes him a true descendant of the poet he loved. 'As for the principal object of the work, the musical rendering of the characters and the expression of their feelings and passions, it was always the easiest part of my task.' But not only the characters' passions, one wants to exclaim, but the Virgilian ambience itself, the whole environment of the epic, has been absorbed by the composer into his inmost being and given back reborn in his own language. A re-reading of the *Aeneid* with the music of *Les Troyens* in one's mind is a startling revelation of artistic correspondence. Feature after feature of the poem reappears in the score. Certain elements may be isolated. On the level of individual images, we find details such as the violin harmonics which in Act V suggest the electric effect of the apparitions on Aeneas, matching Virgil's graphic description of the hero rigid with fear, his hair standing on end (*arrectaeque horrore comae*, 4.280). At the beginning of the opera the combination of shrill, rapidly pulsing woodwind chords, a texture devoid of bass, the absence of strings, and the curiously jaunty melodic material, at once trivial and possessed, conveying a sense of ritual madness, help to establish from the outset the idea of *fatum*, of a people rushing to ruin. But for the most part the corespondence needs no analysing. It leaps out at us. The Octet (No. 8), for instance, once heard seems the inevitable setting of the dread words *tum vero tremefacta novus per pectora cunctis / insinuat pavor* (2.228f) – a whole people's blood running cold, panic spreading as an inkling of their doom 'works its way' into their minds. How much of Cassandra's music directly echoes, in its piercing sadness, Aeneas's cry of anguish over the horror, the pity of it – *o patria o divum domus Ilium!*

Or what could be more Virgilian than the scene in Act II where Hector, 'recalled to life by the will of the gods', appears before Aeneas and lays upon him his sacred mission, then sinks back to nothingness, his task accomplished – the apparition materializing to the sound of stopped horns groping from note to note, accompanied by pizzicato strings, then uttering its message on the successive notes of a falling chromatic scale above a dim fabric of divided cellos and basses, with occasional interventions from the trombones, at once nightmarish and majestic; Aeneas staring and motionless, except for a sudden lurch in the orchestra, like a missed heartbeat, at the words – the most terrible in the *Aeneid* – *hostis habet muros*: 'the enemy's within our walls (2.290)'. In the orchestral prelude to the same act the very sound and feel of Virgil's lines are reproduced in the rhythm, texture, colour and harmonic movement of the music – *clarescunt sonitus armorumque ingruit horror* (The noise grew clearer and the roar of battle swelled, 2.301): war and rumours of war, the hideous confusion of battle. Again, how true to Virgil are the music's insights into the effect of war and the great national enterprises born of war on the ordinary human being – poignant in the case of the Palinurus-like figure of the young sailor Hylas, eaten with nostalgia for the homeland he will never see again; humorous in the case of the two grumbling sentries who would like to stay in Carthage and have done with the whole senseless idea of Italy; tragic in the case of Andromache, whose grief, though it pales before the cataclysm to come, remains the ultimate comment on the misery of war. How deeply Berlioz has absorbed the example of the humanity of the *Aeneid* – those little touches that mark Virgil out among ancient writers, like the picture of the women and children waiting in a long line beside the piled-up loot in the courtyard of Priam's blazing palace (2.765f). Such sudden shifts of viewpoint give a new dimension to the epic, in Berlioz's music as in Virgil's verse.

Dramatic effects of sharply contrasted colours, textures and rhythms are another common feature of the two works. The moment in Book

1 when the magic cloak shrouding Aeneas is stripped away to reveal him in all his glory (1.586ff) is paralleled by the sudden change that occurs in the music when Aeneas throws off his sailor's cloak and steps forward in shining armour. Acts I and II of *Les Troyens* mirror Book 2 of the *Aeneid* in their alternation of light and dark, their evocation of flaring light amid surrounding blackness – the doomed splendour of the great processional entry of the Horse through the torchlit darkness, the smoky glare, in the opening music of the scene of the Trojan women, shot through with gleams of martial trumpets. The feeling we experience in the opera when the harsh, possessed sound of Berlioz's Troy gives way to the lyrical and sensuous sound of his Carthage is just such as we experience in Book 1 of the poem when Virgil cuts abruptly from the clangorous description of the frescoes depicting the Trojan War in the temple of Juno to the delicate and luminous vision of Dido making her way through the throng, attended by young courtiers (1.456ff, then 496ff).

The criticism sometimes heard of Act III, that the lengthy ceremonies in which Carthage celebrates its first seven years are a distraction from the main business of the drama and a concession to Meyerbeerian grand opera, is in effect a criticism of a too close fidelity to Virgil, for the plan of the opening scenes of the act is inspired by the intensely vital and brilliant first impression of Carthage that we receive in Book 1. Berlioz's purpose in following Virgil, however, is a dramatic one, being both to provide an interval of repose after the concentrated fury of Act II and to emphasize the rising star of the new city so that the tragedy of its fall may be fully felt. To this end, and perhaps also borrowing an idea from Book 7 (the picture of Latium as a kingdom of Saturn, still enjoying the blessings of the golden age), he has made his Carthage something of a matriarchal Garden of Eden, absorbed in the beneficent work of building and cultivation, fearful of the enemies surrounding it, yet defenceless until saved by the hero who is destined to be its destroyer (the limping, melancholy strains of the Trojan March in the minor mode telling not only of Trojan sufferings endured but of Carthaginian disasters to come). But in his development of this gentle pastoral state the composer is, as always, the disciple of the poet – especially the poet of the *Georgics*, who is heard through the mouth of the bard Iopas. In the *Aeneid* Iopas sings of the elements and the movement of the stars (1.742ff), but in *Les Troyens* of the shepherd and the farmworker and the fruits of the well-tilled earth.

In this fourth act, set in Dido's gardens at night within sound of the sleeping sea, Berlioz matches Virgil's mastery of verbal magic in music beneath whose beauties lies the same sense of the pathos of life and the brevity of human happiness. Yet the fifth and final act is in some ways the most profoundly Virgilian of all, both in its heroic sweep and in its classicism: on the one hand the great arches of extended melody in Aeneas's *scena* – the huge stride of the vocal line above the surge and stress of the orchestra, the powerful swing of the rhythmic movement between agitation and serene exaltation; on the other hand the simplicity of Dido's grief. In response to the tragic dénouement of Book 4 Berlioz strips his art to an extraordinary economy of gesture. One thinks of the gentle swell of the sea cradling Hylas to a death-like sleep; the two-note semitone figure which suggests Aeneas rocking to and fro in the anguish of his indecision; the brief shudder in the strings, like a premonition of a life escaping into air (*in ventos vita recessit*, 4.705), that abruptly breaks the trancelike calm of Dido's first words from the pyre; the bareness of the vocal line a moment earlier as Dido, speaking as if in a dream, gives the order for the last rites to begin – a passage whose broken phrases and slow chromatic descent through an octave recall the music of Hector's prophecy which was to be the cause of her grief. (Virgil would have recognized here a poetic device of his own, whereby resonances are set up between pairs of similar or ironically contrasted incidents located in different parts of the epic.) While at work on Dido's recitative 'Je vais mourir', Berlioz wrote of his conviction that the music he was composing had a 'heart-rending truthfulness'. What is even more remarkable is the sense of a calm beyond suffering that he achieves in the aria, 'Adieu, fière cité' (*urbem praeclaram statui*, 4.655), which succeeds the torment of the recitative. Nothing in music is more expressive of utter finality than the aria's concluding bars – the voice dying away, a last flicker of agony (the cor anglais's flattened sixth), then a mysterious peace, with a rustle of pianissimo strings and, on trombones, the quiet beat of the rhythmic motif of destiny, stilled in a cadence of such purity and simplicity that the silence which follows is almost palpable: there is nothing more to be said. Dido accepts her fate.

In the tragic climate of the ancients, redemption is neither demanded nor expected. Alone among Romantic dramatists, Berlioz was able to re-create it because it was his own imaginative world. It had become his natural element. The memory of the emotional shock that Dido's death had been to him, forty years before, and of all that had followed in his adolescent imaginative life, remained with him, fresh and undiminished. To it was added long experience as a composer of dramatic music and a capacity for feeling, for pain, for regret, that life had sharpened to a fine point. He had been waiting for this. His musical style, with its long flexible melodic line and its use of timbre and rhythm as subtly varied means of poetic expression, was ideally suited to the task. So was his temperament. The call of Virgil's heroic world was irresistible. A concept of human existence as it might once have been in some possible dream of a golden age took root in boyhood and grew till it possessed his mind. The Virgilian vision – a vision of grandeur without illusions, of destruction lying in wait outside and within man, and life lived subject to the will of implacable fate but, while it lasts, lived fully and ungrudgingly even in the shadow of doom – answered his deepest longings. It is this heroic outlook that is exemplified in the ardent, exalted music to which Aeneas, drunk with his mission, already part of history, apostrophizes Dido in sublime farewell, before turning to embrace his fate and the knowledge of his death – the same mood that is expressed in Hecuba's proud prophecy in the last scene of *The Trojan Women*:

> We sacrificed in vain. Yet if the god had not seized this city and trampled it beneath the earth, we should have disappeared without trace: we would not have given a theme for music and the songs of men to come.

# 7 *Les Troyens as 'grand opera'*

**IAN KEMP**

The story of *Les Troyens* is powerful, spacious, uncluttered, straightforward. As such, it shows how skilfully Berlioz adapted the complex techniques of Virgil to suit the needs of a libretto. He preserved the spirit and essentials of the *Aeneid*, as well as countless details, but boldly cut, selected from, added to and altered, in order to fashion a five-act whole in which each act has a controlled exposition of character and event and each leads to a dramatic finale: there are no Virgilian narrations or flashbacks (or flashforwards). This broad design was of course typical of works written for the Paris Opéra in the heyday of 'grand opera'.[1]

It might be thought that the commercialized opportunism of that place, the artistic compromises it extorted and the wounding treatment it had meted out to Berlioz personally, would have made him contemptuous of everything to do with it. Yet, as with any French composer of the period, the Opéra was in his blood. He had gained some of his most lasting musical experiences there and he never ceased to be fascinated by what might be done with its lavish resources. The scale of his conception of *Les Troyens* was entirely in accord with the scale of things at the Opéra. Since Berlioz was an intensely practical composer, the restraints and demands of an opera house, the Opéra in particular, meant that he had no desire to effect a radical transformation of the genre of opera, as he had done with that of symphony, for example. On the contrary, they were a stimulus to him. While he transcended them in such a way that it seems the Opéra was created for *Les Troyens* rather than vice versa, it remains true that he relished deploying the massive forces and obligatory theatrical effects expected of an opera composer. They were appropriate to his subject, and experience as composer and as critic had taught him how to use them. Consideration of *Les Troyens* as grand opera may take as its starting-point Berlioz's reworking of those features hallowed by tradition and contemporary practice and typical of the genre. They may conveniently be divided into three categories: the more subtly theatrical, the more obviously theatrical and the spectacularly so.

In the first category, there are the off-stage effects – as in the Act I finale or the *Chasse royale* (cf. the off-stage Alpine horns in Rossini's *Guillaume Tell*); the vision scenes – as in Aeneas's visions of the ghost of Hector in Act I and of the ghosts of the four Trojans in Act IV (cf. the 'Scène des spectres' in Act IV of Halévy's *Charles VI*) or in Dido's vision of Rome (cf. Marcel's vision of the Protestants in Act V of Meyerbeer's *Les Huguenots*); and the use of colourful orchestral combinations and of solo or unusual instruments – as in the Dance of the Nubian Slaves (piccolo, flute and cor anglais an octave apart, antique cymbals, *tarbuka* and *tambourin*, all violins in unison *arco*, violas and cellos in unison *pizzicato*), the solo clarinet in the Andromache scene and solo horn in Aeneas's Act V *Air*, or the saxhorns in the Act I finale (parallel instances are given on p. 97).

Expectations of the more obviously theatrical features of grand opera can be narrowed down to the processional chorus scene and to ballet. Berlioz duly incorporates the most familiar types of chorus scene – the ceremonial-religious, as in the Act I prayer to the gods, the Act I finale or the Act V funereal ceremony (cf. the coronation scene in Act IV of Meyerbeer's *Le Prophète*), and the chorus of acclamation, as in the Act III Carthaginian National Anthem (cf. the 'Chœur triomphale', 'Gloire à la reine', in Act IV of Halévy's *La Reine de Chypre*). In the process he writes not only for a large chorus but also for double chorus (Act I octet and finale, Act III anthem), a characteristic feature at the Opéra, whose chorus-singers numbered about eighty. The *corps de ballet* was even larger, its appearance equally obligatory. Berlioz's ballets accommodate the taste for the characteristic, as in the Act I Trojan dances (cf. the Neapolitan dances in Auber's *La Muette de Portici*), and the exotic, as in the Act IV ballets (cf. contemporary opéras-comiques such as David's *La Perle du Brézil*). They are neatly absorbed into the scenario and prevented from becoming obtrusive by the occasional substitution of *entrées*, as in the Act III distribution of rewards, and, notably, by pantomime, as in the Andromache scene and the *Chasse royale*. Pantomime is a feature stretching back to classical French opera, as in Act II of Gluck's *Iphigénie en Tauride* (when Oreste in a dream sequence is tormented by the Eumenides and the ghost of Clytemnestra) or in Act IV of Le Sueur's *Les Bardes* (when Ossian also in a dream sequence is encouraged by the old heroes and bards).

In nineteenth-century French opera mime could, of course, if the scenario required it, be included in the ballets proper – as in the nuns' seduction of Robert in the Act III ballets of Meyerbeer's *Robert le Diable*. But in general the genres were kept distinct. The most famous example of pantomime is in *La Muette de Portici*, whose heroine, Fenella, communicates entirely in mime. Despite these precedents Berlioz's use of pantomime is markedly individual. That in the Andromache scene reveals his classical roots but in fact owes as much to contemporary theatre as to the opera house; and the *Chasse royale* so extends the boundaries of the genre that Berlioz nearly parts company with it altogether.

The spectacular or *merveilleux*, a feature typical of French opera from its beginnings, when it was associated with the supernatural, was given a fresh and realistic slant in the nineteenth century, especially in final scenes, by such composers as Spontini (*La Vestale*: a flash of lightning), Auber (*La Muette de Portici*: Vesuvius erupting), Halévy (*La Juive*: the heroine burnt in boiling oil) and Meyerbeer (*Les Huguenots*: a miniature massacre; *Le Prophète*: the explosion of a powder magazine). Berlioz certainly provides a substantial quota of the spectacular. Apart from the scenes of the wooden horse, the suicide of the Trojan women, the suicide of Dido and the final vision of Rome, there is the *Chasse royale*, the most original of such scenes and, if Berlioz's stage directions are followed, one which can claim to be the most spectacular of all. This scene also contains horses, a feature dating back to Spontini's *Fernand Cortez* (and to Book 4 of the *Aeneid*).

These parallels with the common currency of grand opera are at once so obvious as to be superficial and so integrated with the course of the work as to be inconspicuous. They reflect Berlioz's pragmatism, maybe, or his natural inclination to belong to the environment he lived in. Whether they reflect a genuine artistic identity with contemporary composers or complete indifference can only be understood with a wider knowledge of the genre itself. It is perhaps too easy to assume that Berlioz's guarded approval of contemporary grand operas concealed disdain. What *was* grand opera? Why did it develop? What were its characteristics? What were its innovations? In the next chapter of this book David Charlton re-examines these questions and makes an assessment of *Les Troyens* as grand opera more feasible, if no more clear-cut.

In some ways his chapter reinforces *Les Troyens*'s relationship with grand opera. All the musical features of the genre, listed on p. 96, are present in it, though to a much more sophisticated degree. Preoccupation with historical authenticity (local colour), in order to make the human predicaments more vivid, is also in evidence, as can be seen in Berlioz's stage directions, his use of antique instruments, such musical techniques as the invented 'Trojan' scale in the Act II scene of the wailing women, and in countless details of the libretto, not to mention his enlisting of Flaubert to help with the design of the costumes (he had read *Salammbô*, set in Carthage, a year before the première of *Les Troyens à Carthage*). And the work abounds in 'Romantic' contrasts. Charlton has pointed out that the most striking of these, that between the Trojan and the Carthaginian acts, has a precedent in the contrast (much admired by Wagner[2]) between the Venetian and the Cypriot acts of Halévy's *La Reine de Chypre*. In his review of the opera in the *Débats* of 26 December 1841 Berlioz made no mention of the effect (Venice and Cyprus carried his thoughts to *Othello* instead), though of course it could have been merely one of several a composer would naturally store in his mind for future and better use. It has been suggested that another such, the final scene from Rossini's *Le Siège de Corinthe*, in which the Greek princess Pamyra, surrounded by her women, commits suicide during the sack of Corinth rather than fall victim to the Turks, was Berlioz's model for the finale of Act II of *Les Troyens*.[3]

By reverting to classical subject matter, Berlioz was certainly and pointedly setting himself against the mainstream. In this respect he was ranging himself with Gluck, whose plots are drawn largely from Greek mythology, and Spontini, whose *La Vestale* is set in ancient Rome, rather than with such composers as Auber, Halévy and Meyerbeer, whose plots are based on actual and much more recent historical events. All the same, an essential motif in Berlioz's scenario re-establishes the parallels. The librettos of Scribe, grand opera's chief librettist, typically portray conflict between rival social and political interests, not without contemporary resonance, whose consequences are intertwined with the resulting tragedies of his principal characters; in *Les Troyens* there is a similar intertwining of Graeco-Trojan and then Carthaginian–Trojan conflicts with the tragedies of Cassandra and Dido. What, in the Second French Empire, might be made of an opera recounting the sacrifice of two noble individuals in the interests of the future Roman Empire? Interpreted in this way, *Les Troyens* is less remote from contemporary practice than its classical subject might suggest; had it been staged in the aftermath of the attempted assassination of Napoleon III in January 1858, which greatly strengthened the imperial position, it might even have been credited with topicality. In addition, its grand historical sweep and epic character link it with one of the most influential forerunners of grand opera, *Fernand Cortez*, and a return to the imperial tone of that opera could reasonably have set a model for opera in the Second Empire. Spontini's librettist, Étienne de Jouy, writing in the First Empire, could confidently assert: 'French grand opera has, to say the least, a greater rapport with epic than with tragedy.'[4] Berlioz could well have been content with an ironic endorsement of that. But of course he never found himself needing to be so.

In any case, it can be seen that despite its manifest, if ambiguous relationship with grand opera, *Les Troyens* is not really typical of the genre. This is due not so much to its classical subject or its ambivalent political resonance, nor even to its covenant with the supernatural, an element excluded from historical grand opera, where events are determined by human hand. It is due first to its dramaturgy, which is fundamentally different from the norm. There is no plotting and scheming, no artful engineering of dramatic tension, no intricate patterning of relationships (Berlioz's principal baritone is dispensed with as early as Act II), no unexpected twist. Instead, a simple but highly-charged story is acted out against the inexorable tread of history, fate, destiny. Berlioz was re-creating Virgil: that was enough for him. To betray Virgil would have been tantamount to betraying everything that was sacred to him: his belief in the transcendent power of love and in man's intimations of beauty, kindness and trust; his contempt for man's folly, treachery, cruelty and blindness to knowledge; his passionate agnosticism in the face of the inexplicable behaviour of the gods (or God) who so abuse their evident ability to control man's destiny; his faith in those feelings and experiences of his own youth which had given and continued to give absolute proof of the validity of his creative imagination; his devotion and respect towards those creative artists who had illumined his understanding, Shakespeare, Gluck, Beethoven – and Virgil. Berlioz put his whole self into *Les Troyens*. As for grand opera, he took what he wanted from it and then with enlarged dramatic resource proceeded to give shape to his own vision in his own way. His opera may, paradoxically, be accounted the finest example of the genre, throwing its contemporaries into the shade. But all these considerations are swallowed up in the crucial fact that everything making up Berlioz's musical personality is fused in this one work, a tribute from one creative artist to another. The uniqueness of *Les Troyens* flows from that.

# 8 *On the nature of 'grand opera'*

DAVID CHARLTON

The Paris Opéra, that temple of art at whose 'solemn ceremonies' Berlioz the student so diligently worshipped, was also the setting conceived by the mature composer for his *Les Troyens*. Even in 1821, when he first attended the Opéra, Berlioz's sensitivity towards acting, scenery, music and dramatic truth was acute, and his experiences there over the next forty years enabled him, as he tells us in his *Memoirs*, to 'calculate' the effects he needed for his opera. These experiences coincided almost exactly with the period, from around 1825 to c.1865, which saw the rise and decline (though not expiry) of an operatic type that was created at and for the Paris Opéra, and which had a universal influence on the art form: the so-called 'grand opera'. The following pages provide a historical enquiry into what this was.

The Parisian phase between 1822 and 1831 was vital in respect of its politics, the evolution of French romanticism and the evolution of opera. These three spheres of action, in fact, were rather closely interrelated; certainly 'grand opera' as an outcome was dependent upon both other factors. The reign of King Charles X (1824–30) politically strengthened the Church and aristocracy, resulting in the inevitable growth of liberal opposition. Newspapers and journals took positions; artists and intellectuals grouped in chiefly liberal associations: it was the period known as 'la bataille romantique'. In 1827 the King found himself obliged to retrace a few steps and relax press censorship. This coincided with the emergence of several fictional works featuring the seventeenth-century revolutionary hero, Masaniello. One was to become the prototype of grand opera – *La Muette de Portici*, with libretto by Scribe and music by Auber, first seen at the Opéra on 19 February 1828. (Another was Carafa's *drame lyrique*, *Mazaniello*, 1827.) Although Eugène Scribe was not destined to be the only librettist of grand opera, he did remain its most sought-after practitioner (by Verdi, for example, who set *Les Vêpres siciliennes*, and even by Berlioz, who began though later gave up setting the gothic melodrama *La Nonne sanglante*, which eventually found its way to Gounod). Scribe wrote the librettos for all four of Meyerbeer's grand operas.

The Paris Opéra was and remains a bastion of the Establishment (although the building itself has changed, that from 1821 in the rue Le Peletier being destroyed by fire in 1873 and replaced in 1875 by the present Opéra, the Palais Garnier). It had mounted a string of pro-monarchist works in the 1820s. But it was gradually forced to take account of new theatrical concepts, simply because Romantically-inclined innovations were attracting audiences elsewhere. Theatres like the Porte-St-Martin and the Ambigu were creating stage settings that were spectacularly realistic, used different levels and new lighting techniques, and through which characters could walk: they thus created a conceptual unity between eye and mind in the spectator.[1] Such techniques were pioneered by P. L. C. Cicéri together with the future pioneer of the 'diorama' and of photography, L. J. M. Daguerre.[2] Some account began to be taken of historical and architectural accuracy in their work, notably in monuments of the Middle Ages. The Opéra became conscious of shortcomings in its décors, in the anachronistic design of its costumes and properties, and the absence of co-ordination between the various disciplines that together should make opera a 'unity of the arts'.[3] (The early 1820s saw Weber's innovations to promote this same ideal in Dresden.) Thus a staging committee (the *Comité de mises en scène*) was set up in April 1827, whose eleven members included the composer Rossini and the architect-designer Edmond Duponchel. In 1828 a staging manager was appointed: he (Solomé) began the long tradition of publishing production accounts of grand operas. Such accounts obviously stress that very unity of detail – sets, production moves, bar-by-bar musical effects, etc. – which became typical of grand opera, but which is today universally disregarded.[4]

Priorities did change. Traditionally the Opéra had spent more on costumes than on scenery, indeed re-used old scenery where possible, as in *La Muette de Portici*. But Rossini's *Guillaume Tell* (1829) had entirely new sets, while Meyerbeer's first Paris opera, *Robert le Diable* (1831) now had more spent on scenery than costumes: over 37,000 francs.[5] It was this work that marked the birth of grand opera in the sense of something created and perceived as a phenomenal totality; it was described as such by Berlioz's former teacher, J. F. Le Sueur, in a letter to Meyerbeer of 24 November 1831:

. . .it is so true that [this] theatrical music gives pacing, movement and life to all the details of a great dramatic event, just as it does to all the other arts that are united with it . . .Your great singers, also perfect actors; your energetic and assured choruses; your wonderful miming actors and dancers; your superb orchestra, and your picturesque décors which correspond to them: all, through their closely-woven unity, by their amazing ensemble, have, last Monday, so to speak surpassed perfection itself. . .

As for the visual and the spectacular, political history soon saw to their maintained priority. The new government of the 'bourgeois monarch', Louis-Philippe (1830–48), decreed that the (state-run) Opéra should return to a system of entrepreneurship in order to cut down excessive financial losses. The man who bought control of the Opéra was a doctor and pioneer of patent medicine, Louis Véron. From 1831 to 1835 he pursued a policy of buying in the best talent and marketing the most attractive operatic products with suitable managerial efficiency.[6] Thus some of the most spectacular massed effects of grand opera date from this period, involving about eighty chorus members, extras, dancers, child actors and sixty *machinistes* for shifting the sets about. Higher artistic ideals readily became corrupted in this atmosphere, but we do not detect official recognition of a decadence until 1854, when a report was highly critical of recent examples of 'superficial attractions of noisy passions' and 'the charlatanism of forced expression'.[7] One culprit was probably Gounod's *La Nonne sanglante* of the same year. The *Revue et gazette musicale de Paris* commented: 'Opera librettos are decidedly on the decline. . .and *La Nonne sanglante* is there to prove the fact.' However, it is certainly wrong to dismiss Scribe as a mere hack: artists and public alike acknowledged his ability to use the physical resources of grand opera to maximum and apposite dramatic advantage. And Scribe, if overworked, was compliant up to a point in coping with the habitual alterations demanded by composers, especially Meyerbeer, in the course of a work's completion.

Definitions of grand opera are inadequate if limited to purely external features or to purely musical formal ones; both must be considered. External features are roughly as follows: use of four- or five-act structure (as in the Baroque; Gluck and Spontini, for example, had favoured three-act librettos); incorporation of one or more ballet sequences, though in any act and at any suitable juncture; a spectacular final scene either with or without use of stage machinery; use of visual media for local colour, historical or otherwise; a different stage setting for each act, or even each scene. (Some operas, *La Muette de Portici* included, used alternate sites of action in order to articulate a basic dramatic point.)

Certain purely musical traits may also be identified. Karin Pendle mentions that Scribe's first and last acts mostly 'begin and end with large scenes featuring soloists with one or more choruses'.[8] Often the inner acts do the same. She also mentions that solo items in strophic (verse) form, such as *ballades* or *couplets*, gradually became scarce over the years. The chorus as an entity was vital to grand opera, becoming almost a character (or characters) in itself: it existed as a dramatic as well as a musical force, coming to the fore in tableaux, processions or festivals. It was frequently combined with principal singers in ensemble scenes. An easily-overlooked point is that the duet superseded the solo as the basic musico-dramatic unit. Duets could contain almost any amount of action in forwarding the plot, or none; and for all its large dimensions, grand opera placed a premium on the presentation of action. Concerning purely musical form, the standard outlines of ABA′ or Italianate A (slow) B (fast) can often be found; but these are frequently disguised (especially by Meyerbeer) as a result of manipulation of pacing for dramatic purposes. Concomitantly, the linking segments of grand opera were handled with increasing flexibility: while Halévy's *La Juive* (Scribe, 1835), for example, contains relatively old-fashioned recitatives, the same composer was writing fluid, arioso-like passages for the equivalent sections of, say, *La Reine de Chypre* (C. and G. Delavigne, 1841).

Both opéra-comique and recitative opera made use of new instruments in this period and, not infrequently, of stage bands. Stage bands dated back at the Opéra to Act I of Spontini's *La Vestale* (1807), with twin parts for flutes, oboes, clarinets, horns, trumpets and bassoons – Simon Mayr, incidentally, had already put a small band on stage in *Zamori* (Piacenza, 1804). This tradition, most familiar today perhaps from *Aida*, involved increasing numbers of instruments; the coronation scene of Meyerbeer's *Le Prophète* (1849) uses a stage band including eighteen saxhorns, sometimes in antiphony with the pit orchestra. Less common instruments such as the organ, tuned bells, the glockenspiel, the bass clarinet and the viola d'amore were occasional visitors; the two anvils in *La Juive* proved as transient, however, as Halévy's use of the melophon (a type of accordion) in *Guido et Ginevra* (Scribe, 1838) or of the musette in *La Reine de Chypre*. Halévy included a quartet of saxophones (soprano, two tenors and bass) in the stage band for his *Le Juif errant* (1852) and a saxophone part was added by Fétis to Meyerbeer's *L'Africaine* (1865), a posthumous première, before the (alto) instrument was 'officially' heard as soloist in Thomas's *Hamlet* (1868). The harp's use (as also that of the tam-tam) was regular in grand opera: the use of both dated back to later eighteenth-century Paris Opéra works.

So much, then, for external features. We noted earlier the connection between grand opera and the French Romantic movement; now we must pursue literary matters further in order to develop additional criteria for defining types of grand opera.

Although Scribe's depiction of character on the spoken stage was unsubtle purely in itself, taking second place conceptually to the invention of situations and intrigue, in serious opera this limitation fitted fortuitously well with certain basic qualities of French Romanticism itself. That is, the Romantics in Paris placed definite importance on the role of the individual within society; they believed (to paraphrase Victor Hugo) that what was depicted in art as personal was, in reality, a reflection of what was general.

History might be their chosen field of interest. In taking great trouble to achieve documentary precision, the Romantic artist aimed to portray the human predicament more accurately in its social context, the better to reflect the anatomy of that same context. Both history and the social predicament of the individual were central to the principal type of grand opera. In writing historical opera librettos Scribe often appears to have followed certain traits in Sir Walter Scott's historical novels. These immensely influential works placed individuals in a specially active and psychologically authentic relation to a given society. Yet for all the greatness that Lukács, for example, accords Scott, it is still the case that his characterization can be called 'banal and conventional'. In a parallel manner, Scribe's characterization in his historical librettos is merely one aspect of a totality. Conventional it is, but for that same reason well fitted to mediate between the expressiveness of music and the social milieu of the particular drama.

Scribe's grand opera dramaturgy itself has been seen to reflect the vogue for Scott. It has been suggested that Scott was the root of grand operatic 'piling up of strong contrasts' and 'picturesque tableaux', because his novels were conceived as an 'effective contrasting row of historically exact, painterly, "dramatic" scenes'.[9] And there might be a comparison to be drawn between the new consumer-readers of Scott and the new consumer-audiences of Véron. However, not one French grand opera was created from a Scott source, pure and simple.

For important aspects of grand opera Scribe drew on other Romantic preoccupations: the concern with artistic contrast (in place, in scale, in tone); with local colour (historical and geographical); or with choice of themes that involve morality and religion (cf. the French Romantics' 'persistent search for an empirical, undogmatic alternative to theoretical excess'[10]).

Scribe brought to bear on grand opera, as on opéra-comique, years of experience of writing for the spoken theatre. So distinctive did his techniques become that critics have been able to formulate them as technical ingredients of the 'well-made play'. These comprise (i) a 'delayed-action plot' that relies on a supposed event before the curtain rises (cf. Sophocles's *King Oedipus*), whose implications help bring the drama to its climax through a carefully contrasted progression of successes and failures in the fortunes of the leading figure(s); (ii) a central misunderstanding or secret 'fact' revealed to the audience but not to all the characters in the play, and which bears crucially on the action; (iii) the preparation of the audience for what will occur, by scrupulous authorial attention to plot detail and motivation; and (iv) strong directional exploitation of suspense and action not only overall, but within the acts.[11] In writing opéra-comique librettos, since 1821, Scribe had found ways of synthesising musical and dramatic strokes effectively. But the path to his first recitative opera, *La Muette de Portici*, was not straightforward, as we shall see.

Let us attempt to relate grand operas before Berlioz to one another as well as to their surrounding culture. They can usefully be divided into two, the division cutting across all the above conventions equally, and also across quite celebrated works: those lacking an expression of public political interest, and those containing such an element. The division might have little significance, were it not that we find marked differences of dramatic structure between one class of opera and the other. We can understand this more clearly by first glancing at those lacking this element: they include *Robert le Diable*, *Gustave III* (Scribe and Auber, 1833); *Guido et Ginevra* and *L'Africaine*. Donizetti's *La Favorite* (1840), stemming from an Italian original, was revised by Scribe: it also basically belongs with this group. All these are set at a definite historical time, and all involve the death of one or more of the main characters. But they lack uniformity of construction: in fact only *Robert* comes near satisfying the Scribean 'well-made' criteria, relics of its *comique* origins. *Gustave III* certainly hinges on the secret of the king's lover, Amélie (wife of his chief minister, Ankastrom) but we find little audience preparation and much sense of a doom-laden, unified plot direction, culminating in the murder of Gustave during a spectacular ball scene. The tendency towards episodic structure, held together simply by a love-affair, is most apparent in *Guido et Ginevra* and *L'Africaine.* The former would not actually have been out of place serialised in a Victorian weekly. *L'Africaine* remained in essence the story of one man, Vasco da Gama, and two women: Inès (the Portuguese) and Sélika (the 'African' queen), with the added spices of a sea voyage, a love-potion, and a narcotic-induced death, for Sélika dies by consuming a leaf from the poisonous manchineel tree. Vasco's fortunes certainly fluctuate, but this opera contains the minimum of intrigue and entertains through the passing sensations in its loose panorama of events. This class of opera ought not perhaps to be termed 'grand' at all.

The other main class of 'grand' opera – its works containing an expression of public political interest – shows Scribe as influential innovator in dramaturgical terms. Analysis shows that this class contains first the factor of the *historical episode*, which acts as the framework for the 'public' element or theme; and secondly, the factor of the *private drama*, usually but not always that of love, which is set against and entwined with the historical events themselves. Since 'history' on the stage was ubiquitous, what is important here is the presence of political and social opposition, and the way the librettist makes the private dilemmas of his participants reflect and play against the simultaneous political drama. Perhaps one can go further. In *Gustave III* a husband and wife are ultimately united; in *Guido* there is a happy end; in *L'Africaine*, Vasco goes back to Europe with Inès; in *Robert*, evil is defeated and princess Isabelle wins Robert to the path of righteousness and, indeed, to marriage. These plots result in the death of a principal actor, but the life of a surviving couple. In this sense they are akin to classical period operas (e.g. by Gluck) as well as transitional works like Spontini's *Fernand Cortez* (1809). However, in the other category, mutual love is almost always doomed. Its failure, and the death of one or both parties, are produced as a result of public and historical circumstances. The latter, moreover, are consistently characterised by the opposition of two racial or political groups, one a subject group, the other a dominant one. Sometimes this involves religious opposition, but not always. The essential point seems to be not that an opera shows the natural enmity of two peoples actively at war, as for example in *Fernand Cortez* between the Spaniards and the Mexicans, or in

Rossini's *Le Siège de Corinthe* (1826) between the Turks and the Greeks. Rather, the opposition is manifest through certain moments of crisis that are generated from clashes within a given society. (For this reason, the most significant transitional work was Rossini's *Moïse et Pharaon*, 1827.) In some cases, these 'moments of crisis' are revolutionary, as in *La Muette de Portici* (the seventeenth-century uprising of Neapolitans against their Spanish masters) or Verdi's *Les Vêpres siciliennes*, which in 1855 exploited a parallel theme, the uprising of Sicilians against their Norman masters in 1282. But other cases sprang less obviously from civil conflict. In *La Juive* and Meyerbeer's *Les Huguenots* (1836), a persecuted religious minority becomes the focus of opposition at a politically sensitive moment. In *Le Prophète*, a revolutionary religious minority, the Anabaptists, attains temporary political control, only to fall victim to successful counter-revolution. In *La Reine de Chypre* the insidious power of the Venetian ruling council is only brought fully to light at the end, though its agents have controlled events from Act I. In *Charles VI* (C. and G. Delavigne and Halévy, 1843) the English are poised to take political control of Northern France but are actively repulsed off-stage at the end: division in the French ranks provides the real subject-matter. These five operas all have precise historical settings and datings. The rhetoric of battle scenes, whose vogue even before the French Revolution had persisted to the 1820s (in *Le Siège de Corinthe*, for example), gave way to subtler, internalised depictions of social ill-health.

These, then, were the 'public political interests' of grand opera proper. What of their relation to the private dilemmas of its main characters? This, it seems, is where Scribe made signal advances. In fact, we can almost see him picking his way towards a certain solution. *La Muette de Portici* was apparently initially designed as a three-act work, probably in 1825.[12] In its first known version the Spanish viceroy's son Alphonse loves the mute girl Fenella, and is loved. Social difference prevents their union and, after Alphonse's mother brings him a Spanish noblewoman to marry (late in the opera), Fenella commits suicide. There was thus neither initial nor organic connection between this tale and the revolutionary uprising of 1647. This the opera depicted with historical accuracy as being provoked by the imposition of higher taxes, and by the friendly removal of Fenella to the viceroy's palace by Alphonse's mother, an act which the Neapolitan people misconstrue.

But in the definitive opera, now in five acts, Fenella has been loved and then abandoned by Alphonse before the curtain rises. Her story becomes the emotional touch-paper for popular revolt. By developing the libretto so that Fenella is trapped between her continued love for Alphonse and her loyalty towards Masaniello, her brother, leader of his people, Scribe cemented his themes together. (Since she can love neither in the conventional operatic sense, she becomes as it were the silent spirit of popular feeling.) Further, he dramatized their interaction in a particular way in Act IV. This proved to be an enduring stroke, because it juxtaposed the 'public' and the private elements in a focal scene, using near-maximum resources of stage spectacle in a climactic build-up of ensemble, choruses and orchestra. Through revolutionary circumstance, Alphonse and his new wife Elvira find themselves sheltering, with Fenella's assent, in Masaniello's own dwelling. Out of a sense of honour, Masaniello opposes his co-revolutionaries, who want vengeance on these enemies, and lets the latter escape. At the same juncture, the common people enter to acclaim Masaniello in triumph as leader in a supremely emotive finale, though it is a climax punctured by irony. And in Act V Masaniello is defeated and dies, while his sister commits suicide by jumping from a high terrace; Vesuvius begins to erupt in the distance.[13]

The evidence is that Scribe consciously developed this type of large, pivotal scene, and achieved his greatest effects not simply by projecting an ironic relation between 'public' and private, but by welding these together more closely by means of an absolute, even shocking dramatic intersection. Amassed grand opera forces would thus gain dramatic validity through the value of the irony in each given case: this irony reflected variously on the 'public' and the private spheres. In the next-performed example, *La Juive*, Scribe adapted an old stage trick as it had been developed for some decades: the interrupted ceremony. (A notable precedent was Act I of Spontini's *Olimpie* (1819), where the build-up of stage and musical tension over many pages (Olimpie's wedding) is halted by an act of simple recognition.) The tragic heroine of *La Juive*, Rachel, has – like Fenella – been in love with an influential member of the enemy camp. She, of course, is a Jew; her lover Léopold has wooed her as a Jew also. But Léopold is actually a Christian military hero; the setting is the historical Council of Constance in 1414, convened to heal schism in the Church brought about by the spread of heretical Hussite beliefs. Religious emotions are sensitized. At the height of the Act III state ceremony for Léopold, Rachel recognises him and denounces him for the actual crime he has committed: of having relations with a Jew. In the end, though, he lives and she is executed, which focuses emotional and moral sympathy towards the Jewish minority, even though there are balancing features. Scribe's pivotal climactic scenes show that he drew strength from the most essential quality of historical Romantic drama and novel: the concept of a 'collision' between sections and classes of society, made supremely manifest through the character and fortunes of carefully selected individuals.

> In the dramatic collision [of spoken drama] individual initiative occupies the foreground. The circumstances which, as the result of a complex necessity, give rise to this initiative are indicated only in their general outlines. It is only in the collision and its consequence that the human deed is shown to be restricted and limited, to be socially and historically determined.
>
> (Georg Lukács: *The Historical Novel* (Harmondsworth 1964), p. 173)

It is self-evident that the category of grand opera we are discussing conforms to this generalization, within the limits imposed by the medium. Published modern opinions seeking to make this art polemical miss the point.[14]

The Delavigne brothers took over many of the essentials we have described in creating *La Reine de Chypre*. The opera portrays the gradual destruction of happiness as caused by the ruthless policies of the Venetian Council of Ten. Gérard de Coucy, fiancé of Caterina Cornaro (1454–1510), is displaced – without realising why – for political reasons. In Act III he follows her from Venice to Cyprus, where she is being installed as the wife of Lusignan, the ruler Venice has nominated. As the newly-married couple emerge in state from Nicosia Cathedral, Gérard goes to kill Lusignan, but is arrested. Lusignan is, however, slowly poisoned by Venetian agents for identifying with the Cypriot cause. Caterina finally leads the Cypriots to victory.

In *Charles VI* the Delavignes disrupted the ceremonial scene in which Lancaster (the future Henry V of England) is due to be declared successor to the mentally unstable Charles VI; the French king rallies himself, refuses to sign the papers, and the scene ends in chaos. But the greatest 'intersection' scene was by Scribe, in *Le Prophète*: irony, spectacle, unification of dramatic themes, even the course of history itself were distilled into a single episode. The Anabaptists are about to crown John of Leyden as son of God in Münster cathedral (it is based on events that occurred in 1534–5) when his mother, who has been travelling far and wide in search of him, recognizes him and calls out, 'My son!' It is indeed a shocking moment, but eternally effective because the multiple ironies are developed operatically: the public ceremony dramatized through the use of enormous musical forces, and the private truth through the single voice of the mother. In this case too, moral indignation is directed against the party (Anabaptist) symbolized by the ceremony.

Verdi was much inspired by grand opera of this type and in particular by the scene we have just described. He badgered Scribe into expanding *Les Vêpres siciliennes* from four to five acts, and in fact helped Scribe in the task of formulating a parallel 'intersection' scene in his own fourth act: this is where, in order to save the lives of the Sicilian patriots with whom he identifies and one of whom he loves, Henri is obliged to confess publicly during their execution ceremony that he is the son of the French governor, Montfort. And in *Don Carlos* (1867), which exists in an oblique relation to the grand opera tradition, Verdi was still concerned to compose a grand focal scene, that of the *auto-da-fé*, built on the collision of 'public' and private dilemmas.

One cannot claim that grand opera pursued moral enquiry to any great depth. But equally, one cannot dismiss it as a circus. If one might, perhaps, re-label those works containing an expression of public political interest as 'French historical opera', and see them in contrast to works like Spontini's *Fernand Cortez* or even Rossini's *Guillaume Tell* (which although obviously about an uprising, nevertheless does not place the Swiss principals in any sustained position of ambiguity), then one could acknowledge that such works do differ morally from earlier historical operas. Earlier works present history as a straightforwardly closed book, whether in background or foreground. Grand opera with a public political interest, however, comments upon history, repeatedly, through the dramatization of opposition groups acting within a given society. The illusion is created, by the usual suspension of disbelief in the theatre, that history could have been different. Thus the spectator must consider why it was not different, and can analyse history as something in the making. The processes of power themselves are under scrutiny.

The concern with 'process', of course, makes 'French historical opera' an equivalent of the historical novel as developed by Scott. It also helps to explain why Wagner treated the mythic Nibelung material in the way that he did. Subsequent directions in works for the Paris Opéra were to spring from new literary sources: Shakespeare, *Faust*, the classical poetess Sappho in Gounod's eponymous opera (1851). But it ought not to be overlooked that Scribe's influence remained potent into the era of *Les Troyens* and beyond into the 1880s, e.g. Massenet's *Hérodiade* and Saint-Saëns's *Henry VIII*.

# 9 *The unity of* Les Troyens

**IAN KEMP**

The most plausible reason why Virgil's influence on Berlioz was so deep-rooted is that it was Virgil who had introduced him, at the age of twelve, to Dido; and it was the fate of Dido which transfigured the boy's hopeless love for the eighteen-year-old Estelle and enabled him to contain it. Berlioz was not special in falling in love so young. But he certainly was in drawing such nourishment from the experience. The story of Dido affected him for the rest of his working life; it was only when *Les Troyens à Carthage* had been performed, that is, when he finally had paid proper homage to her shade, that he could lift the veil over Estelle and enter into that profoundly moving relationship with her in his old age. In the interim Dido was rarely far from his thoughts. His own copy of the *Aeneid* (now in the Bibliothèque de l'Opéra in Paris) bears witness to what became almost an obsession. He never wrote in his copy or made marginal annotations, but he did fold over the top corners of pages he wanted to refer to. Many pages are folded in this way but none so often as that describing the death of Dido. Dido must have represented to Berlioz everything a woman could be: beautiful, courageous, wise, generous, inspiring, compassionate – and passionate, which made the terrible outcome of her passion so agonizing to behold. In fact, his conception was a 'Romantic' one. To Virgil's contemporaries Dido was less than admirable – *infelix*, which meant not unhappy but unfruitful, and thus an affront to her nature; in addition she had ugly dealings with the black arts. This part of her Berlioz ignored. He created an ideal. All the same it is the humanity and vividness of that ideal which strikes us now. It is easy to understand Berlioz's excitement at making his Dido take on flesh and blood, actually be there on the stage in front of him and experience all the delights and torments he knew were hers. Easy too to understand his excitement at making the context come alive. He had lived in this imaginative world for forty years and recreated its grandeur and its tiny details with loving fidelity. Here *are* the palaces of Priam and Dido, the rivers of Troy, the African forest, Aeneas's helmet, Helen's veil, even the bare foot of Dido – and the wooden horse. It is all there. But Berlioz's focus remains on his characters. He knew Virgil's characters so well, he wrote, that he felt they must have known him.

If Aeneas did not engage his sympathies to quite the same degree as Dido this did not mean that he was indifferent to him. Aeneas's heroic moments are as powerful as any in the opera and his separation from Dido draws from Berlioz an anguish of soul so acute (far more than in the *Aeneid*) that it is difficult to escape the impression that Berlioz is here drawing on his own experience of wretchedness when separating from Harriet Smithson. Aeneas must go, return to what is necessarily a less prominent role in Berlioz's drama, for he is the one principal character who does not rebel against the brutal machinery of religion and state (though only just) and who therefore retreats into that relentless movement of 'history' which gives the drama its momentum and which forms its lowering background. Another reason for Berlioz's treatment of Aeneas is simply that he is a foil to, and a link between Dido and Cassandra.

Cassandra, a character vividly sketched out by Virgil, is made into a real, complete and believable human being only through the power of Berlioz's creative imagination. He might have drawn a little from the pathos of Creusa in the *Aeneid*, far less from the fearful portraits in the *Agamemnon* and the *Trojan Women*, certainly nothing from the caricature in *Troilus and Cressida*. He really had to invent her himself. No doubt this was because, in the opening acts, he needed a counterpart to Dido – someone of comparative but not pre-emptive strength, a kind of dark reflection who sees only dread, whose single-minded obsession contrasts with an absorption in everything, who also has a hopeless love but who experiences none of its joys, who tells her lover to go rather than stay; but with the twist that at the end it is Dido who is the dark reflection, for her prescience is blind rather than true and her suicide despairing rather than honourable. Another reason for the creation of Cassandra may be detected, which is that through her Berlioz projected a kind of self-portrait: the passionate prophet with god-given messages who was always spurned but who, actually, was right. He identified with her almost as intensely as with Dido, and eventually more so, for the prophecies of his Cassandra were not even uttered: 'Oh my noble Cassandra, my heroic virgin, I must then resign myself: I shall never hear you.'[1]

Berlioz's personal involvement with his characters ensures that they are not symbols or types but living individuals. It also accounts for the care and sheer labour he expended on a project whose outcome was at best uncertain. Too close an involvement however brings its dangers. Of these Berlioz was well aware. 'That is not good. One must try to do fiery things coolly.' What he meant by this is explained in part by an earlier comment in the same letter (see p. 50). 'The hardest task is to find the musical *form*, this form without which music does not exist, or is only the craven servant of speech.' Tantalizingly, he left no record of precisely which form or forms he found for *Les Troyens*, nor of how he approached the problem of giving shape to such an enormous canvas. But the example of Virgil, and of Shakespeare (Berlioz was insistent that his opera was 'Virgil Shakespeareanized'), as well as the formal integrity of the work itself can go some way towards understanding what his reasoning might have been.

The *Aeneid* is an epic, an incomplete but nevertheless vast part of an even more vast historical narrative whose beginnings are lost in the mists of time and whose ending is unknown. How could Virgil have treated his narrative other than by, as it were, slicing a representative chunk out of it, beginning *in medias res*, as Horace noted of the *Iliad*, and, rather than concluding, stopping abruptly, on an 'unresolved discord'?[2] Berlioz follows this tradition by plunging straight away into the middle of things – into his opening chorus of frenzied Trojans. This was a bold and indeed unprecedented tactic,[3] even if it was not so radical as that in, for example, Méhul's *Uthal* of 1806 or, especially, in Gluck's *Iphigénie en Tauride* of 1779. *Uthal*'s 'overture' depicts a calm and a storm (which in fact bears some resemblance to Berlioz's own *Orage*), includes a part for the principal soprano and ends on an imperfect cadence in a new key. The beginning of Gluck's opera also depicts a calm and a storm, the principal soprano entering in the midst of the tumult with an impassioned arioso, the scene then continuing imperceptibly into the rest of the act – a rejection of formalities and a revolutionary emphasis on dramatic truth which Berlioz greatly admired but did not emulate. He simply cut the overture out. Otherwise his sequence of opening chorus followed by aria is perfectly traditional. The reason he gave himself for his novel opening (see p. 51) was that he wanted to reserve the strings for Cassandra's aria, a decision which necessarily eliminated an overture (which could hardly not have had strings) and postulated an opening scene scored for wind and brass only, as indeed is the case. If, therefore, he was not consciously following

Virgil, it may be suggested that his profound understanding of the poet made him do so all the same.

Berlioz's ending is not so easy to interpret, perhaps because he himself was placed in difficulties by its complex demands. He could not dismiss the tragedy of Dido too brusquely, since that was the real, the human ending of the opera. But neither could he renege on his, and Virgil's, overriding theme of the fate-driven Trojans eventually triumphing in Roman grandeur. The question here was what tone to adopt. It is in the nature of epics that however affecting the individual episodes, everything ultimately is subordinate to the greater power of fate, or of the gods, benevolent or malevolent as the case may be. For Berlioz it was usually the latter, and continual dicing with the caprice of the gods was for him an unavoidable fact of existence. Yet, in the epilogue of his original finale (see p. 64), he apostrophizes their purpose, without a hint of irony or of the misery and brutality that has brought it about. He allows the passing of Time to dull the memory of Dido and then sets out his vision of a resplendent Rome and of various of its luminaries, accompanied by the full and unequivocally triumphant strains of the Trojan March. Of course Virgil had written the *Aeneid* with the same object in mind; but he had been less sure of the justice of it. He slips in his own vision of the future grandeur of Rome in an extended parenthesis (8.608–731) and his ending is of Aeneas effecting a nasty killing of his not ignoble rival Turnus. Perhaps Berlioz was more forgiving by nature or perhaps, as a child of the First Empire, he responded to 'gloire' more than he cared to admit. In any event the music of the (still unperformed) original finale looks magnificent. It seems that he scrapped it not because he felt he had misinterpreted Virgil or his music was inadequate but because his apotheosis was an inflated dramatic cliché. His second finale is unconvincing musically: it is brash, unsubtle and too short. It gives the impression of being written with impatience. On the other hand Berlioz could have been attempting a more faithful recreation of Virgil, and indeed of himself, by ending on an 'unresolved discord', a music whose tone jars with the wondrous utopianism on stage or pits the grinning face of history against the individual agony of Dido. If this is so, and in order to compete with the music, the stage spectacle needs to be uncommonly powerful. The original finale is still worth performing, since it provides a more satisfying conclusion to what, after all, remains an opera. (Concerning the second finale, see also p. 149.)

Whatever Berlioz thought of the gods, he did not doubt the prudence of Virgil in making them an integral part of the scheme of things. Divine influence could not be gainsaid. As if to prove the point, he allows a fleeting appearance to Mercury (the god with whom creative artists most readily identify) and, in the original finale, to Iris, Mercury's female counterpart. But to have included Virgil's deities in any systematic way would have been to destroy the essentially human world he was creating, as well as ludicrous. Berlioz's deeply serious solution to this problem was to turn the gods into something actually more awesome than in the *Aeneid* – a purely musical presence, symbolic and abstract, insinuating itself into the fabric of the opera unpredictably yet intimately. The gods are collectively swallowed up into an idea, Virgil's *fatum*. This is an ambiguous idea, as the English equivalents of fate and destiny imply (and as Virgil himself implied, by almost always using the word in the plural, *fata*). Berlioz represents it with a complex of musical material of comparable elusiveness and diversity, the individual components of which are striking enough to act as reminders of the superhuman power they embody, but not so dominating as to deflect attention from his main focus, which remains on his characters' human predicaments. Thus it is only in Act V that the listener realizes that what is by far the most conspicuous component in this complex, the Trojan March, belongs to it at all. As the opera proceeds it acquires a much wider significance than its initial appearance in Act I would indicate: then it seemed no more than a theme (albeit a memorable one) composed specifically for the climactic procession of the wooden horse. In the Act III entry of the Trojans it functions as a kind of passport, while in Act V it is a talisman (*Tableau* 1) and finally the proud bearer of an idea – the divinely-inspired assurance of Trojan (Roman) prosperity. The theme cannot be tied down to particular stage events; it acts subliminally, at strategic points breaking surface as a sign of the idea.

The Trojan March may be said to embody *fatum* as destiny – a positive aspect of the word. Its more ominous aspect as fate is embodied in a component of Berlioz's complex that behaves in a comparable, though more far-reaching way, the theme marking the entrance of Cassandra (see Ex. 10.3A). Initially it seems that this theme is Cassandra's orchestral *Leitmotiv*; certainly it and its many transformations cluster around Cassandra when she is on stage. But later it is also associated with Mercury, and with Dido, at her moment of prophecy, and thus with more general intimations, especially of dread. Berlioz finds extraordinarily rich potential in it, generating a large number of transformations, some close, some remote, some deliberate, some perhaps accidental, which continue to echo across the opera long after Cassandra herself is dead. Ex. 9.1 illustrates the extent of these transformations. (They, along with several other motives and their transformations, are discussed in detail in Chapter 10.)

Ex. 9.1

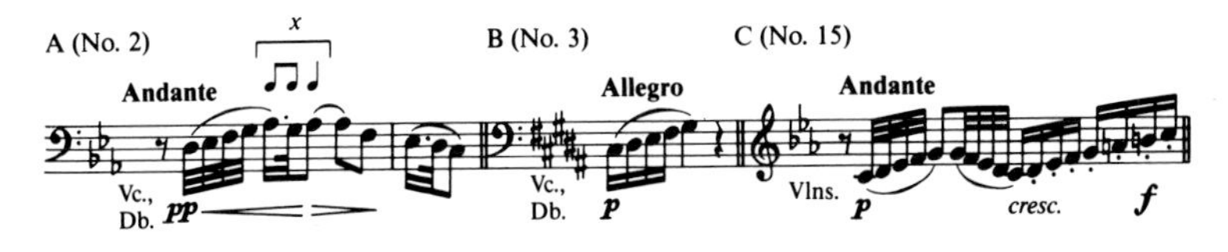


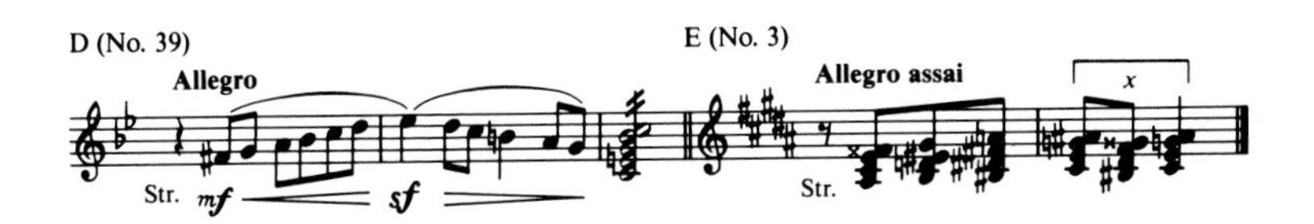


One other component embodies fate – now in its more peremptory manifestations. This is a short and usually threatening rhythmic motif, first appearing in the opening scene on the timpani as Achilles is mentioned (see Ex. 9.2A), then in Cassandra's first aria when she is thinking of Coroebus, thereafter in several other places, notably at the appearance of the ghost of Hector and the funereal ceremony just before Dido mounts the pyre. The motive is fixed in rhythm yet variable in everything else (harmony, orchestral colour, dynamic, tempo). It is also variable in context, sometimes being conspicuous, sometimes not so; and it is also capable of sudden and radical disguise, to such an extent that its identity can be totally absorbed in the general language of the opera (see Ex. 9.2B and C).

Remaining components include 'Italie', a vocal, rhythmic motif deriving from the French pronunciation of the word (and as such more a product of the libretto than the music) and a melodic motif associated with the promise of a new Troy. This latter is so much part of common currency that it might seem almost anonymous; but Berlioz's treatment makes it extremely eloquent. It first appears as Cassandra encourages the Trojan women in Act II, later in several places in Act III and eventually, with supreme dramatic irony, as Aeneas is racked between his divine mission and his love for Dido (see Ex. 10.15, p. 233).

Ex. 9.2

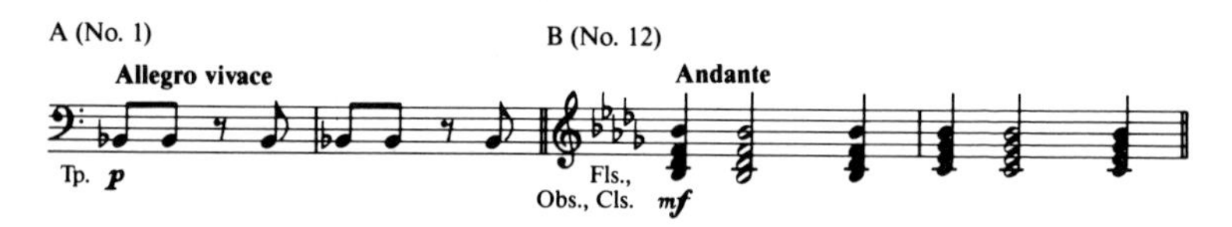

Of the other components, one of the most subtle is Berlioz's transference of the most idiosyncratic harmonic progression in the Trojan March (see Ex. 11.6, bracket) to the Septet and Duet of Act IV, where it acts as a reminder of the ineluctable pressure exerted by destiny even in moments of pure rapture. It is already clear that Berlioz's apparently arbitrary and sometimes even unconscious musical processes are in fact metaphors of their conceptual content: fate pervading the opera in an unpredictable, often obscure, appropriately protean and deliberately unschematic manner. It is as if Berlioz were admitting that the workings of the gods lie beyond the control of the human intellect. And as if by way of reward for his compositional courage, and for his piety, Berlioz gains an advantage, for in the process he finds a solution to the problem of how to unify an opera of such immensity. His *fatum* material establishes, or at least contributes to some kind of unity automatically.

It contributes to a unity of tone. But it hardly contributes to formal or structural unity, an equally important requisite in *Les Troyens*, since the re-creation of an epic brings with it an inherently episodic and even scrappy mode of progress which can result in dramatic stagnation or arbitrariness – in effect, disunity – unless the composer takes active steps to prevent it. Berlioz certainly does so, but not before he has kept faith with his epic vision and allowed himself room both to elaborate situations and, in particular, to incorporate those subsidiary episodes typical of epics. They are of course also typical of Shakespeare. In this lies the real Shakespearean inheritance, which therefore is to be measured not so much in terms of borrowing from *The Merchant of Venice* (see p. 49), or in the presence of ghosts (which had been common enough in opera before and did not need the sanction of *Hamlet* or *Richard III*), but in the mixing of genres. The predominantly exalted tone of the opera is sometimes interrupted by little scenes which sharply lower the temperature, advance the action not at all and run the risk of seeming incongruous, but which lend colour, precision, truth. The most obvious is the low-life dialogue for the two sentries in Act V, about which Berlioz wrote the following: 'In France it has been found that the mixture of tragedy and comedy in the theatre is dangerous and even indefensible – as if *Don Giovanni* wasn't an admirable example of the fine effect produced by the mixture, as if a host of plays produced daily in Paris didn't offer excellent applications of the system, as if Shakespeare had never existed.'[4] Other examples are Hylas's song, and the episode in Act II where Ascanius is too frightened of his father to wake him up. The realism of the presentation of gifts to Dido in Act III is also Shakespearean, as are especially those scenes which admit the grotesque or the supernatural, such as Aeneas's description of the devouring of Laocoön in Act I and the peculiar sounds accompanying the ghosts in Act V.

The essential (Shakespearean) outcome of these episodes is contrast, a procedure which if it can lead to disintegration can also create its own connections (one thing calls forth its opposite). Berlioz's bold use of this phenomenon is the fundamental means by which he unifies his opera, lending coherence to what after all are two separate episodes in the *Aeneid*. Thus two 'dark' Trojan acts are contrasted with two 'light' Carthaginian ones, the first two tense and claustrophobic, the second two fresh and relaxed, the final act integrating the contrasts by a form of inversion – the Trojans now in the ascendant and the Carthaginians in decline.

Within these very broad contrasts Berlioz places lesser though scarcely less significant contrasts of procedure. Act I proceeds in a sequence of isolated, self-contained scenes, without any obvious organic development within or between them. It comprises a set of 'tableaux'. It might almost be called a series of 'effects without causes' (as Wagner diagnosed the operas of Meyerbeer) and it has indeed prompted the observation that Berlioz lacked that instinctive sense of dramatic pulse of the true opera composer. To this he could have retorted that a cultivated audience would not want its causes spelt out for it. Yet, setting aside the fact that *Les Troyens* belongs to an illustrious if not well-known French operatic tradition, Berlioz certainly was interested in 'effect'; and he was deeply interested in his characters, the truthful depiction of whose fates and temperaments obliged him to present them in isolation, with little real interaction and thus in 'tableaux'.

All this misses the point however, which is that Act I is deliberately static in character so that it may be contrasted with Act II. Act I is 'static' – rather bumpy in progress and with abrupt and stark contrasts between scenes; it is long and in one *Tableau*. Act II is 'dynamic' – continuous and of a sustained increase in dramatic tension with minimal contrasts in its two, short *Tableaux*. It reflects the speed of events on that fateful night when Troy was destroyed. When Berlioz wanted his drama to move forcefully he was perfectly capable of achieving it: after all, Act I is not entirely static, for in its last ten per cent or so it gathers a momentum of its own.

The pattern is repeated in the remaining acts. Act III is static, Act V dynamic. Act IV, which functions as an enormous dramatic interlude, is both: dynamic in *Tableau* 1, static in *Tableau* 2. If Acts I and III also comprise an opposition (the one agitated, the other confident), their musical contents restore the connections. Both acts start with short choruses, both include early arias for the mezzo-soprano, duets, ballets or *pantomime* or *entrées*, ceremonial choruses, national anthems, and both give the tenor a late, unprepared but highly-charged entry. Both lead, also very late in their courses, to stirring martial finales. Similarly with Acts II and V. The two 'dynamic' *Tableaux* of Act II are, respectively, for male and female voices. The first two *Tableaux* of Act V are the same. The additional third *Tableau* is structurally a means of integrating the procedures and thus of concluding the opera.

Given the nature of Berlioz's drama these correspondences could hardly be exact: they embody what may be called interior parody technique. But they are clearly audible and their recurrent patternings create a powerful sense of interdependence between the Trojan and the Carthaginian acts. They also of course underline the division between the two. In this respect Berlioz has not yet uncovered his means of unifying the total organism. Whether he consciously applied one is not known, but the opera certainly contains perceptible evidence of a solution to this problem which both ensures unity and allows its composer freedom of action. This is a tonal design of great subtlety.

The most obvious feature of the tonality of the opera is that the Trojan March is always in B flat. It then becomes apparent that B flat is more than the tonality of the March: it represents the Trojans themselves, their fate and destiny. Its influence is at its strongest when they accept that destiny, as in Acts II and V, weakest when they veer away from it in the middle acts, or when the focus is simply not on them but on the Carthaginians, as at the beginning of Act III. Even in this latter case however the expressive meaning of B flat is so powerful that Carthaginian defiance (in No. 19) sounds like a revival of Trojan defiance.

The three collective decisions in Act I are to rush out of the city (No. 1), to give thanks to the gods (No. 4) and to bring the wooden horse into the city (No. 9). The three tonalities involved are a descending cycle of fifths: G, C, and F leading to B flat – a symbol, it may be deduced, of inexorable descent into destruction and of course, with destruction, into rebirth. The Trojans discover their destiny, symbolized by B flat, the pervasive if precarious central tonality. An extension of this process reveals that the more the Trojans lose touch with their destiny, the more the tonality sinks into the descending cycle. Thus the Trojan women in Act II sink into A flat, fate having decreed that destiny leaves them behind. As soon as the Trojans encounter the Carthaginians in Act III, the tonality again sinks, a process continued into the warm, forgetful tonalities of D flat and G flat in Act IV. In Act V Aeneas returns to B flat, while Dido's tragedy takes her back over the descending cycle again. Deliberately or not, Berlioz has created a fundamental structure of great strength and flexibility. Its main pillars, the descending cycle of fifths, support the course of the whole opera. At the same time they are strong enough to accommodate those tonal insertions which might otherwise have threatened its stability. This second consideration is of major significance, for it allows Berlioz the freedom to elaborate the tone of a scene in whichever way his creative imagination directs and, in particular, to include the digressions, parentheses and tangential scenes central to his conception.

In Ex. 9.3 the theoretical basis for this interpretation, the descending fifths, is indicated at the top by large noteheads connected by beams. Its workings are indicated underneath in the same way. (White notes represent major-key tonalities, black notes minor ones.)

Interpretation of the workings of the other tonal areas must be more speculative. The characteristic progressions of downward-moving major thirds (marked $x$ and $x^1$) form parts of major-third axes. 'Axis tonality' is a phenomenon of whose expressive effects no coherent theory has yet been developed; but it is clear that a tonal process which circles back to its starting point comprises not modu-

Ex. 9.3

ACT I
1
2
3
4
y
5
6
6a
7
8
9
10
11
x
z
x
ACT II i
12
13
ii
14
15
16
x′
ACT III
17
y
18
19
20
21
22
23
24
25
26
27
28
x
z
x
x′
x′
ACT IV i
29
ii
30
31
y
32
33
34
35
36
37
ACT V i
38
39
40
41
42
43
44
ii
45
46
47
48
iii
49
50
51
52

lation but what might be called inner revelation. As such, Berlioz's major thirds represent stages in his drama when its progress is suspended in favour of the elaboration of its content. Thus the major thirds between Nos. 1, 2 and 3 and within No. 10 represent an elaboration of the character of Cassandra, those within Nos. 19 and 27 that of Dido. The expressive difference between a progression of two major thirds and just one ($x^1$) may be said to lie in the qualitative difference in revelation between two, which is on a scale of increasing predictability, and one, which is not. Thus the effect of a single major-third progression is more dramatic, as at the entry of the Greek soldiers after the Trojan women's hymn to death in No. 16, or the introduction of Aeneas, and his return to the battle-hymn in No. 28. The difference between these downward-moving major thirds and upward-moving ones (marked *y*) results from the fact that the first are on the flat side of a tonic, the second on the sharp. Thus the second create an effect less of revelation than of outward ambition, the objective as opposed to the subjective.

Berlioz also writes minor-third axes (marked *z*), which are more closely related to their tonics and thus correspondingly less flat and less sharp. In these cases upward-moving minor thirds are on the flat side, downward on the sharp. This form of axis tonality is used when the situations are, as it were, more tight-fisted.

A final consideration is that Berlioz also chooses tonalities simply for expressive or colouristic effect, whether or not they fit into a structural scheme. The tonalities involved are those printed in small notes in Ex. 9.3. In his *Grand traité* Berlioz himself provided a list of tonal analogues which, however, apply only to the violin and have minimal relevance to *Les Troyens*: B flat, for example, is described as 'noble but without brilliance [éclat]', which hardly describes the excitement of No. 43, where violins have a prominent role, let alone the other B flat scenes, where the characteristic sound is of the combined resources. Nevertheless B flat does set up particular associations and this is even more true of those tonalities which are independent of the main tonal structure. E major (Nos. 3 and 24) suggests an otherworldly purity; B major (Nos. 3 and 28), fiery resolution; A minor (Nos. 6 and 45), grief; F major (Nos. 3, 25, 34 and 36), pastoralism. The most conspicuous use of tonality of this type occurs at the end of Act II, where Berlioz wrenches the Trojan women's hymn to death from A flat to A, that is, from determined acceptance of an appointed end to a vibrant, ecstatic identification with a world beyond death. A major means brightness and promise.

The concluding C minor is an evocation of a Beethovenian doom-laden C minor. These final minutes of Act II highlight Berlioz's ability to make tonality float, or be driven by imperatives far more powerful than itself. (On tonal associations, see also pp. 123–4.)

The foregoing sketches out the principal means by which the opera as a whole is unified and characterized. As for its individual parts, Berlioz 'finds forms' which are either adaptations of traditional models or entirely new, but which in both cases keep to his central article of faith – that music should at one and the same time uphold its own abstract logic and its capacity for expressiveness. He met these demands by conceiving forms which in themselves were metaphors of his dramatic situations. Some of them have been referred to in the Synopsis above. Chapter 11 of this book examines three further examples in greater detail, ranging from a complete *Tableau* to a Finale and then to a solo 'aria'.

# 10 *The musical structure*

JULIAN RUSHTON

## Epic and tragic aspects

Any consideration of the musical structure of *Les Troyens*[1] must be reconcilable to the obvious fact that Berlioz's huge conception is not simply a piece of music; it is an epic and tragic work designed for the theatre. It is a critical commonplace to call it epic; yet the structure of a theatrical work is more evidently conducive to the forms characteristic of tragedy, at least within the neo-classical tradition to which Berlioz must inevitably be referred. In tragedy, a narrative is presented concisely and tends to a definite conclusion. The natural structure of epic, on the other hand, is a long, discursive poem.

If one lays aside their origins in drama and poetry, the essential difference between tragic and epic rhythms lies in their handling of narrative. In epic, there is a constant authorial viewpoint; in tragedy this is lacking (for even a Greek chorus has its own viewpoint). If tragic pleasure is derived from pity and fear, inspired by direct experience of an action, epic pleasure is the exhilaration of imagined heroic deeds performed in a world theatre (in which supernatural elements are readily included, since the Greek gods, like the God of Israel, were considered to have acted in history). Neo-classical tragedy is confined within bounds of space, time, and action (the 'unities'); epic knows no bounds. Whereas both genres, in handling time, can use 'this happened next', in epic the qualification 'because' is less necessary; epic, too, can make use of 'meanwhile'. The workings of destiny are not perceived step by step but cohere in retrospect.

Despite the varieties of presentation available to it, musical drama is a distinct genre, one of whose characteristics (as Herbert Lindenberger has pointed out) is the synthesis of elements borrowed from other genres.[2] Although in Berlioz's case the way ahead from neo-classical tragedy and Virgilian epic was pointed by Shakespeare, it may be that to present epic material within a dramatic framework is in any case well within the capabilities of nineteenth-century opera; particularly when, as in *Les Troyens* or *Der Ring des Nibelungen*, the resources peculiar to opera are fully exploited. These include visual effects, integral to most types of serious opera from its inception, and the orchestra, which in the nineteenth century achieved new levels of independent expressiveness. *Les Troyens* is worked out as a theatrical action, but it demands leaps of the imagination in time and place, and like an epic it maintains our memory of one set of characters while dealing directly with another (as in the opening of Act III and the close of Act V). In the final scene Berlioz uses simultaneity, mounting scenes many miles and centuries apart by means of theatrical spectacle and instrumental music; and he thus reconciles the dramatic genres to which the work primarily refers (a point to which I shall return).

Mixing genres came naturally to Berlioz and is indispensable to the character of such works as *Roméo et Juliette* and *La Damnation de Faust*, which are at least as important, as forbears of *Les Troyens*, as any strictly operatic traditions. In all these works, Berlioz had to forge techniques suited to the particular subject. Among them is what, without pejorative intent, may be called a 'loose' technique of association, distinct from such 'tight' techniques as comprehensive tonal schemes, the number-and-scene conventions of Italian opera, or a quasi-symphonic structure based on referential motives. Organization by tonality and motives undoubtedly exists in *Les Troyens*; but it is not comprehensive (see however p. 114) and much of it is undoubtedly the result of unconscious processes resulting from the intensity with which Berlioz composed. These elements are discussed in the later parts of this chapter; their efficacy depends upon one element absolutely unique to opera, the audible strand of continuity provided by orchestral music, which may be considered as a replacement for the normal conventions of poetic or theatrical narrative.

The orchestra is varied in size and structure; in many scenes it is reduced to intimate groupings reminiscent of *Les Nuits d'été*, and bowed strings are totally excluded from No. 1 so that their entry, with Cassandra, has all the impact Berlioz hoped for.[3] Nevertheless orchestral sound is a constant and it emerges not from the scene of action, but from the pit. The occasional use of stage instruments does not affect this, since the changed direction of the sound integrates them with the action. The point is underlined in No. 11, where stage bands form a procession with the chorus, while the pit orchestra adds a commentary in sympathy with Cassandra.

As he moves between recitative, lyrical declamation, and aria, Berlioz never questions the convention that the singer takes the principal part. Conventionally enough, the orchestral music is nearly always concerned with what is happening on stage, doubling or supporting the voice without conflict of mood or motive. The advantage of an orchestral continuum is its flexibility in interpolating or superimposing commentary of its own, without placing these other functions in jeopardy. Passages where this happens are of particular importance in Berlioz's scheme, providing a network of cross-references which convey more complex meanings than are available from stage-pictures or words: more, at times, than the characters are aware of. In adopting this stance of authorial omniscience, Berlioz assumes – in this more like the author of a tragedy than of a poetic epic – that the outlines of the story are familiar; his musical texture, with its continuities and discontinuities, its new ideas and reminiscences, marks out the significant narrative line.

Whether in its simple roles of supporting the voice or preparing the ground for a vocal utterance, or when adding a commentary combined with or following a vocal utterance, the orchestra can function independently; it can underline, point an irony, or even contradict the apparent meaning of a situation or the words. This potential is not confined to the overtly symphonic type of opera but exists wherever modern orchestral groupings are employed; it is certainly present in earlier composers whom Berlioz admired, such as Gluck, Mozart and Weber, as it is in his contemporaries Verdi and Wagner. The constant presence of the orchestra is particularly helpful when the verbal narrative thread is fragile, as in operas like *Alceste* or *Tristan und Isolde*, in which there are few events, or in *Il Trovatore* and *Les Troyens*, in which conventional narrative connections are dangerously tenuous. In symphonies, mixed-genre works, or operas, Berlioz's preference was to engage with the situations which inspired him to the fullest musical development, allowing no time for the unfolding of continuous narrative or the development of characters for its own sake. In a conventional opera, or indeed in a poetic epic, more time would have been devoted to building up the role of the hero (Aeneas's first, admittedly striking, entry is in the humble capacity of messenger), or to the death of Coroebus, in view of his major role within Act I. There is no attempt to bridge the gulf between Acts II and III by reproducing Virgil's account of intervening events. Aeneas's short narration in Act IV (No. 35) is markedly different from his encounter with Andromache in the *Aeneid*, and it would seem perfunctory were it not carefully designed to affect Dido's mood and motivate a connection, subtly pointed by the orchestra, between her music and that of Cassandra (see below).

The tragic element in *Les Troyens* is the story of Dido, presented concisely within Acts III to V. A sovereign over a devoted people, she is nevertheless isolated within the whole action, sacrificed beneath the merciless tread of Trojan destiny. If a tragic figure must have a flaw, it is her excessive love for Aeneas, which leads her wilfully to repress knowledge of what fate holds in store for him. That the other heroine, Cassandra, is dead by the end of Act II, inescapably marks the division between the Trojan and Carthaginian acts. Cassandra, however, is more than another tragic figure. Cruelly marked out by the god, a prophetess never believed until it is too late, she finally foresees and thus in a sense participates in the glorious destiny of the 'New Troy'. This is the epic theme of the whole, and Berlioz took care to ensure that ideas associated with Cassandra, and thus with Trojan destiny, play a role in the Carthaginian acts. The disaster of Troy and the heroic destiny of Aeneas's race form the epic plan which embraces all five acts. Berlioz reconciles the dual rhythms of tragedy and epic in the final scene by a device peculiarly suited to musical drama; the simultaneous presentation of Dido's tragic death and the culmination of the epic theme in the vision, which she shares with the audience, of Imperial Rome.

## Form and tonality

The overt form of *Les Troyens* is Berlioz's subdivision into five acts, nine *Tableaux*, and fifty-two numbers. The reasons for distinguishing numbers are not consistent, either by dramatic or musical criteria. Some numbers correspond to scenes in a dramatic action, and some of these embrace closed musical forms (as does No. 3, with three short airs and a strophic duet). A single dramatic scene (defined by entrances, exits, and events) may involve more than one number (Nos. 7, 8 and 9; most of Act IV; Dido's soliloquy, Nos. 47 and 48). Musically, most numbers are closed in that a definite cadence is attained, but tonal resolution may be only momentary (Nos. 25 and 50), or it may coincide with the first bar of the next piece and be interrupted at once (Nos. 15, 27); sometimes it is missing (Nos. 10, 40, 51). Even if we discount recitative numbers with no clear tonal centre and the group of movements (Nos. 7, 13, 19, 38, 41, 43) which end in the relative major or minor, there are still numbers which end in tonal regions different from the opening: No. 6, a tragic pantomime, and No. 40, a comic duet, both recapitulate their opening melodies to end in 'wrong' keys (see also Nos. 10 and 28). Many numbers begin with a feint at a 'wrong' key, such as No. 13 where the first thematic statement is in C minor (see Ex. 10.1); G minor quickly emerges (in accordance with the key-signature), and the piece finally establishes B flat major.

Such flexibility may be expected in the 1850s but does not explain why larger units defined by tonality are occasionally at odds with those suggested by subdivision in dramatic terms. For example, the second part of Act I proceeds abruptly from the C major chorus (No. 4) to the E major ballet, although they form part of the same celebratory ritual; a simple dominant–tonic move (E to A) is made for Andromache's scene (No. 6), which is still ritual but hardly a celebration. This ends in F sharp minor, in which No. 7 begins and which remains the key throughout No. 8 to the start of No. 9. Yet No. 7, Aeneas's narration of Laocoön's death, comprehensively disrupts the ritual atmosphere and marks a new dramatic period. Tonality suggests grouping from No. 5 to No. 9; dramatic reversal suggests Nos. 4 to 6 and 7 to 9 or even 11 (the end of the act). The missing link is the 'Sinon' scene (No. 6a), tonally fluid and dividing the F sharp minor of Andromache from that of Laocoön's death. Berlioz establishes B flat major during No. 9, and reintroduces it at the end of Cassandra's aria No. 10, ready for emphatic use in the Trojan March; this time long-term tonal and dramatic planning are co-ordinated.

The inescapable conclusion is that Berlioz used no consistent formal or tonal systems for dramatic articulation (but see p. 114). There is no doubt, however, that certain keys are privileged in *Les Troyens*. The prevalence of B flat major and its immediate cousins (G and B flat minors) is consistently striking. All possible major and minor keys are used somewhere, but with a surprising neglect, for so ordinary a tonic, of D, especially D minor. Only some tonics present a consistent pattern of affective usage.[4] B flat is the principal key because of the recurrences of the Trojan March, whose tonality had to suit Sax's novel brass instruments. The B flat major/G minor complex, despairingly heroic in No. 13, is also used for Hylas's nostalgic song, No. 38. The latter, however, is exceptional in a physiognomy of B flat almost consistently heroic and martial. The keys of C and G majors are affectively neutral, much of their use being for ritual and *divertissement* (including the admittedly crucial *Chasse royale*). Of their relatives, E minor is used for various purposes but

A minor occurs almost entirely in contexts of feminine distress: this is apparent in the numbers which begin in this key (6, 45, 47), and also from passing references: in Act IV (NBE p. 544) the orchestral interlude is voluptuous, but also suggests Dido's underlying anguish; in Act V (p. 622) Aeneas uses A minor when referring to Dido's suffering, in an aria in F and A flat. E flat major is neutral – Nos. 2 and 17, for instance, are wide apart in mood – and if C minor is a key of heroic defiance (Nos. 15–16), it shares this mood with other flat minor keys, notably G and B flat (as at the end of Act I). Although E flat minor begins the tender yet confident 'Chers Tyriens' (No. 19), it is soon absorbed into G flat major, and elsewhere joins B flat minor as a key of despair (Nos. 10 and 47 at 'Je vais mourir'). F minor is used for comic and tragic dilemmas in Act V (Nos. 40 and 41). Its relative major, A flat, enters into closer association with C minor (Nos. 15–16); its role here and in Nos. 41 and 48 suggests a connection with defeat, even death.[5]

With favoured and neglected tonalities, however, consistent connotations are difficult to sustain, and although games of key-association could be extended down to the finest details such as passing references in Dido's rapidly-modulating outburst of terrible hatred (No. 46: for instance the use of B flat major and minor on pp. 694–7), they quickly lose touch with musical perception. We are far more likely, in the course of an opera, to be struck by recurring harmonic progressions or melodies than by absolutes such as exact pitch-levels; we recognize the return of the Trojan March by its tune and instrumentation, rather than its pitch, and transposition is no obstacle to recognition of the Carthaginian *Chant national* when it recurs during Nos. 19 and 32.

The background structure of *Les Troyens* cannot be neatly characterized. Categories exist for the complex forms of Verdi and Wagner: *ottocento* conventions or the symphonic idea. With Berlioz there are none. *Les Troyens* has aspects of Franco-Italian grand opera but does not take from it any set of structural expectations. It opens with a typical formula, the introductory chorus being followed by a solo for the *prima donna*, but the pieces stand in harsh contrast to each other; the aria consists of a single movement and both it and the recitative contain motivic working which proves to have a long-term function (see below). In No. 3 Berlioz uses short airs from the French tradition – for him the obvious source is Gluck – followed by the strophic duet. Brief transitions link Nos. 1 to 3, but they are essentially discrete musical units with a common expository purpose.

Yet part of this basic situation – Cassandra's love for Coroebus – is subsequently almost ignored. The two are not seen together again (except in the 'Sinon' scene), and Cassandra's lament for him (No. 15, p. 248), while deeply affecting, is very brief.

It has already been remarked that Nos. 4 to 6 constitute rituals, interrupted by No. 7, and that this interruption conflicts with the timing, though not the general direction, of a tonal movement from sharp regions to the B flat of the finale. Every movement up to and including No. 8 is clearly cadenced, despite undisguised musical transitions (the held G between Nos. 1 and 2, the dominant seventh on E added to the end of No. 5, the more extended modulatory passages which end Nos. 2 (p. 46) and 3 (p. 94)). Thus Berlioz accustoms us to a structure of self-contained units with a minimum of connecting matter. The musically formless genre of recitative appears within Nos. 2, 3 and 6, but only after a thematic and tonal exposition; it is used for introspection or agitated dialogue. There is no 'simple' recitative. No. 9 breaks this mould: Berlioz entitled it 'recitative and chorus', and later he called several numbers merely 'Scene' (Nos. 12, 13, 15, 42, 43, 45, 46, and 50: three in Act II and five in Act V). Comparable sections of Italian opera, combining solo and chorus, recitative and lyricism, would be placed as introductions or intermediate sections within a larger unit (a *cavatina* or duet). In such parts of *Les Troyens* the apparent subdivision into scenes belies the actual continuity of action and music in performance.

No. 9 has the first simple recitative ('Que la déesse nous protège'), and a brief chorus determining to take the wooden horse into the city. This resolution coincides with the establishment of B flat major, and its associated dotted rhythms (the accompaniment as Aeneas proposes action and a theme to the chorus, p. 153) and arpeggiated melodies (chorus, p. 154). Above the cadence, Cassandra's cries of 'Malheur' use the flat sixth (G flat), here violently dissonant, but preparing the key of E flat minor for No. 10. Both Nos. 9 and 10 change tonal orientation (despite the signature of three flats, the end of No. 10 is in B flat, not E flat major). The radiance of B flat major fills the processional part of No. 11, but Cassandra, in the foreground and supported by the pit, contrives to end the act in B flat minor.

There is thus a tonal link to the opening of Act II: the same key is used for the realization of Cassandra's prophecy.[6] Moreover this forms part of a B flat major–minor opposition established in No. 11 whose recurrences plot the curve of Trojan fortunes: B flat major in

No. 13, minor in No. 26 (the March in the 'mode triste'), major and minor in Act V. In Act II B flat minor is quickly undermined (see Ex. 10.10), but it is used for the speech of Hector's ghost, the only closed unit within No. 12. With his exit the music modulates, to find a new key only at the fifth bar of No. 13; characteristically Berlioz provides another link between these numbers by accelerating a common rhythmic motive at the arrival of C minor (Ex. 10.1). The key of

Ex. 10.1

No. 13 continually fluctuates so that, with the scene unchanged and Panthus only entering after a dozen bars, the effect is of a change of tempo within a larger unit (12–13: *adagio–allegro*); in a further cross-reference, the same rhythmic motive is used for the two entries of Ascanius (Ex. 10.2). Similarly, the second *Tableau*, after the self-contained prayer No. 14 (which nevertheless echoes a fanfare from No. 12), consists essentially of a single scene. No. 15 begins with the last A flat chord of No. 14 but plunges to C minor; No. 16 reverses this progression (bars 1–4) and its new tempo and closed form (the first verse of 'Complices de sa gloire') are as much a resolution as a new start. Before the second verse the recitative uses a motive from No. 15 (cf. pp. 256 and 267; both passages concern suicide).

The first two acts taken together show a consistent progression from discrete musical numbers towards larger wholes formed of

Ex. 10.2

short, interlinked units and 'free' areas like recitative. This pattern is repeated within Act III, and then on a larger scale over the last two acts. Act III begins with an introductory chorus, followed by a complex unit of a type favoured by Gluck, extending from No. 18 to No. 23 and including recitative, aria, chorus and ballet, structured by reprises of the *Chant national*. The next scene is a self-contained duet, yet two of its motives recur in Dido's short aria No. 25, as if to point a relationship between speculation about love in No. 24 and the arrival of a lover among the storm-tossed strangers (cf. pp. 365 and 384; pp. 370 and 388). A dominant–tonic relationship allows No. 26 to follow without a break, but it is fully cadenced and No. 27 refers to Dido's regal authority, as she prepares to greet the new arrivals, by citing the opening of the *Chant national* in its first three chords (p. 395, bars 1–3). Thereafter No. 27 consists of recitative, although the orchestral commentary is beautifully elaborated. No. 28 interrupts the cadence; Dido reaches G but Narbal bursts in with bad news, his music contrasted in tempo and instrumentation as well as key (E flat). Although this finale has one predominant tempo, it only attains its final tonic (B major) at bar 162 (out of 415).

Act IV consists almost entirely of discrete musical units, a strategy clearly intended to enhance the effect of its extraordinary conclusion. The numbers are mostly connected by short orchestral links (as in Act I) or by functional recitative; but since there is little action, each piece stands apart from its neighbours. Mercury's entrance, wrenching the key from G flat to the seldom-used D, then to E minor, derives part of its violence from the very solidity of the preceding closed forms.

Act V, on the other hand, is fluid almost throughout. The opening song is fully cadenced (although Hylas falls asleep, the orchestra completes the third strophe), but No. 39 begins in the same key; it introduces a syncopated figure which reappears at its close, and then again to link No. 40 to No. 41. The sentinels of No. 40 are heard during Hylas's song. The network of connections among these numbers reminds us that they all bear, from different angles, on a single dramatic idea: the necessity of the Trojans' departure. Aeneas's 'Inutiles regrets' thus begins in mid-thought, on diminished harmony, and its vagrant tonalities match the hero's bewilderment. Nevertheless, its overall design is clear: the *primo tempo* centred on F minor, the *cantabile* ('Ah! quand viendra l'instant') in F major, and the Allegro in A flat.[7] A unifying element within No. 41 is the extensive use of echo, and later pre-echo, of vocal phrases by the orchestra, seeming almost to mock the hero; whereas the fluid counterpoint of No. 43, after Aeneas has given decisive orders, functions as a strand of commentary (see Ex. 10.4 below).

Continuity, however, is broken by an exceptionally emphatic final cadence to No. 41 (p. 638). Aeneas's high tessitura, and a brief orchestral uproar, invite (and receive) applause, and the singer is no doubt grateful for a breathing-space; but Berlioz may well have desired us to experience a *frisson* when he juxtaposed this glaring cadence in A flat to a single, ghostly bass D, which acts as an intermittent pedal in the tonally ambiguous No. 42. Since continuity has become the norm in Act V, this is an uncomfortable moment, suggesting uncertainty of intention. Although Aeneas remains on stage, the division is emphasized when Nos. 42 to 44 run into each other to form a single unit; although No. 44 was a later addition it ends, like No. 43, with a reprise of the Trojan March.

Tonality and texture, the triumphant B flat and the nervous A minor, mark the gap before the second *Tableau*. Its four musical numbers (45–8) play without a break, using the types of overlap to which we have become accustomed, although midway in this *Tableau* Dido is left alone and Nos. 47–8 form an especially tight unit (see p. 161 below). A dominant–tonic relation links No. 48 to the final *Tableau* (A flat to C sharp minor). Although No. 49 ('Cérémonie funèbre') reaches a cadence, Dido enters before it ends; and No. 50 (marked 'Un peu plus animé' rather than being given a new tempo) twice uses the main theme of No. 49. There is no further interruption to musical and dramatic continuity, the only real cadence being that of the renewed, triumphant Trojan March.

This growth from numbers which can be heard as such towards increasing continuity and co-ordination of action and music is intrinsically satisfying, and represents a powerful cohesive force in performance – although it may be noted in passing that the cumulative continuity of Acts I and II tends to accentuate the division between the Trojan and Carthaginian acts. Nevertheless *Les Troyens* is one opera, not two. Its dramatic design is geared to two major crises in Trojan fortune: the destruction of the city in Act II and the near-loss of a sense of purpose through Aeneas's weakness in Act IV. The second, before its climax in Act V, needs additional exposition (in Act III), because its epic drive is counterpointed to the tragedy of Dido. The successive crises increase in significance, and resolve in a conclusion which cost Berlioz much trouble but which in its final form contrives to tie together the epic and tragic themes.

## Musical detail: the orchestral commentary

The effect of the broad structural processes outlined above is in large part dependent on surface events, including the orchestral 'narrative' or commentary. This may be partly resolved into recurring musical images which tend to cluster in crucial scenes, underlining their significance, pointing to otherwise inexplicit connections with other scenes, and adding an ironic commentary for the audience alone. These images are not necessarily musical ideas of distinction. They work because they are short, flexible, and capable of assimilation into longer melodies; as textural, melodic, harmonic, or rhythmic gestures they are unambiguous, despite the great variety of forms they assume. Together they form a network of signs, an aspect of authorial omniscience; moreover – and this makes them peculiarly apt for an epic – some of them at least signify in much the same way within whole traditions known to Berlioz or contemporary with him.

Berlioz was not necessarily conscious of using all these motives. Many recurrences could hardly escape the attention of the most unobservant composer, but to assume an intention behind every detectable instance is to assume also an intention to disguise, for no discernible purpose. There is no question of *Leitmotiv* (in the Wagnerian sense) in *Les Troyens*. Cross-reference and reminiscence are part of the traditions relevant to Berlioz, but there is no symphonic application of motives, nor do most of them have any fixed denotation. These motives are images which nevertheless permeate the orchestral commentary, and are all the more persuasive because they arise in counterpoint to the number and *Tableau* structure of an opera dominated by the voices.

Before turning to this group of motives or images, conscious reminiscences need to be taken into account. Berlioz's clearest symbolic element is the Trojan March. The *Chant national* of Carthage also extends beyond Nos. 19–23 into Act IV (No. 32, delicately transformed into an instrumental entry for the court). These are, in origin, extended compositions. Among the shorter signs, the summons to 'Italie' stands apart in that it is confined to voices. It arises from the dénouement of Act II (p. 292), providing a brief but powerful moment of stability within a context of tonal fluctuation. 'Italie' frames the idyll of Act IV, when the mêlée at the climax of the *Chasse royale* is echoed by Mercury. In Act V 'Italie' recurs more frequently as the Trojans prepare to depart; the ghosts sing it in No. 39 and use its rhythm in No. 42 for the words 'Pas un jour, pas une heure'. Finally we hear it from Aeneas himself, and from the Trojan chorus in Nos. 43 and 44.

The frequent cases of transference of musical ideas between adjacent numbers, of which some have already been observed, assist the growing continuity of Acts II and V especially (between Nos. 12 and 13, 15 and 16, 39, 40 and 41). More distant reminiscences are best if not over-used. Berlioz achieves great poignancy by first hinting at the love-duet (No. 37) in a moment of repose in Aeneas's aria No. 41; in the A flat passage in the *andante* at 'Lutter contre moi-même, et contre toi, Didon', three bars (p. 628, bars 119–21) use a softly-moving string accompaniment over a pedal, backed by flutes and clarinets, the exact orchestration of the last reprise in the duet (p. 585, bars 103–5); the melodic movement is very similar. This seed blossoms in the explicit reminiscence, also in A flat, during Dido's aria, No. 48.

Personal motives are another well-established technique which Berlioz uses only sparingly. Besides that for Coroebus (see pp. 20–1 above), Cassandra's is a case in point. After Coroebus's first *Cavatine* (p. 53) we recognize a roughly fragmented form (Ex. 10.3B) of the motive which introduced Cassandra in No. 2 (Ex. 10.3A). This spawns the scales and dotted rhythms which punctuate the recitative until a new declamatory motive takes over (p. 56). After Coroebus's second *Cavatine*, a return of his motive (p. 66) and his *andante* in F, the declamatory motive proves to be the theme of the duet (p. 72); Cassandra's motive plays no further part until it greets her entry, with an abbreviated version, in Act II (Ex. 10.3C).

Ex. 10.3

Aeneas has no personal motive, perhaps because almost throughout he is seen as the representative, and eventually the leader, of the people with whom his destiny is inextricably entwined. When he loses sight of it, he is in thrall to Dido, and the musical atmosphere is hers. She too has no personal motive. Indeed, it may appear from what follows that the identification of Ex. 10.3 with Cassandra *as a person* is too straightforward; while close investigation does reveal a concealed motivic basis to the musical characterization of Dido (see p. 176).

Table 10.1 lists a selection of identifiable images, most, but not all, of which might also be called motives. They are characterized musically in the left-hand column, and dramatically, but with deliberate vagueness, in the central column. Reference is made in the right-hand column to tabulation in the appendices to my 1985 article (see note 1, p. 232). In addition this column refers to examples in the present chapter and/or to numbers in the score.

The melodic images attain a virtual apotheosis in the eloquent orchestral commentary to Aeneas's farewell in No. 43 (Ex. 10.4).

Table 10.1

| | | |
|---|---|---|
| **I Melodic images**([8]) | | |
| A Sweeping scales upward, mostly upbeats | Agitation; dire prophecy; animation of musical texture | [1985: App. 7] Exx. 10.3, 4, 8, 9, 10, 12, 13 |
| B Lower auxiliary, often in dotted rhythm, usually upbeat | Similar to A: agitation, fate | [1985: App. 8] |
| C Arpeggiated melodies, especially rising | Heroism, even joy; national hymns; militarism | [1985: not listed except those in B flat, App. 3] *Marche troyenne, Chant national,* Nos. 4, 9, 12, 15, 17 |
| D Upper auxiliary, often appoggiatura, falling a semitone (often flat sixth to dominant) | Conventional image of suffering | [1985: not listed] Exx. 10.4, 11B, 13; in voice, No. 9 ('Malheur'); in oboe, No. 3 (pp. 63–4), end of No. 6; many others |
| **II Harmonic images** | | |
| A The key of B flat major and its relations (G and B flat minors, whence D flat major) | With arpeggiated melody and dotted rhythm, military, heroic; minor keys, resistance, suffering | [1985: App. 3] |
| B Juxtaposition of major keys, the second a major third lower | Entry of new characters; dramatic revelation | [1985: App. 4] Ex. 10.10 Nos. 1, 2 and 3 are in G, E flat, and B; see also Nos. 27–8; end of Act IV |
| C The diminished seventh chord[9] | Agitation; uncertainty of harmonic direction symbolizing dramatic crisis | [1985: not listed] |
| **III Rhythmic images** | | |
| A 2–4 very short notes, usually upbeat to a longer note | Death[10] | [1985: App. 5] Ex. 10.5 |

| | | | |
|---|---|---|---|
| B | Short repeated notes recurring on down-beats, preceded by upbeat of same value | Fate | [1985: App. 6] Exx. 10.6, 11B |
| **IV Timbral and textural images** | | | |
| A | Pedals combined with muted sounds or harmonics | Ghosts | [1985: not listed] Nos. 2, 13, 42 |
| B | Melodic commentary in middle or bass registers | Mood dependent on context; texture draws attention to cross-references | [1985: not listed] Exx. 10.4, 9, 10, 13 |

Ex. 10.4

Ex. 10.4 (*cont.*)

The passage begins with an obvious reference to the Quintet (cf. Ex. 10.13, bars 37–8), using a scale-fragment and melodic image B; there follows a B flat arpeggio (melodic image C, picked out by trombones), falling semitones (bars 94–5 and 98, melodic image D), and a sweeping scale (melodic image A, bar 101) suggestive, in this form, of No. 39 (p. 601). The two rhythmic images can only be selectively illustrated here. The 'death' rhythm (Ex. 10.5) is liable to escape attention since it too readily appears in conventional figures such as fanfares; an obvious case is the opening of the Trojan March. But the

Ex. 10.5

March does bring death to Troy, and in No. 11 the orchestral commentary from the pit begins with the more highly charged version of the rhythm shown in Ex. 10.5B and there referring to the death of Coroebus. Ex. 10.5A and 10.5C are bass figures in the two heroines' arias which contemplate death. The 'fate' rhythm (Ex. 10.6) has a more marked character; in Nos. 2 (p. 42), 12 (p. 213) and 50 (p. 728) it appears in a form identical to Ex. 10.6A, the first two on violas, the last two on brass. Another form from No. 12 (Ex. 10.6B) belongs to a ghost scene (cf. Ex. 10.12B), and in No. 26 (Ex. 10.6C) a variant of

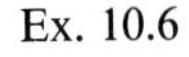
Ex. 10.6

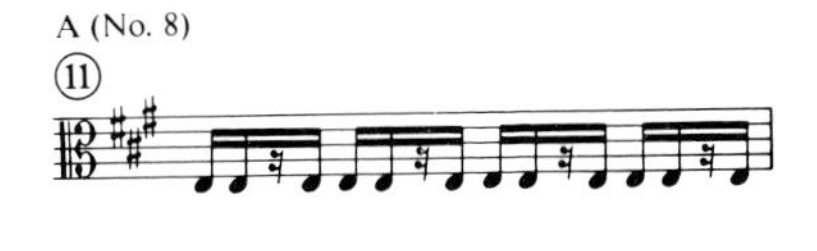

the rhythm accompanies the last reprise of the Trojan March in the 'sad mode', with obviously fateful implications.

Short of classifying every bar of the opera, any such list as Table 10.1 is necessarily provisional. It is possible, however, to attempt a survey of the whole work in the light of the fateful musical imagery. This will be undertaken in order of composition; although my concern is not with compositional processes but with results, such an approach sheds some light on the possibility of Berlioz's mind, consciously or otherwise, having ordered these images for a dramatic purpose.

Berlioz began with the Act IV duet, the epitome of a love which nearly destroys the epic. The threat derives from its sheer beauty, its transcendent lyricism; images of fatality form no part of its principal material. Yet even here Troy is not forgotten. In lines closely modelled on Shakespeare, Aeneas sings of Troilus, son of Priam, awaiting Cressida beneath the walls. The line is set in the relative, E flat minor, elsewhere a key of black despair. At first (p. 579) the bass syncopation suggests 3/4 against the prevailing 6/8; as the music modulates to B flat minor, key of Troy's fall, the bass changes to a rhythm clearly related to the 'fate' rhythm (Ex. 10.7), in exactly

Ex. 10.7

the note-values used at the end of Dido's aria, a few bars after the reminiscence of this same duet (p. 712). Berlioz may have added this detail only after composing Act I, at the orchestration stage, since it does not appear in the sketches.

When he turned to Act I, Berlioz must soon have reached the entry of Cassandra, compelling in its fateful temper. For No. 2 the key drops a major third (G to E flat: harmonic image B). Her first words are punctuated by shorter up-beat scales and the dotted returning-note (melodic images A and B), audibly related to the later part of her motive (see Ex. 10.3A and cf. Ex. 10.8). Whether Berlioz conceived the musical details of the end of Act IV (Mercury's interven-

Ex. 10.8

tion) before or after composing Act I, he at one stage intended to use Cassandra's motive in full as it appears in No. 2 (but in D: see p. 943). Again, the key-change is an abrupt fall of a major third. Eventually he replaced Cassandra's ghost with Mercury and removed her full motive, but he retained the key-change and the scale, following it with pulsing chords referable to the fate rhythm; the final, equally abrupt, modulation to E minor is clinched by the returning-note figure.[11]

Berlioz plants the scale, returning-note, fate and death rhythms and the falling major third into No. 1. The last three are all associated with the reference to Troy's most terrible enemy, Achilles. The scale and subsequent descent from a high tonic by thirds to the supertonic defines not only Cassandra's motive (Ex. 10.3A) but the first thematic shape of the opera, No. 1 from bar 3. These elements are pointedly recalled when Dido assumes Cassandra's mantle of prophecy in Act V.[12]

Cassandra's foreboding spills over from the recitative into the main section of her aria (Ex. 10.9). Her first line is a short up-beat scale, too lyrical, perhaps, to relate to melodic image A, but used pervasively within the freely imitative texture. At 'Tu ne m'écoutes pas' the melody is reduced to a declamatory ascent; the integrated

Ex. 10.9

counterpoint of voice and bass is replaced by an accompanimental continuum (upper strings and wind) with a marked bass commentary of instrumental character (Ex. 10.9, bars 53ff). This refers to the dotted rhythm of Cassandra's entry; moreover it binds into one motive melodic images A and B, heard separately in the preceding recitative (Ex. 10.8). Aria style and mood are thus threatened by a point of musical integration within the orchestral commentary.

Most remarkably, the same image-cluster marks the event Cassandra fears, the death of the 'malheureux roi' Priam, which must occur near the start of Act II (Ex. 10.10). This passage, one of the most potent in the opera, is further connected to No. 2 by the use of a

Ex. 10.10

'half-diminished seventh', not a particularly common harmony in Berlioz (Ex. 10.9, bars 53 and 57; Ex. 10.10, bar 2). Act II continues with harmonic image B: after the chord of D flat (bar 4), a moment of silence and a crashing chord of A major.

I have anticipated these prominent cross-references because they are easy to hear and interpret; whereas throughout the rest of Act I, perhaps for the better effect of the opening of Act II, the fateful images recur in a less integrated fashion. In No. 3 they appear as gestural material, punctuating the recitative: melodic image A deriving from Ex. 10.3B; melodic image D frequently, built into the minor-mode form of the declamatory duet theme, p. 56; A, again, adding a layer of commentary in sympathy with Cassandra to the repeat of Coroebus's *Cavatine* (p. 64). During the ritual scenes which follow, fateful motives are understandably not conspicuous. Both rhythmic images are, however, incorporated into the texture of No. 8. The first response to Laocoön's death is a melodic line doubled by violas, whose shuddering demisemiquavers form an 'on-beat' version of the death rhythm, and Ex. 10.6A punctuates the music between vocal entries (bars 11, 21 and 31). Cassandra's anguish at this turn of events brings the 'Malheur' semitone of No. 9 and the death rhythm as an ostinato bass to her aria No. 10 (Ex. 10.5A). Scales and returning-notes, sometimes combined, are included in the sporadic but forceful commentary from the pit during the March, No. 11 (Ex. 10.11A–B).

Ex. 10.11

Berlioz turned to Act IV after completing Act I. This seemingly erratic process may in fact have allowed him to take stock of his materials, and to resist the temptation to apply certain figures mechanically in unsuitable contexts. Certainly the fateful images are suppressed during most of Act IV. Figures related to them in the *Chasse royale* (except for the intentional sign of the cry of 'Italie!') are swamped by its exuberance; the real portent of disaster is the combination of metres at the climax (p. 467) which forms an image of disorder, shattering the neo-classical calm of Act III. It may be worthy of note that a version of the 'fate' rhythm used here (the downbeat crotchet–minim in a quick tempo, woodwind and horns on p. 467) corresponds to that used in Nos. 16 (p. 286, all the orchestra), 28 (p. 441, timpani) and 51 (p. 737–8, all the orchestra), passages concerned with the downfalls, respectively, of Troy, Iarbas, and Dido, whose real downfall, however, is the event which takes place during this climax of the *Chasse royale*. Narbal's fears (Nos. 30–1) refer in passing to harmonic image B and melodic image B (which is built into the melody of his aria: several vocal occurrences of this motive, however, I have neglected because they may simply result from word-setting). Until Mercury's entrance, only the Quintet (No. 35) clearly refers to the fateful images, which naturally do not occur in the extended *divertissement* formed by Nos. 33–4.

The Quintet is crucial because it brings Dido directly into relation with the past history of Troy. When she asks Aeneas to resume his narrative, a doleful string figure anticipates the ghosts' music in Act V (Ex. 10.12). The tale of Andromache's infidelity affects Dido

Ex. 10.12

deeply, as is shown at once when she echoes Aeneas's last line of recitative, just as the first phrase of the Quintet becomes more sustained and establishes its key of D flat (Ex. 10.13; compare bars 25–6 and 29–31). This delay in clarifying the tonic is unusual within Act IV. As Dido cadences (bar 33), the orchestra comments in a middle-register melody which suggested to Ernest Newman 'a secret thought threading its way silently through the Queen's mind'.[13] That may well be so. Her second phrase, however (from bar 37) is counterpointed to a mobile bass-line which, with the orchestral continuum

Ex. 10.13

Ex. 10.13 (*cont.*)

32
et mon cœur est ab - sous!
36
An-dro-maque é - pou - ser l'as-sas - sin de son
40
pè - re, Le fils du meurtri - er de son il - lus - - tre é -
44
- poux!
f

between, is the texture of Ex. 10.9 from bar 53; Dido's bass owes something to the 'secret thought' melody but, like Cassandra's, it is formed from an up-beat scale and dotted auxiliary note (melodic images A and B). Since she refers to the death of Priam, the relevance of these images here needs no underlining. The modulation to A flat is coloured by the flat sixth above its dominant (melodic image D, bar 43) and marked by a repeat of the 'secret thought' melody. Perhaps understanding the effect his story is making, Aeneas repeats this last phrase. From his cadence (p. 558, bar 55) the 'secret thought' melody in B flat minor is quickly snuffed out by Dido's new idea ('Tout conspire à vaincre mes remords'); as her heart is absolved the bass counterpoint becomes more languid, its upward scale (bars 60 and 62) expressively smoothed and losing any residual relation to melodic image A; the auxiliary note is forgotten. When the other voices enter the fateful commentary in the bass remains only a memory; attention shifts to Ascanius's theft of Dido's ring, at which point the fate rhythm in the woodwind teasingly marks this turning-point in Dido's tragedy (p. 559, bars 75ff).

In the Septet which follows, the serene night is barely disturbed by an intermittent sound, like the breaking of waves. This is usually followed by an oscillation in the dominant treble pedal from C to D flat; but the tragic power of this flat sixth auxiliary seems no more than a tinge of melancholy here, dissolved in the pedal which persists throughout, preventing more than passing modulations. In retrospect the D flat is also heard as structural, since it is used to modulate to G flat for the love-duet. The paucity of fateful images in this movement again enhances the peculiarly shocking effect of Mercury's appearance. We see nothing of Aeneas's reaction to the god's summons, but when Act V begins we are fully prepared for the tragic outcome of his love for Dido; further narrative connection would be otiose.

Berlioz next wrote Act II, whose most powerful reunion of images has already been described (see Ex. 10.10). The images figure severally, as in No. 3, during the recitative-like No. 15: the death rhythm for Coroebus, followed by a new combination of scale and auxiliary note reminiscent of parts of No. 11 (Ex. 10.11C). All later references to this material inevitably bring to mind the prophecies of Cassandra, and her role as the conscience of Troy. In No. 42 her own motive does not reappear with her ghost, perhaps because it now means so much more than a sign for Cassandra herself; she sings in unison with Hector (whereas Coroebus and Priam sing alone), but the climax of Aeneas's horrified exclamations is his identification of her ('Gods of Erebus! Cassandra!'), whereupon he yields, to 'immolate Dido while looking the other way' (pp. 643–4).

Act III creates difficulties of interpretation when images associated with Troy occur in scenes preceding the arrival of the Trojans. No. 19 makes use of martial rhythms in the key of B flat, reached by a major-third leap from D (harmonic images A and B), with the arpeggiated melody supplied by the *Chant national* (pp. 324–6). Dido is speaking of the war with Iarbas which she can win only with Trojan help; the death rhythm has already accompanied her allusion to the god of war (p. 319). This fateful imagery is relaxed, however, until the Trojans enter and the fate rhythm accompanies their March (Ex. 10.6C). In No. 27 Ascanius reverts to B flat minor, key of Trojan misfortune, when mentioning his father ('un chef pieux', p. 396). Harmonic image B becomes a feature of his gradual revelation of the Trojans' identity and colours Dido's murmured 'Strange destiny' (p. 399; A flat replaces an expected C chord). This progression (G to E flat) opens No. 28 and rings out again (A flat to E) when Aeneas finally reveals himself (p. 412).

Berlioz wrote Act V last. In its first *Tableau* the fateful images recur sporadically, but with some frequency; several of these have already been mentioned (from Nos. 39 and 42). There are passing allusions to them in No. 44, which Berlioz added some time after completing the rest. In the second *Tableau* the death rhythm underlying No. 45 is almost alone until melodic image B and the fate rhythm are sensitively integrated into Dido's farewell aria, No. 48 (see p. 170). But the image-clusters return as Dido's death is prepared amid public ceremonial. The auxiliary note forms part of the instrumental melody of No. 49, and the funeral tread, not unlike the earlier ritual chorus, No. 4, refers to a dactylic version of the death rhythm (timpani). The central section is punctuated by swirling scales (melodic image A), and the reprise is burdened with a disturbed triple metre (strings, bass drum) superimposed on the prevailing 4/4, a device which may be heard as a distant echo of the fatal climax of the *Chasse royale*. When the reprise of the funeral ritual in No. 50 (p. 728) is accompanied by the fate rhythm in its original semiquaver form (cf. Ex. 10.6A) the allusion is inescapable; here it presages the downfall of another city. When Dido ascends the pyre, a chain of suspensions in the clarinets (p. 731, bars 36–41) recalls a moment of impotent passion in her last confrontation with Aeneas (p. 667, bars 99–107) – recalls, that is, in performance, since No. 50

was composed before No. 44. The instrumentation is similar but the disruptive effect of metrical expansion in No. 44 (bars of 3/2 sound, although the metre is duple) is regularized in No. 50 to match Dido's resignation.

In No. 50 Dido alludes directly to the prophetic style of Cassandra, with melodic image A and dotted rhythms (from p. 732). As she stabs herself harmonic image B appears in the drop from D flat (her cadence) to A in the first bar of No. 51. The frantic chorus is accompanied by blurred, almost hallucinatory references: as well as the fate rhythm the screaming violin triplets (p. 738, bar 8) recall the *Chasse royale* textures, melodic image B springs out in bar 15, and the last two harmonies for chorus reproduce harmonic image B (C flat to G, bar 26).

As Dido foresees the defeat of Carthage by Rome, her cries of 'Ah!' echo her momentary loss of self-control at the beginning of No. 47 (p. 742; cf. p. 705); in both the harmony is a diminished seventh completed, in No. 51, by Anna (Ex. 10.14A). A strangely dis-

Ex. 10.14

Ex. 10.14 (*cont.*)

42
No. 52
Allegro non troppo e pomposo ♩ = 138
- ge. . périra. . .
Ro - me. . . .
Ro - me. . . .
p
3
4
immor - tel - - - - le. . .
B
21
CASSANDRA
ah!
je cache à vos yeux
Le trouble affreux dont mon âme est rem-
24
pli - e!
quitte moi
Cas - san - dre. . .
Viens
Allegro
Mesuré

sonant sequence (bars 39–42) returns to the same diminished seventh, its spelling altered (A flat for G sharp) ready for a chromatic resolution to B flat in bars 3–4 of No. 52. Dido's prophecy is uttered in an ascending sequence of falling semitones which was previously heard as early as Act I, divided between Cassandra and Coroebus in No. 3 (Ex. 10.14B).[14] Into No. 52, Dido's rising sequence of falling minor thirds ('Rome. . .') is reminiscent of Aeneas's plea for 'grace' in No. 44 (p. 670); both derive from the Trojan March, into which Dido herself seems about to launch ('immortelle. . .'). Her dying word, therefore, forms a heroic B flat arpeggio; images of fate, death, and suffering are suddenly dissipated. As at the very end of Act II, explicit motives of death or mourning would be tautological, since Dido is dying on stage – such signs are for the spectator, and are most useful when the orchestral commentary, without being necessarily incompatible with the stage-picture, refers outside the moment to surrounding events. At the end the Carthaginians are accordingly given no music specific to themselves. No. 52 is headed 'Imprecation', but its musical substance is the Trojan March. A melodic bid for independence by the chorus lasts only four bars (p. 747, bars 19–22); their first dissonant entry on a flat seventh (p. 745, 'Haine') merely anticipates the invariable modulation to A flat within the March; there are no further harmonic clashes and the choral melody fits easily with the orchestra. It was not beyond Berlioz to have repeated the idea of the end of Part II of *La Damnation de Faust*, where the soldiers' song in B flat is combined with the students' song in a different metre, beginning in D minor. But *Faust* is a 'concert opera'. In the theatre such a musical *tour de force* would be superfluous; true opera allows us to witness the glory of Rome, symbolized by the orchestra, which ends its commentary by taking over the stage music of No. 11. Meanwhile the angry Carthaginians' musical impotence signals their inability to combat destiny. Thus an apparently heartless abandonment of motives of suffering at the moment of Dido's death contributes to a dénouement of terrible tragic power, as well as of epic grandeur.

# 11 *Commentary and analysis*

## (a) *Chasse royale et orage* (No. 29)

IAN KEMP

When, in Act III, Aeneas is first revealed to Dido, Berlioz is echoing the *Aeneid*, 1.586ff, where Venus lifts the cloud concealing her son and reveals him in startling beauty. Berlioz invented the Numidian invasion and sailor's disguise, in order that Aeneas could announce himself to comparable dramatic effect: in both cases Dido is immediately and profoundly attracted (evident in *Les Troyens* particularly in the orchestral coda). If it suited him Berlioz was quite happy to alter Virgil. But he had no need to alter the episode in which Dido's passion finally ignites. The scenario for the *Chasse royale* is (barring the omission of goats and stags) in every essential Virgil's. Earlier controversy over the scene was largely over its positioning. It arose firstly from ignorance of and indifference to what Berlioz had prescribed. Secondly, it was due to prudery: you could have passion (or marriage, as the scene could be said to represent) only after respectable preliminaries, and so it was thought correct to have the *Chasse royale* after the love-duet, and therefore to switch the order of *Tableaux* in Act IV. There was a third reason, which did have some logic. Virgil's banquet, where Ascanius disguised as Cupid first enchants Dido with the gifts and then inflames her with desire (and where Iopas sings and Aeneas narrates the story of Troy), takes place before the royal hunt – which is the climax of a period, including the scene with Anna, of frantically unsatisfied desire. Berlioz's banquet equivalent (the Act IV diversions and the Quintet) takes place after the hunt. He could be said to have got it wrong and therefore to need correcting, again by switching the order of the *Tableaux*. But he had not got it wrong: he was only altering Virgil again – this time admittedly for more than practical reasons. Virgil's picture of Dido in love may be unforgettable but it is not really sympathetic. He regarded love almost as an illness, possession by irrational and even distasteful forces which when unleashed lead to disaster. Berlioz thought differently. 'Love or music – which power can uplift man to the sublimest heights? It is a large question; yet it seems to me that one should answer it in this way: love cannot give an idea of music; music can give an idea of love. But why separate them? They are the two wings of the soul.' Love to him was not a disaster; it was a gift. What he understood was that its physical expression uncovered the sublime. He proceeded therefore to have the *Chasse royale* first, the love-duet second.

Of course the *Chasse royale* can be heard as a piece of music, pure and simple, and unless it holds up under this guise discussion is otiose. Berlioz writes a sustained crescendo and diminuendo (the form of, for example, Wagner's *Lohengrin* prelude, which he admired as a 'symphonic' piece regardless of its relationship with the opera). All the musical elements involved, and none are not involved, are designed to build up, to *be* this clear and straightforward shape. It is a seamless whole with a riding momentum – though it is not without its breathing spaces, ingredients Berlioz thought essential if a composer were to respect his listeners' sensibilities rather than take them by force. Berlioz's compositional craft in this respect can be observed in his manipulation of its basic shape. The large-scale crescendo is given its breathing space by the adoption of a form like an introduction and allegro, which is a helpful way of saying 'this is the situation, and this is what is to be done with it'. In fact the 'allegro' (marked *allegretto*) begins in the middle of the 'introduction' (by means of a subtle tempo change); when the 'allegro' seems to begin, it actually is in the same tempo as before. So the punctuation which could have arrested the momentum is elegantly bypassed.

Other technical means by which the crescendo is sustained are, obviously, dynamics and, in particular, orchestral textures. Dynamics do not just get louder, nor textures thicker. In perpetually new ways textures gather substance and thin out, become dense and then airy, sharp-edged and contoured, arresting and relaxing, all the time controlling the weight of those accumulating waves of movement which are the real shape of the piece. Sometimes these waves are held in suspended animation – in order that a new event may be introduced or that a lull may occur (a breathing space). Ex. 11.1 illustrates both eventualities. From one point of view the music is simply a prolonged chord of B flat, marking a point of rest where a wave has sunk to a middle register there to take in a new theme (not illustrated) and a second new one. But the texture is not simple. Its principal component is a web of high string sounds, alive with points of articulation and structured in rhythmic canons (of prophetic originality) – a fascinating sound in its own terms and one of which Berlioz himself was obviously proud, for in his simplified orchestration he cut out the theme altogether and left the sound to itself.

Ex. 11.1

[Original in ¢ , except for saxhorns in 3 (𝅗𝅥. = 𝅝)]

If the theme in Ex. 11.1 does not look very thrilling, it has to be remarked that with its original sounds for two tenor saxhorns it would be. In his simplified orchestration Berlioz scored its immediate predecessor for his characteristic doubling of cornets and horns in octaves and undoubtedly made that thrilling - or, in other words, made the point that the effect of a theme is created by its sound and function, not its appearance. Here a crucial consideration has to be taken in account. There are altogether seven themes in the piece. They are all designed to lead into one another while at the same time remaining vividly individual. None of them can be assertive enough to threaten their collective balance and so all have a certain modesty. This is a notable example of compositional self-discipline.

Although the seven themes are never heard in the same way twice, they remain individual enough to map out the course of the whole. Their functions are as follows. The first is slow, fugal and open-ended (Ex. 11.3A); the second lyrical, apparently complete and self-contained but in fact evaporating into the third, which is a genuinely complete theme (Ex. 11.3B), if strangely elusive in mode and phrasing; the fourth is motivic and developmental (Ex. 11.4B), the beginning of a fast section which generates a number of subsidiary motives; the fifth is powerful and concise, signalling the appearance of the sixth and seventh, which are, as it were, its younger twin brothers. Once he has presented his fifth theme Berlioz begins to loosen up his material by introducing a non-thematic, impressionistic sound, which is a means of setting the stage for a gradual process of integration - here a recurrence of the third, the most stable of the themes. The non-thematic sound continues, to prepare for the entry of the sixth and seventh, at which point the process generates a version of the dynamic fourth theme and a drive to the first climax. A lull. Then the tumultuous main climax, which is not only a revelation of something new (the introduction of the chorus), as is proper in climaxes, but the culmination of the integration process. Themes five, six and seven are heard all at once, and in extended forms (see Plate 8). The most powerful of them, theme five, carries the chorus with it; in the bass there is a recurrence of theme one. As if to compensate for the ineluctable strength of the crescendo, Berlioz's diminuendo is exceptionally rapid. It reaches the calm of theme two and dies away with an echo of the most memorable, theme three. In the process it returns the tonality to the opening C major. This procedure may be called traditional. But Berlioz's use of tonality

8 A page from Berlioz's autograph full score of the *Chasse royale et orage*, at the point marking the climax of the *Tableau*, and showing the alterations he made for the Théâtre-Lyrique performances. He crossed out the parts for his off-stage brass and transferred them to instruments in the main orchestra: thus the part for the first pair of tenor saxhorns is taken by four bassoons, four horns and two cornets all in unison, that for the second pair is omitted altogether and that for the three trombones is taken by trombones. The previous page is illustrated in NBE, p. 782.

elsewhere is profoundly original. He makes it float. It is unstable, his originality lying in his use of the rich sounds of E flat (notably at the climax) and the brilliant sounds of D major for non-structural, expressive purposes. All this amounts to an astonishing display of creative imagination – the writing of a piece of music which is universal in its basic design, unique in its working out.

The *Chasse royale* can be heard in another way, the one Berlioz presumably intended to carry the most immediate effect. It can be heard 'visually' – beginning in the steely light of morning with the birds twittering and the sun shining (themes 1 and 2), continuing with hunting calls (3) and huntsmen galloping along (4) with their friends not far away (5), until a storm builds up with its rain (Ex. 11.1), thunder and lightning and rallying calls from other huntsmen (6, 7). It concludes with a spectacular climax which soon dies away leaving a clear sky and the huntsmen disappearing into the distance. It holds up very well in this guise as a self-contained piece of descriptive music for the concert hall; when presented in the opera house and with Berlioz's scenic requirements (or some of them) it becomes that much more graphic – even if it leaves the audience slightly mystified. What, exactly, was it all about? Why did it begin with the theme heard at the end of Act III? What are those naked nymphs doing? That first horn solo (3): why dreamy and alert at the same time? If Dido and Aeneas are to consummate their love in a cave why does Berlioz give them only fifty seconds to do so? These are reasonable questions and suggest that there is more to the *Chasse royale* than at first appears.

A third way of hearing it can be offered, which takes as its starting-point the fact that the main dramaturgical purpose of the *Tableau* is to represent the passion that has sprung up between Dido and Aeneas. If the remainder of the opera is to depend on this, it seems hardly likely that Berlioz could have disposed of it in just fifty seconds. It is at least possible that he used the whole of the *Tableau* to represent their love-making, drawing on the subliminal power of music to complement the stage picture. In this connection it could be mentioned that the hunt as a symbol of the sexual chase is as old as the hills, as is the storm of emotional turbulence. Here is an interpretation of what Berlioz might have meant his music to portray.

At the opening the theme, on the violins, is in a high register: Aeneas looks into Dido's eyes. He caresses her face. As he slowly finds her whole person, the theme winds downwards and her tremulous responses are heard in the woodwind (Ex. 11.2). She begins to sing. He responds. A saxhorn solo, deriving from the first theme though soon taking on its own elusive character (Ex. 11.3). The symbolism of the horn is also old. Stirrings in the lower strings begin to take charge, derived from the earlier woodwind responses (Ex. 11.4). Bolder more decisive movement, and bolder symbolism in which the saxhorn theme is transformed into a new one for trombones, leading to the first surging wave of delight. The urgency quickens and, eventually there is a shrill cry on the piccolos, a signal of the climax, which comes with the sound of multitudinous voices and of all the themes together, a kind of cosmic embrace. A dark forbidding colour and then she sings again.

Ex. 11.2

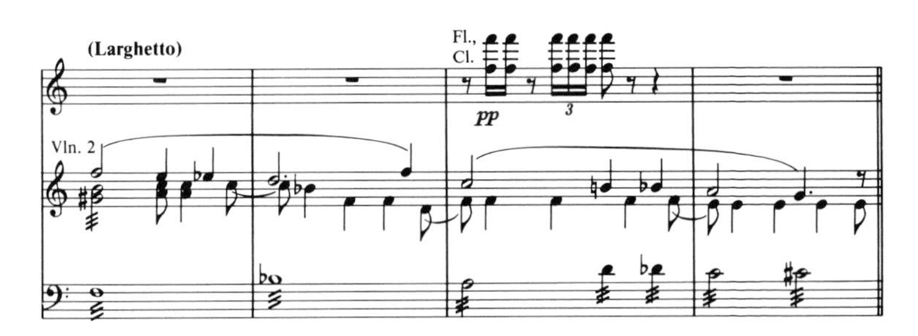


Ex. 11.3

Ex. 11.4

Berlioz was, in the best sense of the word, a *naïf*, and an interpretation along the lines above would not be out of character. But it is only one interpretation and the enduring fascination of the *Chasse royale* lies in the fact that its meaning cannot be circumscribed.

## (b) The Act I Finale

**IAN KEMP**

Because it contains the scene of the wooden horse the Act I finale is the most famous number in the opera. The question remains however of whether Berlioz actually meant the horse to appear. Originally he certainly did so. In his autograph libretto, stage directions include the following: 'The gigantic horse appears and crosses the back of the stage.' And his autograph full score indicates the following: 'The whole chorus enters, ranging itself to left and right at the back, while the horse, and the procession which follows it, cross the stage.' (See Plate 9.) The score indicates the precise bar at which this should start happening (183.112). It does not indicate the point at which the procession should have left the stage; but since the band of saxhorns enters with the procession it can be assumed that their exit, which Berlioz marks at 191.150, is that point. Later, he seemed to have changed his mind and decided the horse should not appear. In a copyist libretto with corrections in his own handwriting he crossed out the directions which include the sentence quoted above from the full score and added that the procession should be 'invisible to the spectator'. This seems conclusive, though he never removed the relevant sentence from his full score.[1]

However these directions are interpreted, the music for the scene indicates that the horse *should* be seen. It is a carefully planned crescendo, culminating when the full performing resources are heard for the first time and with Cassandra singing 'La voici!' (see Plate 9). This also seems conclusive, though the ways of producing the horse on stage or of producing the effect of the horse on stage are obviously infinite.

Berlioz's musical structure is simple, a march tune with the traditional 'trio' sections between its various recurrences. In every other respect it is unique, planned for the particular stereophonic effect he had conceived of a procession slowly approaching from a distance and suddenly being present in dazzling splendour. All his compositional resources are brought to bear on the achievement of this aural

9 A page from Berlioz's autograph full score of the Act I finale, at the point marking the entry of the wooden horse

illusion. His most subtle device is to have 'trio' sections of rapidly diminishing length (of respectively 46, 30, 16 and 7 bars), so that the march tune seems to get closer and closer. The trios contribute to the sense of anticipation through Berlioz's ability to make the music float, as if the horse itself were waiting, pawing the ground (see Ex. 11.5). In addition they spawn a large number of subsidiary themes, which preserve the momentum while not challenging the pre-eminence of the march tune.

Ex. 11.5

The Trojan March itself (see Ex. 11.6) is exactly geared to its expressive purpose. It is stirring and memorable, coloured with particular idiosyncrasies which symbolize both the Trojans' fateful destiny and their inherent vitality. The former is evident in the tune's plunge into the darker side of its tonality (bar 4). Its attempt to rise out of that produces its most striking progression (bars 6/7,

Ex. 11.6

Ex. 11.6 (*cont.*)

bracket), although it does not quite succeed in restoring a stable B flat tonic. A question-mark is left, a tension which Berlioz uses as the justification for the emergence of the trio sections. These therefore do not stand out as such, but form parts of an organic process, eventually completed when the Trojan March, after the alarm from within the horse, is given final, clinching and stabilizing phrases.

Berlioz implied that he had borrowed the structural idea of his finale from the 'Marche triomphale' in Act III of Spontini's *Olimpie* (see p. 53) – a remarkable instance of how composers can influence one another, for the paltry material of the Spontini is worlds apart from Berlioz's. All the same the Spontini does contain an imaginative structural idea, his 'trio' sections (far less tightly integrated than Berlioz's) gradually *expanding* in length (respectively 8, 20, 48, 66 and 72 bars).

The most conspicuous feature of the finale is Berlioz's deployment of the very large forces involved. Apart from the main orchestra and Cassandra, who have nothing to do with the March, there are two choruses and three stage bands or 'groups', as he called them. The latter are carefully distinguished in sound and function (see Appendix B under 'Saxhorns') and also in placing. The first group, the most penetrating, is placed furthest away from the stage, because it can be heard well from a distance and can make a dramatic impact as its players move forwards. The second group, comprising eight of the recently invented but now obsolete saxhorns, to evoke the sounds of the 'Phrygian trumpets' of the libretto, is placed closer, so they can be ready to march on stage at the climactic point. The least penetrating of the groups, and the one which has to be in a fixed position, is placed in the wings: oboes and harps, representing the 'double flutes' and 'Trojan lyres' of the libretto. Berlioz employs these groups judiciously, neither overexposing nor squandering their potential. The saxhorns, for example, are allowed to warm up in the second march, take a short rest, play properly in the second trio and then make their dramatic stage entry in the third march. This is the point at which all forces converge on stage. The two choruses (one of sopranos and basses, the other of contraltos and tenors) had sung independently of each other but now sing the march tune together (see Plate 9). By the fourth march, when the procession is on its way out, the sharp focus created at the climax has begun to break up and accordingly the choruses now sing not the tune but a counterpoint to it.

Superbly handled as the March is, the essence of this finale lies in its daring irony: Cassandra and the orchestra reacting as to the horrific. These unresolved tensions are entirely appropriate in a finale, in which respect its originality can be swallowed up in its dramatic power. It remains true however that Berlioz's music of pure gesture is without precedent. What is its legacy?

## (c) Dido's *Monologue* and *Air* (Nos. 47 and 48)

**JULIAN RUSHTON**

### The *Monologue*

Despite the beauty and pathos of her death scene, the quintessence of Dido's personal tragedy lies in her only soliloquy, formed of these two numbers. The monologue opens with a short *allegro* which may be compared to one of Berlioz's most feverish and syntactically radical passages, the opening of the tomb scene in *Roméo et Juliette*; melody, harmony, and rhythm are dislocated to match the raging against fate of Romeo and Dido. For the first time, we see the Queen alone. Yet having flung aside all restraint, she quickly controls herself and examines her situation: all she can do is die, and die unavenged.

The text is laid out in Table 11.1 with my own line-count but in accordance with Berlioz's musical interpretation and his own vocal score. It falls into no neat poetic shape. There are several rhymes or near-rhymes, and those of lines 2 and 3, 7 and 8, and 10 and 12, help to delineate the four main sections. Gradually lines of from six to eight syllables emerge as a structural basis for contradiction. The music mainly determines the structural divisions, I to IV, but they are also poetically distinct. Line 13 stands alone; its futile apostrophe to the goddess, while it echoes line 12 musically, also generates the next thought, and it has therefore been included in section IV. Sections I to III all begin with isolated four-syllable lines. Lines 1 and 4 cor-

Table 11.1 *Dido's Monologue and Air (1)*

| Section/line | | | Syllable count | |
|---|---|---|---|---|
| | | *(Didon parcourt la scène en s'arrachant les cheveux, se frappant la poitrine, et poussant des cris inarticulés)* | | *(Dido rushes across the stage tearing her hair, beating her breast, and uttering wordless cries)* |
| I | 1 | Je vais mourir. . . | 4 | I am going to die. . . |
| | 2 | Dans ma douleur immense submergée | 11 | Drowned in my overwhelming sorrow |
| | 3 | Et mourir non vengée! | 7 | And I die unavenged! |
| II | 4 | Mourons pourtant! | 4 | Yet die I must! |
| | 5 | oui, puisse-t-il frémir | 6 | yes, perhaps he will tremble |
| | 6 | A la lueur lointaine | 7 | At the distant glow |
| | | de la flamme de mon bûcher. | 8 | from the flames of my pyre. |
| | 7 | S'il reste dans son âme | 7 | If there is still a spark |
| | | Quelque chose d'humain, | 6 | of humanity in him, |
| | 8 | Peut-être il pleurera | | Perhaps he will weep |
| | | sur mon affreux destin. | 12 | at my terrible fate. |
| III | 9 | Lui me pleurer! | 4 | But for *him* to mourn me! |
| | | *(Avec un retour de tendresse)* | | *(With renewed tenderness)* |
| | 10 | Enée, Enée! Oh, mon âme te suit, | 10 | Aeneas, my soul follows you |
| | 11 | A son amour enchaînée, | 8 | Chained to its love, |
| | 12 | Esclave, elle l'emporte | | A slave, it bears its burden |
| | | en l'éternelle nuit. | 12 | into eternal night. |

Table 11.1 (*cont.*)

| Section/line | | | Syllable count | |
|---|---|---|---|---|
| IV | 13 | Vénus, rends-moi ton fils! | 6 | Venus, give me back your son! |
| | 14 | inutile prière | 7 | futile prayer |
| | 15 | D'un cœur qui se déchire; | 7 | Of a heart torn asunder; |
| | 16 | à la mort tout entière | 7 | to death alone devoted |
| | 17 | Didon n'attend plus rien que de la mort. | 10 | Dido desires nothing other than death. |

respond musically; line 9 is a brief access of indignation, after which returning tenderness precedes the period of highest intensity (lines 12–13). In section II Dido considers Aeneas's reaction to her death; in section III she seems to address him directly. Both these sections end with pure Alexandrines. Lines 5 to 7 and 13 to 16 consist mainly of half-Alexandrines, since the seven-syllable lines end with 'mute E'. Lines of ten or eleven syllables (line 2 also ending with 'mute E') act as gathering-points of thought; lines 2 and 10 are in corresponding positions within their sections, and line 17 provides a conclusion.

Ex. 11.7 reproduces Berlioz's own vocal score. Berlioz did not call the monologue a recitative, and despite a considerable amount of word-setting to repeated notes, the vocal line uses a lyrical rather than a functional style of declamation. Berlioz prescribes a unique notated *rubato*: two tempi, *moderato* and a considerably slower *andante*, alternate regularly at first; then each is extended until, in the middle of section III, the *moderato* seems to have been abandoned; it returns for a moment of determination near the end. These tempo changes do not subdivide the poetic or musical thought. The only distinct orchestral commentary, confided to the bass clarinet, is first heard *andante* (bar 22), but thereafter *moderato*, until at bar 41 it blossoms into an arpeggio (not shown in Ex. 11.7). Words and music are governed by a single obsession; Dido's thoughts move from herself to Aeneas and back, but her mind is always on death.

Ex. 11.8A breaks the vocal line down into motivic units. It can be read in the normal way from line to line, but the vertical alignment clarifies the taut motivic structure which Berlioz imposed on apparently free declamation. Motive A, the descending arpeggio, initiates sections I and II, and marks the cadence; the climactic period is also marked by descents (motive $A^1$). Motive B, an ascending scale, is used only at the beginning and end. Most of the line derives from the much less clearly-defined Material E (why it is E not C will become apparent). E may have its origin in Dido's second aria, No. 25, and it is used in recitative (No. 35) for 'en mon inquiétude extrême' (Ex. 11.8B). Material E is characterized by note-repetition, a dotted rhythm, a tendency to fall through a third (marked by broken slurs in Ex. 11.8A), and a sighing semitone; the latter, melodic image D (see p. 132), takes on a major role throughout the monologue.

After the *allegro*, No. 47 adheres to the key of E flat, moving from minor to major. Despite continual tonal fluctuation, relatively few key-centres are implied; all are unstable, and only E flat is cadenced. Section I seems to be returning to E flat minor from a subdominant

Ex. 11.7

No. 47
Monologue
All° assai. (132 = 𝅗𝅥)
Didon parcourt la scène en
mf Tutti.
f
417
s'arrachant les cheveux, se frappant la poitrine et poussant des cris inarticulés
ff
DIDON.
f
Ah! ah!
Elle s'arrête brusquement
Modto 100 = ♩
Andte un peu plus lent.
Modto un peu plus vite.
Je vais mourir...
Dans ma douleur im_
pp
Vons
Clar. Basse.
Andte plus lent.
Modto plus vite.
Andte plus lent
_men_se submer_gé_e
Et mourir non ven_gé_e!
mou
m.d.

Ex. 11.7 (*cont.*)

Mod^to plus vite.
-rons pourtant! oui, puisse-t-il fré - mir A la lueur loin
And^te plus lent.
-tai - ne de la flamme De mon bu-cher. S'il res - te dans son â - me Quelque cho - se d'hu
(Avec un retour de
Mod^to plus vite.
-main, Peut être il pleure - ra sur mon affreux destin. Lui me pleu - rer! E - née, E -
tendresse.)
- nee! Oh! mon â - me te suit, A son a - mour enchainé - e, Es -
Cres
A.C. 988.

Ex. 11.7 (*cont.*)

419
Andte Plus lent
-clave, el-le l'emporte en l'éternel-le nuit. Vé-
sf
f
p
Cres.
Ped.
nus, rends moi ton fils. i-au ti-le priè-re D'un cœur
p
qui se dé-chi-re.... à la mort tout entiè-re, Di-
Modto Plus vite.
Un poco cres.
don n'attend plus rien que de la mort.
Andte Plus lent.
Rit.
Cres.
p Andte Plus lent.
A.C. 98

Ex. 11.8A



An asterisk (*) indicates abbreviation by the omission of repeated notes.

Ex. 11.8B

No. 25

No. 35

excursion (implying a lowering of energy) when interrupted by the C flat major of section II (bar 28). The next bars are relatively stable, despite dominant (energizing) inflections (F natural leading to G flat). Section III begins with the chord-progression F flat to C natural, which wrenches the tonality from C flat to F natural, a tritone's distance (the *allegro* also encompassed a tritone, from A minor towards E flat). The period in F major (bars 41–3) is relatively sharp, thus 'bright', but the light is not optimism but the clear vision of despair: *Quaesivit coelo lucem ingemuitque reperta* (Sought light from heaven and moaned at finding it, *Aen.* 4.692). After the immediate return to F minor the pressure of dissonance thrusts the music in the dominant direction, so that the second occurrence of the highest vocal pitch, $f^2$ ('Vénus'), belongs to a dominant of C. The cadence in C is interrupted (bass G to A flat, bar 46); when A flat is resolved back to G (voice, bar 47) the tonal context is E flat major, in which the movement cadences at bar 54.

The sparing use of $f^2$ reflects the very careful disposition of vocal register. Motive A outlines a tonally-defining fifth (e $flat^1$–b $flat^1$), extended to a sixth in motive B (note the expanded rhythmic values of 'immense'; the *andante* minim is the longest note until bar 41). The thought, rather than hope, of revenge brings a range-extension in bar 26, after which the line remains within the octave e $flat^1$–e $flat^2$ until bar 40. Berlioz avoids monotony by subtle changes in key, instrumentation, and disposition of motives. Section II changes texture only slightly by silencing bass clarinet and horns. Motive B does not follow A, and the forms adopted by E which persist until bar 36 assist a shift of tonal centre so that G flat is heard both as a dominant and a tonic. Then comes the first D of any kind (d $flat^2$, bar 29); the tonally-defining fifth is thus now a third higher, g flat$^1$–d flat$^2$. The descending third becomes the main motive, falling by stages to the initial g flat with two chromatic inflections (bars 34–5). Section III at once completes the chromatic octave by introducing the missing pitches (C natural, D natural). If a general ascent to a high note seems an obvious ploy, this approach is harmonically ambiguous and gains force from its lack of relation to the tonic.

Berlioz actually extends the range at the climax, but in the orchestra. Before bars 43–4 the highest orchestral notes are all within the vocal octave and are seldom heard above the voice. The bass clarinet, emerging from the depths in bar 41, enters the vocal octave (reaching a natural$^1$), and perhaps inspires the ascent beyond f$^2$ in bar 43 (violins, flute, clarinet). By then the voice has sunk through a ninth to e natural$^1$, and this note is handed, in a lower octave, to the basses (with bass clarinet), and collides, as a diminished fourth, with the a flat$^2$. Dido's second descent from f$^2$ (from bar 45) proceeds more slowly, the scale inflected to C minor, then E flat. It reaches f$^1$ only after vacillating between G natural and G flat. The last phrase (bars 50–2) covers the whole range in a majestic ascent, before the awesome drop of a major ninth on 'plus rien'. At the last moment a semiquaver d natural$^1$ (bar 53) enlarges the range at the cadence. Dido is a mezzo-soprano; her range elsewhere extends from c$^1$ to a thrilling b flat$^2$ in No. 19. By confining the monologue and aria to a more limited range, Berlioz is able to exploit numerous resources for expression without abandoning the essential intimacy of soliloquy.

### The *Air*

In contrast to the monologue, the text of No. 48 (Table 11.2) uses only a slight variation in line-lengths, on the basis of the opening Alexandrine and the eleven-syllable lines with final 'mute E'(lines 2, 3, 5 and 7). The third 'Alexandrine' is divided by a comma, evading the elision ('Afrique astres'), and so has thirteen syllables. All the Alexandrines end 'strong' until the last line, which the 'mute E' again extends to thirteen syllables. Although the metre remains free, the consistent use of long lines conveys a new certainty and dignity, which correspond to the music despite Berlioz's free handling of the text (e.g. the repetitions in lines 3 and 4, bars 12–16; the splitting of line 6 by the echo of 'Adieu' on 'astres'). Ex. 11.9 again presents Berlioz's own piano reduction.

The musical restrictions exceed those of the monologue. The prin-

Table 11.2 *Dido's Monologue and Air (2)*

| Line | | Syllable count | |
|---|---|---|---|
| 1 | Adieu fière cité,<br>qu'un généreux effort | 12 | Farewell proud city,<br>which a noble effort |
| 2 | Si promptement éleva florissante, | 11 | Raised so quickly to prosperity, |
| 3 | Ma tendre sœur qui me suivis errante; | 11 | My gentle sister who followed me, wandering; |
| 4 | Adieu mon peuple, adieu rivage vénéré, | 12 | Farewell my people, farewell holy shore, |
| 5 | Toi qui jadis m'accueillis suppliante; | 11 | Which once greeted me, a suppliant; |
| 6 | Adieu beau ciel d'Afrique,<br>astres que j'admirai | 13 | Farewell lovely sky of Africa,<br>stars which I loved to see |
| 7 | Aux nuits d'ivresse et d'extase infinie; | 11 | On nights of rapture and endless ecstasy; |
| 8 | Je ne vous verrai plus,<br>ma carrière est finie.<br>(*Elle sort à pas lents*) | 13 | I shall see you no more,<br>my race is run.<br>(*She goes slowly out*) |

Ex. 11.9

No. 48
Air

421
Riten
a Tempo.
m'ac - cueillis suppli - an - te; Adieu beau ciel d'A - fri - que, as - tres que j'admi -
Riten.
a Tempo.
Poco f
Appassionato.
- rai Aux nuits d'i - vresse et d'ex - tase in - fi - ni - e;
Altos.
Una corda.
Flutes.
Tre corde
Je ne vous verrai plus, ma carrière est fi - ni - - e.
Altos.
Cres
Quat
Vclle
Tromb.
A.C.988.
La scène change.

cipal motives, A and B, are readily identified; the motivic handling is of extraordinary concentration (see Ex. 11.10), although the third element, motive C, is more freely handled, like material E in No. 47. Motive B re-emerges near the end in its original shape, but it appears in compressed forms, covering only a fifth (bars 11–12), then a fourth (16–17), in which form the chromatic insertions suggest identification with the first part of motive C (hence it is repeated in Ex. 11.10A, line 3).

The instrumentation is again very restricted. Trombones appear at the very end, taking over from the bass clarinet which is the last survivor from the wind group of the opening. The oboe, apart from the citation of the love-duet where it doubles the voice, has barely a dozen notes. The horn and bassoon parts are equally sparse; although horn tone is present throughout, there is only one incidence (bar 4) of three horns playing together. Even the cor anglais, which does so much to colour Berlioz's melancholy music (notably Marguerite's 'Romance' in *Faust*) has no melodic independence; the clarinet accompanies except for a brief melodic flowering; the muted violas, who make a melodic commentary, are the only strings until bar 24.

The tonality is still more confined. Indeed, 'Adieu, fière cité' does not modulate at all; a momentary inflection to the supertonic (bar 9) proves only a step towards the second imperfect cadence (bar 14, cf. bar 8), and the ambiguous diminished sevenths of the next phrase quickly return to dominant harmony (bars 18 and 22). Yet despite the opening pedal and the tonic-rooted citation from the love-duet (bars 27–30), there is not a single perfect cadence until immediately after the end of the voice part – a miracle of musical poise which prevents any hint of monotony within this masterpiece of negative climax.

The vocal range, still e flat$^1$–f$^2$, appears freshly conceived. The idea of range-extension, crucial within No. 47, is simply ignored (the voice begins on e flat$^2$ and f$^2$ is reached as early as bar 7). The tonally-defining fifth (a flat$^1$–e flat$^2$) now lies near the top of the range, so that the opening phrase sounds like a downward unfolding of overtones from the distant bass. Apart from the slight instability imparted to the pedal bass by the returning-note motive, the first pitches foreign to this dream-like tonic belong to motive B (violas), lingering on the b flat$^1$ into bar 6. Thereafter the tonic is clouded rather than undermined, to return clearly twice, in the parenthetical allusion to the love-duet, and after the cadence.

Ex. 11.10A

Motive A

3

A¹

Motive B

Motive C

6

10

15

19

21

23

25

27–30: citation from No. 37

31 Violas

32 Voice

33 Violas

35 Voice

Ex. 11.10B

No. 45

Motive B generates, and motive C completes, a scale over the entire range. Berlioz's motivic economy is more what one expects here, in a lyrical genre, than in the monologue. Musical repetitions correspond to those in the poem; but much of the fragrance of this aria derives from their inexactness. The second 'Adieu' (bar 15) moves down only to $f^1$, initiating the first ambiguous harmony (the diminished seventh, bar 16). The third 'Adieu' has a new melodic shape, while the fourth (bar 23) is rhythmically displaced (accent on the first syllable), and set to a melody derived from 'Ma tendre sœur' (bar 10). Its repetition ('astres'), with a lengthened first note, adheres to the characteristically prolonged subdominant harmony, marked by the entry of string basses and by the soaring clarinet line which again emphasizes the interval b flat–a flat (cf. bar 6). As in No. 47, the motives are redisposed, and Berlioz again reserves his most telling stroke for motive B. Its three final statements (from bar 31) build up chromatically (f flat–f natural–g flat$^2$) as if influenced by motive C. Dido sings only the diatonic second version; as in No. 47 she is momentarily silenced and the melodic high point is confided to the orchestra, coinciding with the most acute dissonance. The viola line falls back chromatically to the principal melodic note of the aria, e flat$^2$, then diatonically to cadence on $c^1$, effecting a dissolution of motives B and C. Dido's counterpoint to this, floating up to the initial e flat$^2$, is virtually the same as her closing phrase in No. 45 (Ex. 11.10B). The dominant note, onto which the first violins twice sigh in a last recall of the semitone motive (bars 36–7), is retained by the second violins to the very end, effecting a type of melodically open form very characteristic of the most intense Berlioz. The last orchestral arrivals, the trombones, join the basses in quietly reiterating the tonic and dominant pitches; the rhythm may be that of Dido's reluctant footsteps, but it is also a version of the 'fate rhythm'.

### Dido's 'personal motives'

It remains to establish whether the musical imagery of this two-movement soliloquy, in which the 'fate' elements are so reticent, forms part of a larger pattern. In fact, a cluster of motives quite different in shape and presentation from those discussed on pp. 129–49 threads its way through Dido's principal utterances, to reach a convincingly integrated conclusion in the aria; thereby we can make distinctions between the two heroines of the opera, despite Berlioz's indifference to personal motives, or to distinguishing Dido from Cassandra by using different tonalities or instrumental colours. Texturally, colouristically, and even (despite Cassandra's preference for flat keys) in terms of tonality, there is more differentiation according to mood within each role than between them; both, for instance, are enhanced by mobile and expressive bass lines, by string orchestration backed up by flutes and clarinets, and by the use of extremely flat keys, particularly E flat minor and G flat. The only evident contrast is in metre. Dido uses 6/8 in Nos. 24, 37, and 48, and this metre dominates the scene in her gardens in Act IV (Nos. 33a, 33b, 34, and 36 as well as 37); but Cassandra never uses 6/8, nor, indeed, does it appear after No. 1 until the Carthaginian acts.

Cassandra and Dido sound most alike, inevitably, in their most emotionally exacerbated recitatives. Nevertheless an elaborately-worked continuum, as in Nos. 2, 3, 15 and 16, belongs only to Cassandra who, although nearly demented, has a fixed vision, whereas Dido, in her most strident recitative (No. 46), does not know what she can or should do; she is fate's plaything; her disjointed thoughts are reflected in disconnected tonalities and orchestral motives; coherence is only restored when she turns for comfort to the gods of the underworld.

If a distillation of operatic characterization resides in any single place, it must be the beginnings of arias. Here a difference emerges all the more clearly in that the first three (Nos. 2, 10, and 19) all begin in E flat minor. 'Malheureux roi!' (Ex. 11.11A) is based on rising

Ex. 11.11

phrases, strongly directed by the scale over a fourth, with less determinate consequents falling nearly to the bottom of her range. In 'Non, je ne verrai pas' (Ex. 11.11B) the main motive is a descent, aimed with awful finality at the tonic, although it is harmonically interrupted by a bass C flat (bar 6). 'Chers Tyriens', however, begins with a descending arpeggio filled out by a passing-note (Ex. 11.12A): motive A, in fact. The orchestra responds with motive B, falling back by a sighing semitone to the dominant. Subsequently Cassandra tends to build paragraphs impetuously, by transposition and sequence; Dido introduces a third melodic idea ('tant de nobles travaux', motive C). Cassandra's first thoughts, then, tend to a fatalistic accent on the tonic, whereas Dido's prolong the dominant until, in No. 48, this remains the prime pitch-level throughout. Even the rising fourth to the tonic in 'Errante sur les mers' (No. 25), ostensibly similar to 'Malheureux roi!', falls back at once to the dominant. This motive is in any case drawn from the preceding duet, No. 24, which more emphatically prolongs the dominant (Ex. 11.12B); in this Anna may take the initiative, but the music is entirely concerned with Dido's feelings. The duet motive winds its way through even the 6/8 section, where it is inverted; the inversion reappears in Anna's frivolous *Cavatine*, No. 31 (Ex. 11.12B).

Ex. 11.12 shows the network of Dido's motives; it includes extracts from all her principal utterances except those in recitative or those where, as in Nos. 35 (Quintet) and 45, the orchestral commentary is of especial significance. The only other exception is the duet with Aeneas, No. 44, in which Dido's motives are hardly present; perhaps Berlioz did not intend to present her real self in this mood of irrational, even vicious, fury. The pattern elsewhere is strikingly consistent. The second vocal phrase of No. 19 (motive C) reaches d flat$^2$, which within a few bars is confirmed as the dominant; the rest of the melody is in G flat. 'Malheureux roi!' also changes mode, but by way of an abrupt modulation to G minor; the reprise recomposes the opening in E flat major. Thus nervous variation continues throughout No. 2, whereas 'Chers Tyriens', having confidently assembled a melody out of many motives, repeats it exactly with choral backing. Yet No. 2 is as solid a musical form as Cassandra ever has. Dido, in contrast, is involved in an extended two-movement duet (No. 24) as well as the last three ensembles of Act IV, so that the informal 'Errante sur les mers' is an exception within the role, justified by its obviously transitional nature (the time it occupies suffices for her message of welcome to reach the Trojans; and Dido is full of a

Ex. 11.12A

Motive A

Motive B

Motive C

No. 19

No. 24

No. 34

No. 37

No. 45

No. 47

No. 48

32 29 49 112 1 3 6 33 50 114 9 25 27 7 50 21 23 2 5 6

Ex. 11.12B

strange excitement which persists during the minor-mode Trojan March, No. 26).

A group of distinct motives, therefore, none of great complexity, may be seen to cluster in the movements which most represent Dido and which – No. 44 perhaps aside – embody her tragedy. They include even the love-duet, No. 37, where Aeneas is completely under her spell. The litany 'Par une telle nuit', which so strongly develops motive C and also anticipates the repeated-note and dotted-note configurations of Material E, is initiated by Dido. Ex. 11.12 shows this chain of connections which, with the extension of Material E in No. 47 and the reprise of the love-duet during No. 48, make a portrait of the unfortunate Queen of Carthage as fully-rounded as Virgil's. Ex. 11.12 is not comprehensive; and perhaps, in what it may imply about the composer's methods and the signifying powers of operatic music, it raises more questions than it can answer. Nevertheless this compelling economy of means makes a perfect illustration of the inner fire ('l'ardeur intérieur') which Berlioz listed, in a postscript to his *Memoirs* written at the time of work on *Les Troyens*, among the predominant qualities of his music.

# 12 *Performance history and critical opinion*

**LOUISE GOLDBERG**

*Les Troyens* has not been neglected (see Appendix D), though its performance history is a sad one indeed.[1] To this day there has never been a production which followed Berlioz's instructions exactly, for the saxhorns have always been replaced by other brass instruments.

Léon Carvalho's production of *Les Troyens à Carthage*, a cut version of Acts III to V divided by Berlioz into five with a newly written Prologue to replace the scenes in Troy, opened at the Théâtre-Lyrique on 4 November 1863. Cuts were made even within the part presented, some of them before the opening and some of them during the run of twenty-one performances. Berlioz lists ten in his *Memoirs*, and gives reasons for some of them which explain his personal bitterness and his description of the work as mutilated. The *Chasse royale* was cut after the first night: set changes required nearly an hour. This was in spite of the fact that the set was not particularly complicated, Berlioz's waterfall, for example, having been represented by a painted stream, since Carvalho's original plan to divert water from the nearby Seine had almost resulted in disaster at rehearsal when a switch failed.[2] The duet in Act V between Dido and Aeneas was cut because it was too much of a strain for Mme Charton-Demeur, and Hylas's song was cut because of contractual problems: the singer, Edmond Cabel, would have had to be paid overtime after 1 December. And so on . . . In his autograph score Berlioz reluctantly authorized eight of the ten cuts and included necessary musical adjustments. These eight are Nos. 20, 21, 22, 29, 30–1 (counting as one), 34, 40 and 44. What he evidently could not countenance was the removal of Nos. 33b and 38.

Performances after the first production continued the 'tradition' then established, as cut or divided productions have persisted for more than one hundred years. The lack of a complete orchestral score before 1969 and the extreme scarcity of a complete and accurate vocal score made an uncut performance as well as study of the work difficult if not almost impossible. Difficulties have also been created by staging demands. The large cast, multiple changes in scenery, the co-ordination of off-stage bands and chorus, and the movement of the horse have all contributed to problems of production. The problem of the off-stage bands and chorus is now easily solved with television cameras, but the opera remains expensive to produce. It requires both a large stage and a large backstage area, and opera companies have generally accepted the need for lavish sets and costumes.

The Trojan horse creates its own problems (see p. 157).[3] In order to bring the climax out of the wings, producers have had the horse on-stage in most productions. The size of the horse and how much of it is shown depends, of course, on the size of the stage and backstage areas. When there is not enough room, producers have used their creativity to suggest the presence of the beast. One solution, used at Covent Garden in 1957, was to have the legs and belly of a huge horse as an immobile frame for the stage in that scene. And the Metropolitan Opera in New York, although it had room for a horse, used a television projection against part of the Trojan wall in 1973 and just the horse's head showing above the wall in 1983.

Another difficulty is presented by the very unequal lengths of the two parts of the opera. The Trojan acts make a short evening by conventional standards; producers were inclined to fill out the rest with something else. That something else was not the three Carthaginian acts, for the entire opera is longer than many producers considered suitable for one evening.

Productions of *Les Troyens* between 1863 and the present can be summarized by tracing the trends in production during three periods: from 1863 to 1899, from 1900 to 1940, and from 1945 to the present.

*1863–1899.* Although *La Prise de Troie* was not staged until 1890, concert performances were given in Paris in 1879 – in fact two of them on the same day, 7 December (see Appendix D).

On 6–7 December 1890, in Karlsruhe, Felix Mottl conducted the first staged performance of the whole opera. *Les Troyens* was given on two consecutive evenings, sung in German, and using Berlioz's division of the two parts into three and five acts respectively. The production was revived often during the next eleven years, with some of the performances on one day. Mottl took the production to Mannheim in 1899, and then in 1908 conducted another production in Munich, which was revived in 1909. He 'arranged' the music for the production, mainly by placing the *Chasse royale* after the love-duet; his shifting of scenes was to prove sadly influential.

Although the first French production of *La Prise de Troie* took place in Nice in 1891, the two most significant productions during the ensuing decade were those of *Les Troyens à Carthage* at the Opéra-Comique in Paris in 1892 and of *La Prise de Troie* at the Paris Opéra in 1899. At the time of the 1892 production, Carvalho had become director of the Opéra-Comique, and by coincidence, due to a fire in the Opéra-Comique's theatre in 1887, was using the Théâtre-Lyrique, where the 1863 première had taken place. Numerous cuts were made, but the opera received generally favourable reviews. The 1899 production of *La Prise de Troie*, mounted in commemoration of the thirtieth anniversary of Berlioz's death, was the first of any part of his work at the Paris Opéra. (The Opéra's first production of *Les Troyens à Carthage* was not to follow until 1919, in Nîmes.)

*1900–1940.* In contrast to the large number of concert performances in the nineteenth century, the period from 1900 to 1940 consisted almost entirely of staged productions. Separate presentations of one part or the other were given, but the tendency was to give the whole opera in extremely condensed versions, in order to squeeze it into a single evening of the 'usual' length.

The first performance of *Les Troyens* as a whole in French (though of course cut) was staged in Brussels on two consecutive nights in December 1906. It was performed twelve times during in 1906–7 season, some of the later performances being on a single evening.

In Great Britain during this period, both concert and staged productions took place. The first performance of any part of the opera in England had been a concert performance of *Les Troyens à Carthage* in Liverpool in March 1897, followed by another concert performance in Manchester in December of that year. A second Manchester performance took place in 1928. These performances all had the *Chasse royale* after the love-duet, which in 1928 provoked an exchange of letters to the *Musical Times*.[4] A staged production followed in Glasgow in 1935, sung in English. Produced and conducted by Erik Chisholm, this ambitious, largely amateur production was the first time any part of the work had been staged in Great Britain, and it triggered a great flurry of interest (a special train even brought Berlioz connoisseurs from London) which would lead to the intense work done in that country after World War II, both in staging the opera and in publishing the score.

Three condensed versions produced during this period marked

important stages in the changing fortunes of the opera. They allowed the opera-goer to see at least part of all five acts in one evening, although naturally the structure of the work suffered.

The first of them was made in Stuttgart in 1913 by Emil Gerhäuser and Max von Schillings. They changed the divisions between acts (though keeping five) and moved the Anna–Narbal duet and the *Chasse royale* to after the love-duet. Large parts of both Act I and – surprisingly – Act IV were omitted.

The second condensation, made by the Paris Opéra, was first performed in Rouen in 1920 and then seen in Paris in 1921. Parts of Act I, all of Act II, scene 2, parts of Act III, and much of Act V were omitted. Act IV appears to have been nearly complete and in the proper order. The production was revived several times between 1921 and 1939, and during the course of these revivals some music was restored and other sections cut. Whatever its faults, this production at least introduced the idea of *Les Troyens* as a single work to Berlioz's native country.

The third condensation, made for the Berlin Opera in 1930, was a laughable travesty. Julius Kapp, the conductor, not only made cuts, but drastically reworked the story in the Carthaginian acts.[5] Much was cut immediately after the Trojans had landed and Aeneas announced himself; it was love at first sight, for the next music was the Septet and the love-duet. Not satisfied with Shakespeare and Berlioz, Kapp changed the text of the love-duet. The next act began with the *Chasse royale*; the following scene was Aeneas's departure. After Hylas's song and the appearance of the ghosts, Dido appeared on the shore, saw that Aeneas had departed, and stabbed herself as he sailed away. Most of the final scenes were eliminated, including the apotheosis.

*1945–the present.* Since the end of World War II, *Les Troyens* has been finding its way into the repertoire much more widely and much more authentically. The trend now has definitely been toward presenting the opera as an entity; condensations have been made but they have been less characteristic. Besides staged productions, there have been concert presentations as well; many of them, especially those in England, were preparations for a staged production.

Major highlights have occurred during this period. In 1957, Rafael Kubelik conducted a production of *Les Troyens* at Covent Garden with very little music cut, although with the *Chasse royale* still in the wrong place. Sir John Gielgud produced the opera, using television as an aid to the problem of the off-stage forces.[6] The work was revived the following year. Another revival, in 1960, restored the *Chasse royale* to its proper place, but the scene was no longer staged.

1969, the centenary of Berlioz's death, encompassed four memorable events: the first complete *Les Troyens* staged in one evening, uncut, and sung in English (by Scottish Opera in Glasgow and Edinburgh conducted by Alexander Gibson); the first complete *Les Troyens* staged in one evening, uncut, and sung in the original French (at Covent Garden conducted by Colin Davis); publication of the first complete orchestral score; and, crucially, the first complete recording (Colin Davis's Covent Garden performance, released by Philips in 1970). It was finally possible to study and produce the whole work, and to judge it on its own merits.

The French, however, continued to shorten the opera. A production first heard in Lyons in 1958 was probably the most truncated ever made, despite which it was presented with minor variations elsewhere in Europe and in Buenos Aires and San Francisco. Made by Lou Bruder to enable his wife Régine Crespin to sing both Cassandra and Dido in the same evening, the version omitted as many as eighteen numbers and had internal cuts in about half those remaining.[7] A production at the Paris Opéra in 1961 was somewhat less heavily cut than Bruder's. For the centenary in 1969, the Opéra revived the production, restoring some of the music which had been cut in 1961.

The 1969 events in Great Britain set the stage for productions in other opera houses, especially in the United States, which had a fair history of performances of its own. Concert performances dated from 1882, when Theodore Thomas conducted three performances of the second act of *La Prise de Troie* in New York, Cincinnati, and Chicago; the concert in New York was part of his May Music Festival, for which he had at his disposal an orchestra of 300 and a chorus of 3000. These performances were followed in 1887 in New York by one of most of *Les Troyens à Carthage*, sung in English and 'adapted for use on the concert stage by Frank van der Stucken'.

Nothing more was heard of *Les Troyens* (other than excerpts) until 1955 in Boston, where Boris Goldovsky conducted the first staging of the work in the United States, a somewhat condensed version sung in English. The American Opera Company gave two concert performances during the winter of 1959–60, in Washington and New York. Sir Thomas Beecham conducted in Washington, but due to Beecham's illness, Robert Lawrence conducted in New York.

The Boston Opera Company mounted the first uncut staging in the United States in February 1972, conducted by Sarah Caldwell.

10 Scottish Opera, 1969: the opening scene of Act III

11 Covent Garden, 1969: the Act III finale

Sung in French, the first of the two presentations was on consecutive evenings and the second an afternoon–evening split performance. John Nelson conducted a complete and uncut concert presentation a month later in Carnegie Hall and in October 1973 the Metropolitan Opera of New York presented *Les Troyens* with minor cuts (Nos. 20–2 and, inexplicably, Nos. 45–6, half of Dido's final scene). The production was conducted first by Kubelik and in later performances by Nelson. In the summer of 1978, James Levine conducted the Chicago Symphony in a concert performance of the uncut work, and he revived it at the Metropolitan Opera in 1983, now with all the music restored.

Critical opinion of *Les Troyens* during its first century must be viewed with extreme caution. Lack of knowledge of the opera handicapped earlier critics, many of whom did not know that they were seeing truncated versions. Praise or criticism of the worth of *Les Troyens* was made according to what was seen on stage. In spite of the lack of basic information, many critics made serious attempts to understand the opera, and contributed valuable insights. Some twentieth-century critics and writers are conspicuous for their profound understanding of it before the score was generally available, notably Ernest Newman[8] and, in particular, Jacques Barzun, whose classic biography of Berlioz, first published in 1950, exerted a crucial influence on the subsequent rehabilitation of the opera.

A number of trends stand out in the history of critical writing on *Les Troyens*. During the second half of the nineteenth century, the practice of comparing all operas with Wagner's quickly displaced most other aesthetic standards. Since Berlioz disagreed so radically with Wagner's concept of music drama, reception of his work naturally suffered. After the turn of the century, German critics continued to judge *Les Troyens* by Wagnerian standards, while French and English critics began to examine Berlioz's work on its own merits.

Critical opinion in the nineteenth century corroborates views held on Berlioz's music in general at that time, and reviews are thus valuable more as instances of the changing nature of music criticism than as judgements of the opera's musical and dramatic worth. Yet the first performances of *Les Troyens à Carthage* in Paris in 1863 were a considerable success.[9] After a first hearing, most critics were unable to write in detail about the work's intricacies and subtleties but many tried valiantly to convey to the public the greatness they sensed – among them, for example, Auguste de Gasperini:

None of the elements that comprise solid and complete works, as Berlioz has understood it, is lacking in the drama of *Les Troyens*. All the feelings he brings into play are profoundly human; he responds to all the needs of the soul. That is the great secret of art.

He explained further the following week:

In the entire dramatic part of the work, when his characters are on stage, Berlioz makes certain that it is passion, and passion alone, that speaks. We are not watching heroes, sons of gods;. . .make-believe characters, slaves and toys of the Divinity, could not move us or charm us. We want to hear human voices. . .Berlioz is entirely and profoundly human.[10]

Gustave Bertrand, contributor to and later the editor of *La Revue Germanique*, contrasted Berlioz's with Wagner's use of the orchestra:

What is more monotonous. . .than this immense and massive entanglement of symphony and chanting, which reigns unceasingly in M. Wagner's operas. M. Berlioz's style is less full – he almost never uses the whole orchestral mass; his means are better divided and apportioned, there is air and there are open spots.[11]

In 1870, Georges de Massougnes took critics of the 1863 Paris production to task for singling out only a few numbers for praise rather than treating the work (or what they had seen of it) as a whole:

*Les Troyens* is not only a masterpiece, but a masterpiece of rare perfection. I emphasize this perfection, because most of the critics, malevolent or innocent, while recognizing in this work two or three sublime passages 'where genius', they say, 'ran freely', have contented themselves with showing these flashes of *genius* as a stroke of luck for the author, who found them by chance, and with representing them as isolated amidst an immense jumble of senseless laboriousness.[12]

By the time *Les Troyens à Carthage* was next seen in Paris, in 1892 at the Opéra-Comique, the increasing tendency of French critics to judge Berlioz by Wagnerian standards had taken root and enabled them to hold an incompletely-known *Les Troyens* inferior to whatever Wagner operas they had heard. (In fact, only three had been performed in Paris to date: *Tannhäuser* in 1861, *Rienzi* in 1869 and *Lohengrin* in 1887). The following is characteristic:

Whatever his admiration for certain numbers of an obviously original nature, the music-lover will be disappointed, since he does not for a minute have the sensation of novelty that he has all the time in *Lohengrin*, though it dates from thirteen years before *Les Troyens*; and deception in music is one of the most disagreeable things I know, since it is double because of the disappointment at not receiving the pleasure that one had been promised.[13]

Nevertheless, some critics positively preferred Berlioz:

> Berlioz's opera differs from the Wagnerian type in all its essential elements. First, its subject is as human and concrete as that of the *Tetralogy*, for example, is abstract and supernatural. Moreover, the *leitmotiv*, the cornerstone of Wagnerism, is absent from it . . . Does the psychological expression (the Greeks would have said the 'ethos') of this music lose anything of force and appropriateness? I believe not.[14]

Julien Tiersot (the foremost Berlioz scholar of his time) wanted to reassert the Berliozian aesthetic:

> . . . it is a series of tableaux and distinct impressions rather than an action in the true sense. As a consequence, the music was able to occupy in the work a dominant place that it has not always had in the modern musical drama.[15]

Adolphe Jullien (Berlioz's biographer) wanted to redress the balance. In a review of the 1890 Karlsruhe production, he wrote that it was 'impossible for the discerning and impartial listener not to see how many points in common these two great minds have', pointing out that while France still thought it 'good manners to speak of the incomparable genius of the composer of *Tristan*', but did little about it, Germany actually performed and appreciated Berlioz's music.[16] By way of proving his point, the epoch-making Karlsruhe production had no effect on French theatres. Only a very small number of French critics went to see it. Yet by the time *La Prise de Troie* had reached the Opéra, in 1899, many of them felt that the two parts of the opera should be put back together. Paul Dukas, for example, wrote:

> . . . if *La Prise de Troie* and *Les Troyens à Carthage*, otherwise and more simply known as *Les Troyens*, were presented in one evening, we would see this admirable creation of Latin genius in a completely different light, and we would better realize its imposing proportions.[17]

During the first forty years of the twentieth century, many of the same trends persisted, but the emphasis changed. The Wagner aesthetic persisted but not so strongly. Although ignorance lingered (the composer and critic Reynaldo Hahn, for example, asked in a 1921 review whether Berlioz was right in wanting to join two works which were so different[18]), the feeling grew as the work became better known that its unity was destroyed by splitting it into two parts.

Ernest Clausson, a Belgian critic, had reservations about *Les Troyens* after seeing it in Brussels in 1906, but praised it nonetheless. The Wagnerian in him however led to comparisons:

> The prelude to this scene [No. 12] appears to be a sketch for the prelude to the second act of *Götterdämmerung*, and does not fall short of that in its impact . . . How, for example, can the short procession of the guilds in the beginning of *Les Troyens à Carthage* [Nos. 20–2] be compared to 'the other,' the one in *Die Meistersinger*?![19]

The post-Wagnerian aesthetic developing in France from the turn of the century – deriving particularly from Debussy's *Pelléas et Mélisande* and the early works of Stravinsky – led to judgements such as Raymond Bouyer's, after the performances in Rouen in 1920. He was one of the first to mention the relationship between the influences of Virgil, Shakespeare, and Gluck.

> Do not be so preoccupied with form, for only inspiration counts here; and in its absolutely French form of *tragédie lyrique*, does this opera not present to us the décor or the image of a harmonious yet original sanctuary, where, curiously, the great spirits of Virgil, Shakespeare, and Gluck assemble, reconciled in the splendour of dedication?[20]

After the 1921 Paris performances, many other critics set about judging *Les Troyens* on its own merits and (notably Tiersot) complaining about the number of cuts – which in fact were substantially the work of Adolphe Boschot (author of a three-volume biography of Berlioz). Their main subject was the relationship between music and drama. Ernest Newman, a Wagnerite who had dismissed Berlioz's later music as that of an ill and discouraged man, found the 1921 performances a revelation, deepening his conviction that 'Berlioz has never yet had justice done to him as a composer'. His remarks about the Quintet (No. 35) are among his most telling:

> A man needs to have lived long and to have suffered much to compass a beauty so wistful and so touched with all the humanities as this. This scene alone would be enough to make Dido one of the greatest female characters in opera.[21]

After the 1935 Glasgow performances he was able to write;

> The test of a dramatic composer is not in his ability to write fine music for outstanding lyrical episodes but in his capacity for filling the veins of the action as a whole with living blood; and judged by this test Berlioz, in the 'Trojans', stands out as a genuine musical dramatist.[22]

– an opinion endorsed by Tovey, who called the opera 'one of the most gigantic and convincing masterpieces of music-drama'.[23]

The picture changed after World War II, providing a new background against which critical writing on *Les Troyens* must be viewed.

Not only was Berlioz's music becoming better known, thus affording critics a chance to relate *Les Troyens* to his other works, but operas by nineteenth-century composers such as Meyerbeer, Spontini, Cherubini, and Bellini, among others, were being produced; thus the relationship of *Les Troyens* to operas preceding it and contemporary with it was more easily studied.

Three broad areas of discussion have dominated criticism since World War II: praise for and criticism of the opera itself, comment on the truncated versions, and discussion of the relationship between music and drama.

Not all critics liked the opera, of course – some thought it dramatically weak – but there was a great deal of comment on the effect of the whole (even with some music cut, as in the 1957 Covent Garden production), and especially after the complete productions. Mosco Carner, writing in 1957, expressed feelings which were characteristic of many critics at the time:

> We sat in our seats last week enthralled, stirred, uplifted and wondering again and again how it came about that this work had suffered so sad a neglect since it was written nearly a hundred years ago. In *The Trojans* the greatness of the subject is matched by the greatness of its treatment, displaying a nobility, dignity and grandeur of vision that makes most present-day operas appear no more than *opusculi.* It drew from Berlioz some of the most ravishing and glorious music he ever penned.[24]

French critics, for the most part, continued to be negative, and many called for the continuation of condensed versions which would 'shorten as much as possible . . . the part of the work which is the least good musically'.[25] A few critics disagreed however, notably Jacques Bourgeois (see below) and Claude Rostand (see p. 17 above).

Although the Wagner aesthetic is no longer the dominant factor in discussion of *Les Troyens*, comparison of the two composers can hardly be avoided. Most writers placed at least some of the blame for the neglect of *Les Troyens* on the fact that it is so different from Wagner's works. In 1967, David Cairns took to task those anti-Wagnerites who used Berlioz as their weapon:

> Nothing is more pointless and wasteful than to pit Berlioz against Wagner, to try to use him as a weapon in anti-Wagnerian polemics . . . But antitheses they certainly are; and until the tide of Wagnerism which swept over Europe in the latter part of the nineteenth century had receded, it was vain to expect a work so classical, so French and so – from the Wagnerian point of view – reactionary and primitive to be understood.[26]

With the complete opera finally available, critics have begun to examine more carefully the relationship between music and drama. It was realized that by cutting the work so heavily, producers had changed internal balances of both music and drama, as well as the relationship between the two. Jacques Bourgeois, who had seen an extremely shortened version in Paris in 1939, wrote in 1957:

In that abridged version there seemed to be certain dull passages that I was quite unconscious of in the recent Covent Garden performance of the complete score. This often happens when the balance of a work is tampered with in such a way that the contrast between the climaxes and the passages of lower intensity, so carefully planned by the composer, is missing.[27]

Just before the 1957 production at Covent Garden, Robert Collet examined Berlioz's dramatic ability within the larger framework of opera aesthetics in general:

The criticism is often made that Berlioz was not truly dramatic . . . It is based on the idea that the drama of Opera should, within the limits of what is possible, approach the standards that would be acceptable in an ordinary stage play . . . It was not really true of the older French Opera which on the contrary was first and foremost a drama of *situations* . . . If this basic fact is grasped the much greater emphasis in France on the chorus, the ballet and the orchestra, and the willingness to accept a much more static stage action, become perfectly understandable. *The Trojans* is no doubt the last, and certainly one of the greatest works in this peculiar tradition, which begins in the late seventeenth century with Lully and stretches into the nineteenth through Rameau, Gluck, Lesueur, Méhul, and Meyerbeer. If it can intelligibly be held that their works are undramatic (or perhaps the true word is untheatrical) in the sense that they would be quite unacceptable as ordinary stage works, they are truly operatic in a special sense, in that the music makes possible a kind of drama that humanly can be most deeply impressive, and that would otherwise be impossible on the stage.[28]

One of the major aspects of the drama in *Les Troyens* is the relationship between the epic theme and the characters' personal feelings. Once the overall structure was known, critics could begin to see how the epic theme unified the various episodes. Thus Winton Dean, in 1957:

But Berlioz does not proceed in ordinary dramatic terms. . .The main epic theme does not arise from the drama at all: it is superimposed from without (as of course it is in Virgil . . .). Again and again, Berlioz appeals over the heads of the characters directly to the audience and its acquaintance with literature and history. . .

Berlioz is able to get away with this because the double epic-dramatic vision exactly suits the nature of his genius, and in particular his tendency to project the action in a series of tableaux, like friezes on the pediment of a Greek temple. . .His overall theme, however loosely super-imposed, does help to keep the episodes in focus.[29]

The *Chasse royale* has come under much discussion as to its dramatic place in the opera. At one time it was seen as improper, no doubt because of its suggestion of love consummated before marriage. Perhaps it was for this reason that Felix Mottl moved it to a point *after* the love-duet – which if not representing marriage, was at least a declaration of love. Winton Dean examined the issues from the point of view of Virgilian and Shakespearean concepts. Berlioz, he wrote, expressed the consummation of the love between Dido and Aeneas at two different points in the work because each time it is depicted according to a different dramatic concept.

The climax of the love between Dido and Aeneas is the great central event of the opera, and Berlioz presents it twice, first epically in the Symphonic Intermezzo [the Royal Hunt and Storm] and then dramatically in the garden scene [the love duet], following it on each occasion with the 'Italie!' warning. There is no question of the garden scene representing a second or later consummation:. . .Berlioz wanted to have it both ways: Virgil's storm-consummation as well as his own (Shakespeare-aided) garden consummation.[30]

The careful consideration of *Les Troyens* that has been emerging more recently can be seen particularly clearly in the following excerpts from Alan Levitan's review after the Boston staging in 1972:

*Les Troyens* . . . is not a linearly conceived opera; rather, it is a study in extraordinary juxtapositions. Part I is almost a mirror-prologue to the Carthage section, and the whole opera strikes one as a series of reflected images, echoes, and themes which suffer a structural diminishment if not seen as a totality.

. . . Cassandra, pleading with her lover to flee Troy in the face of her visions of defeat, is – though differently motivated – balanced by the later Dido, pleading with *her* lover *not* to leave the city of Carthage to fulfill his own visions of victory. . .

Lest you think that the structural niceties . . . are in the libretto alone, let me hasten to add that Berlioz makes cunningly organic use of musical mirror-images as well, to underline his contrasts and comparisons. For example, in Part I, when the ghost of Hector urges Aeneas to flee Troy, he does so in a sequence of lines. . .which trace a descending scale;. . .In Part II, when Dido becomes enraged at Aeneas' insistence upon leaving Carthage (her function here is exactly the reverse of Hector's), she sings. . .a sequence that is the mirror-image of Hector's, this time on an *ascending* scale of reiterated notes. . .This is no more accidental than are the closely balanced textures of Shakespeare's plays, which Berlioz knew and loved all his life.[31]

The past thirty years have seen the period of the deepest understanding of *Les Troyens* – both of the work itself and of its interwoven elements, among them the musical and dramatic, the juxtaposition and balancing of the epic and human themes, and the preparations and recalls. It has become a work of perennial fascination, fully justifying Gasperini's prediction after the 1863 première: 'Whatever the destiny reserved for it in our time, it is an important work, one of the glories of the century; it will not die.'[32]

APPENDIX A

# *Glossary of names in the libretto*

**IAN KEMP**

Names are listed in Berlioz's French spellings. Those appearing in the rejected Sinon scene and original finale are included. Details of the references to Berlioz's numberings in the opera are given in the Synopsis. With the exception of Hylas and Narbal all Berlioz's characters are drawn from the *Aeneid.*

**Achille** (Achilles) Son of Peleus and the goddess Thetis. The most famous and fearsome of the Greeks, killed by Paris before the sack of Troy. Recent excavations suggest that Achilles's tomb was on the mainland opposite Tenedos, and not on the banks of the Simois, as Berlioz's stage directions for No. 1 require.

**(Pas des) Almées** (Dance of the Almas, or Alméhs: No. 33a) The letter cited on p. 55 suggests that Berlioz got the idea of almas from Auber's opéra-ballet *Le Dieu et la Bayadère* (1830). Almas, still in existence in the nineteenth century, were Egyptian dancing girls who specialized in voluptuous dances. Their dress included little bells, as indicated in Berlioz's wind parts (e.g. bars 10–13). In his *The Manners and Customs of the Ancient Egyptians* (London 1837) J. G. Wilkinson suggested that a plate in Hippolito Rosellini's *I Monumenti dell'Egitto e della Nubia*, reproduced on p. 206, gave a good idea of what almas originally looked like. Berlioz's initial idea of representing his almas as *bayadères*, Hindu dancers (see p. 55), was evidently abandoned during the course of composition.

**Anchise** (Anchises) Member of the royal family of Troy and, through a union with Venus, father of Aeneas. Anchises boasted about this and as a consequence was lamed. He was carried from the burning Troy by Aeneas but died before the Trojans reached Carthage. (No. 37)

**Andromache** Widow of Hector. She never recovered from his death and grieved for him (No. 6) for the rest of her life. After the sack of Troy she was captured by Pyrrhus, who had just killed Priam, her father-in-law. Pyrrhus took her home to Epirus, forcibly married her and had children by her. Having transferred his interest to Helen's daughter Hermione, he passed Andromache on to her brother-in-law Helenus, whom he had also brought back captive. On the death of Pyrrhus some of his realm was inherited by Helenus. At *Aen.* 3.294ff Aeneas recounts all this to Dido. But in No. 35 Berlioz, in an ingenious gloss, makes Andromache love Pyrrhus and draws a veil over Helenus.

**Anna** [contralto] Dido's sister. In a letter of 7 April 1858 to his favourite, younger sister Adèle, Berlioz wrote: 'You are my sister Anna and I know very well that you would follow me to Carthage and to the end of the world – if it weren't for the children and their father.' (CG V 2295)

**Annibal** (Hannibal) Carthaginian general who after spectacular successes against the Romans in the Second Punic War was eventually defeated by Scipio Africanus and obliged to accept a humiliating peace. Eighteen years later he committed suicide. (No. 50)

**Ascagne** (Ascanius) [soprano] Aeneas's beloved young son (Berlioz makes him fifteen); also called Iulus by Virgil in order to link him with the earlier Trojan king Ilus and with the later Roman family of the Julii, Julius Caesar and Augustus in particular.

**Astyanax** Infant son (Berlioz makes him eight) of Hector and Andromache, and thus heir to the throne; murdered after the sack of Troy. (No. 6)

**(Champs) Ausoniens** (Ausonian fields) An adjective used frequently by Virgil to mean Italian. (No. 41)

**Augustus** The first Roman emperor, for whom Virgil wrote the *Aeneid.* (Nos. 52, 52a)

**Aulide** (Aulis) The harbour where the Greek fleet assembled before setting sail for Troy. In No. 1 the Trojans think the Greeks are on their way back there.

**Bacchus** God of wine (Dionysus). (No. 40)

**Calchas** The chief prophet of the Greeks. (No. 6a)

**Caron** (Charon) The old, unkempt god who ferried the dead across the Styx in the underworld. By crediting Charon with a 'funeral fanfare' (No. 16) Berlioz is probably following the example in Act III of Gluck's *Alceste*, where Charon has a conch. (*A travers chants*, pp. 209–11)

**Carthage** According to Virgil, and most other writers, Carthage was founded by Dido. Evidence suggests that this was in the first half of the ninth century BC, which makes the Trojans' voyage to Carthage even more remarkable, for Troy was destroyed in the thirteenth century BC. Carthage was itself destroyed, by the Romans, in the middle of the second century BC. Dido's Carthage was situated on a narrow strip of land (about two miles long and a mile deep) at the southern end of a peninsula stretching eastwards into the Mediterranean. About four miles to the north-west was a gulf (the present Sebka er Riana), immediately to the south a lake (the present Lake of Tunis with the modern Tunis at the western end).

**Cassandre** (Cassandra) [mezzo-soprano] According to the *Iliad*, the most beautiful of Priam's daughters. She attracted the attention of Apollo, who promised her the gift of prophecy if she would sleep with him. She agreed, but then broke the bargain. In his distress Apollo craved just one kiss, which she vouchsafed, whereupon he spat in her mouth, thus ordaining that her prophecies would never be believed. *Aen.* 2.403ff recounts that during the sack of Troy she was dragged from the shrine of Pallas Athene (elsewhere

Virgil alludes to her rape there by Ajax the Lesser), a blasphemy which so incensed Coroebus that he hurled himself upon the Greeks and was immediately killed. According to the *Odyssey* and to Aeschylus and Euripides, Cassandra was then captured by Agamemnon, whose mistress she became. On his return to Argos, Agamemnon, along with Cassandra, was murdered by his wife Clytemnestra. 'In spite of history', wrote Berlioz, 'I am obliged to kill her off at the end of Act II.' (CG V 2115)

**Cérès** The goddess of corn (Demeter). (Nos. 23 and 24)

**(Combat de) Ceste** Berlioz's title for No. 5 seems to present a contradiction. The *Aeneid* describes both boxing and wrestling. The boxing (5.363ff), particularly nasty, is conducted with a *caestus*, a huge 'glove' made of extremely hard and heavy leather and sometimes stiffened with lead and iron. The equivalent in French, *ceste*, is worse: in *Le Roman de la Momie* (1858, p. 237) Gautier described it as an iron band, held in the left hand (the right holding a stick). Whatever the *ceste* was, it certainly indicated some kind of boxing. On the other hand, Berlioz's subtitle, *Pas de lutteurs*, means dance of wrestlers. According to the *Aeneid*, Trojan games included wrestling: contestants stripped, oiled their bodies and wrestled (3.281f). It must be assumed that, for Berlioz, *Combat de ceste* meant wrestling match.

**Chaos** Berlioz follows *Aen.* 4.510 in ascribing divine status to Chaos. (No. 44)

**Chorèbe** (Coroebus) [baritone] Son of Mygdon, a Phrygian king. Coroebus came to Troy to win Cassandra, with whom he was madly in love, and to whom he became betrothed. He was killed during the sack of Troy.

**Citadelle** (Citadel) In the *Aeneid*, Virgil uses the Latin word for citadel, *arx*, to indicate both the fortified, walled city of Troy and, in particular, an inner citadel at the summit, where Priam's palace was situated. In Latin the survival of a city and the safety of the *arx* were indissolubly connected. Berlioz follows Virgil in this respect (stage directions for No. 1, and in Nos. 13 and 15). In fact no such inner citadel appears to have existed.

**Clio** [contralto] The muse of History. (No. 52a)

**Cupidon** (Cupid) Son of Venus and thus the god of love. At *Aen.* 1.657ff Venus disguises Cupid as Ascanius and has him inflame Dido's heart at a banquet – by presenting her with the Trojan gifts, and by nestling in her bosom and gently removing Sychaeus from her mind. Berlioz's adaptation of Virgil, in No. 35, was inspired by a painting (see p. 56).

**Cybèle** The mother-goddess of Phrygia and Asia Minor (No. 14), goddess of the powers of nature, also called *Magna Mater*. Aeneas's first wife Creusa became her spirit votary (*Aen.* 2.788). Cybele was worshipped on Dindyma on Mount Ida. Her ecstatic rites are described by Lucretius in *De Rerum Natura* (2.600–43) – though without mention of the double flutes referred to at *Aen.* 9.618 and employed and referred to in the opera (Nos. 1 and 11 respectively).

**Cythérée** (Cytherea) Venus (*Aen.* 1.257). Cythera, an island lying off the southern coast of Laconia, was where the goddess, rising naked from the sea, first stepped on dry land. (No. 37)

**Diane** (Diana) By having Dido, in No. 29, costumed as Diana, the chaste goddess of the hunt and of the forests, complete with bow and arrows, Berlioz was echoing Virgil's opening description of her – she was to be compared with the tall and graceful Diana (*Aen.* 1.498ff). He was also indicating that Dido was impelled by divine forces and would thus capture her prey (Aeneas). In fact, the goddess herself never made love with anyone; the nearest she got to it was with Endymion, who was always asleep. Aeneas's reference to this legend in No. 37 is teasing (or blind) love-talk between Dido and himself, as is his reference in the same duet to Troilus and Cressida (Cressida, in Shakespeare, jilted Troilus).

**Didon** (Dido) [mezzo-soprano] Queen of Carthage and widow of Sychaeus. Sychaeus was murdered by her brother Pygmalion, king of Tyre, for his riches. Dido did not know this until she was told so by the ghost of Sychaeus, who urged her to leave Tyre with a hoard of gold and silver he revealed to her. With a band of followers she eventually reached what is now the Gulf of Tunis on the North African coast, where she bought some land and founded Carthage.

**Dindyme** (Dindyma) A mountain in Phrygia, one of the peaks of Mount Ida, where the rites of Cybele took place. (Nos. 11 and 35)

**Diomède** (Diomedes) King of Argos who was reputed to have stolen and defiled the Palladium. (No. 6a)

**Énée** (Aeneas) [tenor] Son of Anchises and Venus. He married Priam's daughter Creusa (who was killed during the sack of Troy) and was the principal Trojan hero to escape death in the war. This was because he was entrusted with the divine mission (adumbrated in *Iliad* 20.302ff) of founding a new Troy in Italy. His acceptance that this mission transcended everything else, even his divinely inspired relationship with Dido, earned him the epithet of *pius* (devoted, faithful, respectful, pious) – with which Dido bitterly mocks him in Nos. 44 (NBE p. 673, 161–2) and 46 (NBE p. 694, 51–2; Berlioz here added a footnote explaining that this strange word is Virgil's).

**Épire** (Epirus) North-western region of Greece, of which Andromache (q.v.), when she married Pyrrhus, was queen. (No. 35)

**Érèbe** (Erebus) God of darkness, or a region in the underworld. (Nos. 3 and 44)

**Erinnys** (Erinyes) The Furies or Eumenides, spirits of retribution and punishment. (No. 13)

**Hécate** The three-faced triple goddess of heaven, earth and the underworld, worshipped at crossroads. In Dido's magic funeral rites (*Aen.* 4.511) the priestess invokes her along with Erebus and Chaos, i.e. as a death-goddess, as does Berlioz in No. 49. Unlike Virgil, Berlioz does not equate her with Diana.

(Ghost of) **Hector** [bass] Priam's favourite and eldest son, bravest and most respected of the Trojan heroes. He was killed by Achilles before the sack of Troy.

**Hécube** (Hecuba) [soprano] Wife of Priam and queen of Troy.

**Hélène** (Helen) Wife of Menelaus of Sparta. She absconded with Priam's son Paris (q.v.). (No. 27)

**Helenus** [tenor] Son of Priam. Like his sister Cassandra he was a prophet. Berlioz introduced the character only after he had cut the Sinon scene: he needed someone to sing Sinon's part in Nos. 8 and 9.

**Hylas** [tenor] The young Phrygian sailor of No. 38 is Berlioz's invention. He seems to be a conflation of Virgil's Palinurus and the favourite of Alexandrian poets, Hylas. In the opera Hylas falls asleep, which suggests that Berlioz was thinking of Palinurus, Aeneas's helmsman, who was assailed by sleep at the helm and apparently drowned. (Palinurus gives a different account of his death when Aeneas meets him in the underworld, *Aen.* 6.337ff.) The beautiful pageboy Hylas, immortalized in Theocritus's *Idyll* 13 and referred to in Virgil's *Eclogue* 6, was also drowned – dragged down by water nymphs while attempting to fetch water for his lover Heracles. Berlioz told his sailor son Louis that he was thinking of him while writing Hylas's song.

**Iarbas** Son of Hammon (or Ammon), an African god identified with Jupiter, and an African nymph. As king of the Gaetulians he sold Dido the land upon which she built Carthage. He wanted to marry her; she rejected him. Berlioz makes this the reason for his attack on Carthage (No. 28). In the *Aeneid* his fury is not aroused until he hears of Dido's liaison with Aeneas and rather than attack Carthage he challenges Jupiter to get rid of Aeneas. This is why Mercury was sent to command Aeneas to set sail for Italy. Virgil makes a distinction between Gaetulians and Numidians (*Aen.* 4.40f). Berlioz however describes Iarbas simply as a Numidian. (Nos. 19 and 28)

**(Mont) Ida** The high mountain or mountain range to the south-east of Troy, rising above the present Gulf of Edremit.

**Ilione** (Iliona) Priam's eldest daughter. (No. 27)

**Iopas** [tenor] Dido's bard. At *Aen.* 1.742ff he sings of cosmogony and the seasons, rather than the pastoral song Berlioz gives him.

**Iris** The goddess of the rainbow and a counterpart to Mercury. At *Aen.* 4.693ff she was sent to enable Dido to die, by cutting off a lock of her golden hair as an offering to Proserpine (Persephone), queen of the underworld. Normally Proserpine would have done this herself but there was no time for it since Dido dies a sudden, unnatural death. (No. 52a)

**Ithaque** (Ithaca) Island off the west coast of Greece, home of Ulysses and Sinon. (No. 6a)

**Jupiter** The supreme god (Zeus).

**Laocoön** Trojan priest of Neptune (Poseidon). (No. 7)

**Lybie** (Libya) Country to the south and east of Carthage, although Virgil uses it more loosely to mean (North) Africa, including Carthage. (No. 44)

**Mars** God of war (Ares).

**Mercure** (Mercury) [baritone or bass] The messenger of the gods (Hermes).

**Myrmidons** A people who lived in Thessaly, in north-eastern Greece. Achilles was a Myrmidon prince, so 'Myrmidons' in the opera indicates ruthless ferocity. (No. 15)

**Narbal** [bass] The character of 'Dido's minister' is Berlioz's invention. It must be assumed that Berlioz derived the name from Maharbal, Hannibal's cavalry commander (see, for example, Livy 22.51), the alteration making it easier to sing, easier for the audience to take in and forestalling comparison with the real Maharbal, who was far more shrewd than Berlioz's Narbal.

**(Pas d'esclaves) Nubiennes** (Dance of the Nubian Slaves: No. 33c) Nubia was a satellite of Ancient Egypt, lying south of the first cataract of the Nile. Nubian slave girls were tall, very beautiful and much coveted.

**Numide** (Numidian) Numidia was the country lying to the south and west of Carthage.

**Ombrien** (Umbrian) In No. 49 Anna and Narbal pray that two non-Roman peoples, the Umbrians to the north of the city and the Latins to the south, may unite in thwarting Aeneas.

**Olympe** (Olympus) Mountain in Thessaly, home of the gods.

**Palladium** The image of Pallas kept in the goddess's temple in Troy. The city depended on its safe keeping. In No. 6a Sinon reminds the Trojans that it had been torn from its shrine by Diomedes, in atonement for which crime, he said, the Greeks had built an enormous offering to Pallas – the wooden horse. When Berlioz in No. 9 has Aeneas command the Trojans to drag the horse toward the Palladium, he is drawing on the Roman belief that what was stolen was simply a replica on public display and that the genuine Palladium was rescued during the sack of Troy by Aeneas, eventually finding its way to Rome.

**Pallas** Another name for Athene, goddess of wisdom, the arts and (to some extent) war. Pallas Athene (Minerva).

**Panthée** (Panthus) [bass] Trojan priest of Apollo who was killed during the sack of Troy. Berlioz spares him and takes him to Carthage, where he assumes the role of Achates in the *Aeneid.*

**Paris** The beautiful son of Priam, who was exposed at birth because of a sinister prophecy but survived as a shepherd boy and was eventually taken back to Troy. In his celebrated Judgement he awarded the apple to Venus in preference to Juno and Minerva, bringing about Juno's fierce hatred of the Trojans. This was compounded by his subsequent abduction of Helen, which caused the Trojan War. He killed Achilles (No. 1) and was himself killed by Philoctetes before the sack of Troy.

**Pergame** (Pergama) Another name for Troy (not to be confused with the Mysian city of Pergamum situated about a hundred miles south and renowned as a centre of culture). Virgil uses *Pergama* to mean the inner citadel of the city. See under Citadelle. (No. 11)

**Phénicien** (Phoenician) Phoenicia, on the eastern seaboard of the Mediterranean (what is now Lebanon), was Dido's native country.

**Phœbé** Goddess of the moon. (No. 37)

**Phrygie** (Phrygia) Country in Asia Minor flanking the north-eastern Aegean. Troy was its principal city.

**Pluton** (Pluto) God of the underworld (Hades). (Nos. 16 and 44)

**Polyxène** (Polyxena) [soprano] Virgin daughter of Priam. At *Aen.* 3.321ff Andromache relates that Polyxena, after the fall of Troy, was sacrificed by the Greeks on the tomb of Achilles. Berlioz's Polyxena, following the example of his Cassandra, stabs herself during the sack of Troy.

**Priam** [bass] King of Troy, son of the perjurer Laomedon, second cousin of Aeneas's father Anchises, and like him a descendant of the royal line of Dardanus, Tros and Ilus. He was killed by Pyrrhus during the sack of Troy.

**Pyrrhus** (also called Neoptolemus) Son of Achilles. He was called to the war after his father's death, killed Priam during the sack of Troy and later married Andromache (q.v.).

**(La) Renommée** (Fame) The allegorical figure of Fame, a messenger of Jupiter, usually represented as a half-robed, winged woman blowing a trumpet. Virgil provides a famous description of her (*Fama*) at *Aen.* 4.173ff, though in her less attractive aspect as Rumour. Berlioz would have been familiar with several statues and paintings of her in Paris. (No. 52a)

**Scamandre** (Scamander) The principal river of the Troad, called Xanthus in the *Aeneid.* It lay to the south-west of Troy and flowed north-west into the bay (see under Troie).

**(Porte de) Scée** (Scaean Gate) The principal (southern?) gate of Troy. In No. 6a Berlioz makes use of the legend that the great tower next to it was pulled down to allow the wooden horse to be dragged into the city.

**Scipio Africanus** Roman general who defeated Hannibal and thus ensured Roman supremacy in North Africa. (No. 52a)

**Sichée** (Sychaeus) Dido's husband, murdered by Pygmalion (see under Didon).

**Sigée** (Sigeum) The coastal ridge to the north-west of Troy. The 'straits of Sigeum' are the Dardanelles.

**Simois** The second river of the Troad. It lay to the north of Troy and flowed west into the bay (see under Troie).

**Sinon** [tenor] Greek spy, who persuades the Trojans to bring the wooden horse into the city.

**Tartare** (Tartarus) The underworld, or the deepest part thereof. (No. 49)

**Ténare** (Taenarus) A cave, on the southern tip of the Peloponnese, leading into the underworld. (Nos. 16 and 49)

**Ténédos** Island off the western coast of the Troad, where the Greeks hid before the sack of Troy. Just after he had written the libretto, Berlioz's son Louis told his father that he had visited Tenedos (NL, p. 175). (No. 3)

**Thessaliennes** (Thessalians) Women from Thessaly in north-eastern Greece. In the opera a term of abuse, like Myrmidons (q.v.). (No. 16)

**Troiade** (Troad) The region around Troy. (No. 2)

**Troie** (Troy) Michael Wood's *In Search of the Trojan War* (London 1985) convincingly argues that the Troy of the *Iliad* and the *Aeneid* did indeed exist, the sixth of nine cities that had been built at the western end of the high ridge of Hisarlik in the far corner of north-western Turkey, just south of the Dardanelles. Wood explains that Troy VI was destroyed in about 1250 BC. It was a very small city, covering an area of about 200 by 150 yards and housing barely a thousand people, with perhaps five thousand outside. But it was grandly designed and well fortified. It held a strategic position about a hundred feet above the surrounding plain and about a mile from the sea, the bay looping round to the west of it not yet having been silted up. Berlioz wrote *Les Troyens* some ten years before the first nineteenth-century excavations of Troy. In his stage directions for Act I he imagines the city from the north, but with the Simois (instead of the Scamander) to the right of the stage picture.

**Tyr** (Tyre) Dido's native city in Phoenicia. 'Tyrians' means Carthaginians.

**Ucalégon** Berlioz describes him as one of Priam's advisers. Virgil's tiny reference to the blazing house of Ucalegon (*Aen.* 2.311f, quoted by Berlioz in the Preface to his *Memoirs* and used again in No. 13 of the opera) indicates that Ucalegon lived next door to Deiphobus, one of Priam's sons.

**Ulysse** (Ulysses) The cruel and cunning Odysseus of the *Iliad* and the *Odyssey.* (No. 6a)

**Vénus** Goddess of love (Aphrodite); mother of Aeneas.

**Vesta-Cybèle** This compound goddess seems to be Berlioz's invention – perhaps a way of showing that Trojan religion was not, in Virgilian terms, uncivilized. Vesta (Hestia) was the virgin, peaceable Roman goddess of the hearth and home. Both goddesses sustained Life: Vesta through the undying flame of the hearth, Cybele through the passionate fires of fertility. The Romans believed that Aeneas had taken Vesta's sacred flame from Troy and bequeathed it to his successors in Rome. (No. 14)

APPENDIX B

# *Antique and obsolete instruments*

**IAN KEMP**

The following is an attempt to clarify Berlioz's intentions concerning antique instruments. Apart from the well-known *cymbales antiques* (used in No. 33c), his score contains parts for *doubles flûtes antiques, sistres antiques* and *tarbuka*. In the three latter cases he wrote complementary parts for what he obviously regarded as equivalent or substitute instruments from his modern orchestra. This suggests that he introduced antique instruments as a contribution towards an authentic *mise-en-scène* and did not, with the possible exception of the *tarbuka*, intend them to be heard. The illustrations on p. 206 provide some indication of what replicas might look like.

### Doubles flûtes

In No. 1 three shepherds, standing on top of a mound representing the tomb of Achilles, are playing *doubles flûtes antiques* 'or three oboes'. Berlioz's direction in this case makes it clear that the sounds should come from the stage, which leaves open two performance possibilities: oboes (double flutes being left to the imagination of those who have read the libretto) or imitation double flutes somehow concealing the oboes actually being played.

The double flute is mentioned at *Aen.* 9.617f, where Numanus taunts the Trojans before being killed by Ascanius: 'Run over high Dindyma where you're used to hearing the sounds of the double flute' (*ite per alta / Dindyma ubi adsuetis biforem dat tibia cantum*). Numanus is saying that the Trojans are not warriors but effeminate followers of the orgiastic rites of Cybele. Berlioz's double flutes thus indicate that the Trojans' excitement is uncontrolled and irrational. His three (off-stage) oboes in No. 11 indicate a similar emotional disarray: a recall of their opening phrase in No. 1 is combined with the chorus singing 'May the sounds of the flutes of Dindyma mingle with the most exalted of songs'.

The double flute is mentioned by several writers and is not necessarily associated with orgies. The reproductions on p. 206, from J. G. Wilkinson's *The Manners and Customs of the Ancient Egyptians* (1837) and Georges Kastner's *Manuel général de musique militaire* (1848), are, according to the authors, of Egyptian and Greek double flutes respectively. Wilkinson suggests that the left-hand flute acted as a bass while the right-hand one played the melodic part. (In Berlioz's score the lower two oboes play a drone, the upper one a melodic tag phrase.)

### Sistres

Berlioz writes for sistra, *sistres antiques (sur la scène)*, in No. 4, at the point marking Aeneas's entry. According to most writers the sistrum is Egyptian in origin, associated with religious ceremonies and with war. Wilkinson regarded the sistrum as the Egyptians' principal sacred instrument, played by women of royal or noble rank or by priestesses.

What gave Berlioz the idea of using the instrument and what type of instrument he had in mind is not known. It is referred to at *Aen.* 8.696, where Virgil describes the new shield Venus has brought for Aeneas: on it is depicted the future history of Rome, one scene being of Cleopatra at the battle of Actium rallying her fleet with the sounds of her native sistrum (*regina in mediis patrio vocat agmina sistro*). Since Cleopatra was on the losing side and the Trojans were about to lose the war, Berlioz's allusion, if he meant it, carries an ironic relevance.

Berlioz's interest in the instrument could have been awakened by the development of archaeology in the nineteenth century and the consequent increase in holdings of ancient artefacts in museums. Several sistra and sistra fragments are held in the Louvre. A sistrum acquired in 1852/3 is illustrated on p. 206.

Another possibility is that Berlioz was introduced to the instrument by his friend Kastner's *Traité général d'instrumentation* (1837), for in his own *Grand traité* he merely takes note of the sistrum's existence and directs his reader to Kastner. There the sistrum is described as a kind of circle with metal rods fixed from one side to the other, held in the left hand, and made to sound by striking the rods with a stick called a plectrum. By the time he had written his *Manuel général* Kastner had revised his understanding of the instrument: an illustration reveals it as more oval than circular in design, with four metal rods running freely through holes pierced in the frame and prevented from falling out by being bent at the ends. There is a handle underneath. The instrument is said to be of bronze. What the illustration does not show are the small metal rings, discs or bells attached to or threaded through the rods, which together with the oval frame, the freely moving rods (typically three) and the elaborately wrought handle complete the characteristic design of the Egyptian sistrum. It was shaken not struck and must have made a jingling, metallic sound.

The moving rings or discs are particularly relevant features in the present context, since they relate the sistrum to early examples of triangles, which also had rings on their bars. In his *Les danses des morts* (1852) Kastner made precisely this point. An illustration from his book is reproduced on p. 206. Berlioz may have taken note of Kastner's remarks, for in the score of his opera (No. 4, bar 76), immediately above the stave for the sistra is one for what he calls *Jeu de triangles*. Since the two 'instruments' always play at the same time he must have intended the supposed sounds of his sistra to come from triangles in the orchestra. There should be at least seven triangles, since seven pitches are specified – a unique instance of pitched notation for the instrument. In the chapter of his *Grand traité* setting out his ideas for a monumental orchestra of 827 performers Berlioz had included six triangles, remarking that like antique cymbals they could be tuned to different pitches.

### Tarbuka

In the Dance of the Nubian Slaves (No. 33c) Berlioz calls for a *tarbuka sur la scène*. How he came across the tarbuka is not known. What he meant by it is

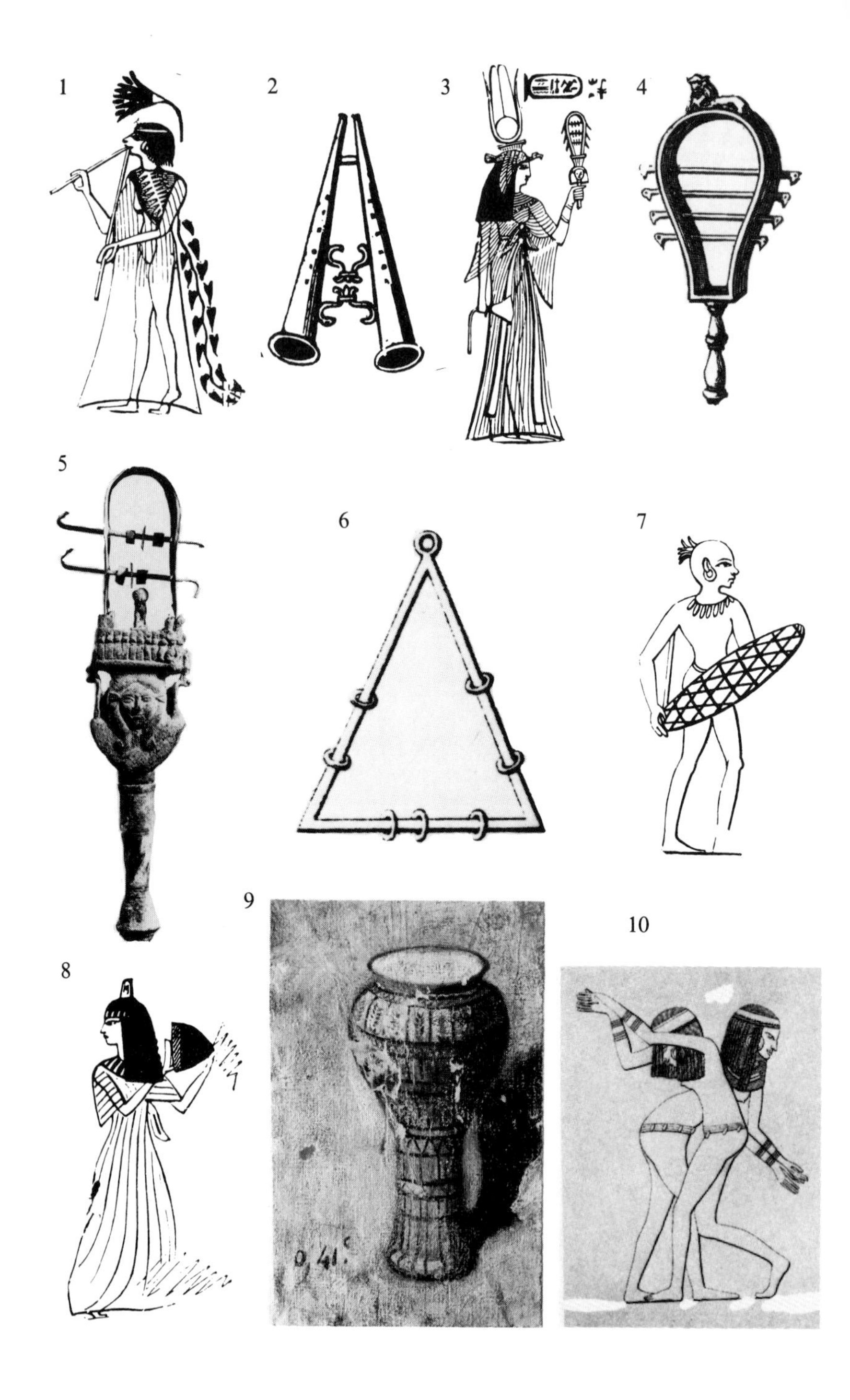
1
2
3
4
5
6
7
8
9
10

the subject of dispute: it has been described as a 'long, narrow drum of Egyptian origin'[1] and as a 'small kettledrum Tarbourka (a drum from North Africa in the shape of a flower pot)'.[2] Berlioz's spelling seems to be unique. The closest equivalent found is 'tarabouk', mentioned by Gérard de Nerval in his *Voyage en Orient* when describing an Egyptian wedding dance performed by Nubian dancers accompanied by almas (see p. 196), singing and playing 'tarabouki'. Berlioz could well have read Nerval's book. The relevant section, 'Les Femmes du Caire', is in fact a translation from Edward Lane's *An Account of the Manners and Customs of the Modern Egyptians* (1837), where the instrument is called a darabukkeh. Berlioz's tarbuka must be presumed synonymous with darbuka, derabucca, tarabuka – a sample from the confusing variety of other names given the instrument, a consequence of its use in the folk music of a great number of countries fringing the north-eastern, eastern and southern coasts of the Mediterranean. (More recently it has been known as the *tambour arabe* or Arabian hand drum.[3])

The instrument is a goblet-shaped drum usually made of earthenware, its head of goat, sheep or fish skin, with a longish neck, open bell and ranging from four to eighteen inches in height. (See illustration on p. 206.) The player, sitting down, lays the instrument on his lap and plays with his hands or fingers, tucking the neck and bell under his left or right arm.[4]

In Berlioz's score the orchestral counterpart is a *tambourin*. By this he presumably meant the long drum with one skin and no snares, associated particularly with the Farandole in Bizet's *L'Arlésienne* music, rather than the tambourine, which he called a *tambour (de) basque*. (It is worth noting however that Lane's description of a darabukkeh is preceded by one of a 'tar', a tambourine.) Clearly the *tambourin* is not a close aural substitute for the tarbuka described above, for which reason the illustrations on p. 206 include an Egyptian long drum and an Egyptian 'darabooka', both from Wilkinson.

12 No. 1: double flute, from J. G. Wilkinson, *The Manners and Customs of the Ancient Egyptians* (London 1837), Vol. 2, Woodcut No. 190, fig. 4, p. 237

No. 2: double flute, from Georges Kastner, *Manuel général de musique militaire* (Paris 1848), Plate 1, fig. 12

No. 3: sistrum, from Wilkinson, Vol. 1, Woodcut No. 8, fig. 5, p. 260

No. 4: sistrum, from Kastner, Plate 3, fig. 12

No. 5: sistrum, from Christiane Ziegler, *Catalogue des instruments de musique égyptiens: Musée du Louvre* (Paris 1979), fig. 68, p. 57

No. 6: triangle, from Kastner, *Les danses des morts* (Paris 1852), Plate 20, fig. 190, p. 309

No. 7: Egyptian long drum, from Wilkinson, Vol. 2, Woodcut No. 201, p. 264

No. 8: 'darabooka', from Wilkinson, Vol. 2, Woodcut No. 195, fig. 1, p. 240

No. 9: painting (1853) of a 'darabukka' by Eugène Fromentin (collection James Thompson)

No. 10: Almas, from Hippolito Rosellini, *I Monumenti dell'Egitto e della Nubia* (Pisa 1834), Vol. 2, Plate 98 (original in British Museum)

### Saxhorns

Apart from the well-documented ophicleide, the obsolete instrument given greatest prominence in the opera is the saxhorn – various types of which appear in the stage bands of the Act I finale, in the *Chasse royale* and in Nos. 44 and 52 of Act V. Berlioz himself never heard what he had written for them. To this day no one else has either: the saxhorn parts have never been played on saxhorns. The most surprising fact is that while Berlioz specified alternatives for the more familiar types of saxhorn used, he did not do so for the least familiar, the *petit saxhorn suraigu* in B flat. He must have considered that for his opera (as for his single other work using it, the *Te Deum*) this sopranino instrument was irreplaceable.

Berlioz met the Belgian instrument maker Adolphe Sax in 1839, when Sax visited Paris in order to promote his new design of bass clarinet. Along with other leading composers Berlioz was greatly impressed and when Sax settled in Paris in 1841 he struck up a warm and lasting friendship. Berlioz became Sax's most ardent champion. His article in the *Débats* of 12 June made Sax famous overnight. Berlioz put his precepts into practice when, in his Salle Herz concert of 3 February 1844, he gave Sax's instruments their first public hearing in Paris and in a work specially written for them – his *Hymne pour six instruments de Sax* (a transcription he made of 'Chant sacré' from his *Neuf Mélodies*). Berlioz continued to write enthusiastic articles, not least when supporting Sax's proposals for the reorganization of French military bands. In 1845, through a government decree, Sax won an assured place for his instruments in infantry and cavalry bands, with saxhorns the essential basis of both. After the 1848 revolution, the decree was revoked; but Sax found a new champion in Napoleon III, who rescued him from bankruptcy in 1852, appointed him imperial instrument-maker in 1854 and private director of music to the Emperor (with responsibility for the band of the Imperial Guard) in 1858, as well as authorizing various new decrees on the use of his instruments in military bands.[5] So their pre-eminence was restored. When writing *Les Troyens* Berlioz must have thought that the victory for Sax instruments was complete and that he could confidently score for them. He could hardly have anticipated that in 1867 cavalry bands (where the *petit saxhorn suraigu* found its special place) would be abolished[6] and that three years later Sax's imperial patron would surrender to the Prussians and the Second Empire collapse, nor that in 1873 Sax would again be forced into bankruptcy and then into a slow decline.

Saxhorns were designed primarily for the military – evident in particular from their upright design, which enabled the cavalry to hold their instruments easily and the infantry to play in closed ranks. But they also became a conspicuous component in scenes at the Opéra (usually marches or processions) involving the stage band, a feature dating back to Spontini's *La Vestale* of 1807. Naturally this was another reason why Berlioz used them in *Les Troyens*. It was underlined by the fact that Sax himself had been appointed director of the 'Fanfare de l'Opéra' in 1847, the year in which saxhorns made their official début at the Opéra in Verdi's *Jérusalem* (his adaptation of *I Lombardi*, first performed on 22 November).[7] Saxhorns also appeared in, for example, Meyerbeer's *Le Prophète* (6 April 1849) and Halévy's *Le Juif errant* (23 April 1852, seemingly the first opera to have used the *petit saxhorn suraigu*). As far as Berlioz was concerned it was not his scoring for saxhorns which prevented *Les Troyens* from being performed at the Opéra. He deleted saxhorns from the Théâtre-Lyrique performances only because he had to. Even the Théâtre-Lyrique had used saxhorns – in the Soldier's Chorus of Gounod's *Faust* in 1859.

Of course, none of these reasons for using the instruments would have carried weight with Berlioz unless he had liked them in the first place. He described their tone as 'round, pure, full, equal, reverberant [retentissant] and of a perfect homogeneity across the whole range from high to low'.[8] Despite his enthusiasm, he used them extremely rarely (as he pointed out himself in his *Memoirs*). It seems that he wanted to reserve them for very particular purposes and not to weaken their effect by treating them as 'normal' members of the stage band, let alone the orchestra. In *Les Troyens* they evoke the other-worldly sounds of the 'phrygian trumpets' of his libretto (Acts I and V) and the hunting calls of divine passion (Act IV).

The saxhorn is a valved bugle, early references describing it as a 'bugle à pistons' or 'à cylindres'. (The saxhorns heard at Berlioz's concert in February 1844 were 'bugles à cylindres'.) It has a tapered bore and an upright bell. Valved bugle horns, notably the flugelhorn, had been made for and used by Prussian and Austrian military bands in the 1820s and 1830s, before Sax had developed his own versions of them. What he envisaged was a homogeneous family of instruments of uniform design, covering the full range, with improved mechanism and with a simple technique (identical fingering) and notation (all instruments in the treble clef) which would make it possible for a player to learn an instrument relatively quickly and switch from one to another; they would replace existing bugles, cornets and ophicleides (his saxtrombas, see p. 211, would replace horns). He took out a patent for them in 1845. His instruments were in fact such an improvement on existing types that he was persuaded to give them a name which would make them easy to pick out. He decided on *Sax-horns* – simply to distinguish his instruments from others and not to claim that he had invented them. All the same he thereby aroused that opposition from rival manufacturers which was to plague him for the rest of his life.

The list below, adapted from Berlioz's *Grand traité* (2nd. edn, 1855), shows the complete family.

1 *Petit saxhorn suraigu* in B flat – sounding a seventh higher than written
2 *Saxhorn soprano* in E flat – a minor third higher
3 *Saxhorn contralto* in B flat – a tone lower
4 *Saxhorn alto* or *ténor* in E flat – a major sixth lower
5 *Saxhorn baryton* in B flat – a ninth lower
6 *Saxhorn basse* in B flat (a wider bore instrument) – also a ninth lower
7 *Saxhorn contrebasse* in E flat – an octave and a major sixth lower
8 *Saxhorn contrebasse grave* in B flat – two octaves and a tone lower (Berlioz also mentions a *Saxhorn contrebasse grave* in E flat and a *Saxhorn bourdon* in B flat.)

Saxhorns 2 to 7 were in Sax's catalogue of 1845;[9] 1 and 8 were added in 1851.[10] In the first, 1843 edition of his *Grand traité* Berlioz did not mention saxhorns, though there are brief mentions of the 'bugle ou clarion' (a bugle with a chromatic attachment patented by Sax – the 'bugle à clefs') and the 'bugle à pistons ou à cylindres'. But in the second edition he did, describing saxhorns in general in the terms quoted above and singling out the *petit saxhorn suraigu* for special praise. 'There is nothing more brilliant, more precise, less strident despite its sheen, than the whole upper octave. In addition the timbre is so clear and penetrating that a single saxhorn *suraigu* can be picked out among a large group of other wind instruments.'[11] As if to prove the point, in the Act I finale of *Les Troyens* this sopranino saxhorn belongs to an off-stage band whose other members comprise two natural trumpets, two cornets, three trombones and an ophicleide. To this band is added another, of two soprano, two contralto, two tenor and two contrabass saxhorns; and there is a third 'band' (Berlioz called them all 'groupes') of three oboes and six (or eight) harps, not to mention the full orchestra. It will be seen that Berlioz used saxhorns 1, 2, 3, 4 and 7 in the table, omitting 5 and 6, the baritone and bass, presumably because he wanted to avoid thickening the middle-to-low register and to keep the three layers of sound made by his twenty-six players distinct. No such precision of aural imagination can be found in the Verdi, Meyerbeer and Halévy scores mentioned above, which employ single stage bands using saxhorns 2 to 7 (respectively, eight saxhorns among twelve instruments, eighteen among twenty-two, and eight among twenty, with four saxophones among the latter); in the second version of the Halévy score the whole family from 1 to 8 is used (twelve saxhorns among fourteen instruments). In *Faust* Gounod included 2, 6 and 8 (three among ten instruments).

What saxhorns look like can be seen on p. 211, an illustration from A. Elwart's *Manuel des aspirants aux grades de Sous-Chef et de Chef de musique de l'Armée* (Paris 1861).[12] (It should be mentioned that the saxtrombas in the illustration were instruments of narrower and more cylindrical bore than saxhorns, producing a more strident tone, comparable with that of trumpets or bugles.)

What saxhorns really sound like is difficult to say. Museum examples can be tested; but the style of playing has been lost – along with the style of so much brass playing (even French orchestras now use those modern mouthpieces which make for more secure intonation and more brilliant tone). If Berlioz's altered orchestration of the *Chasse royale* for the Théâtre-Lyrique performances is any guide, saxhorns must have been capable of playing very loudly. Plate 8 (see p. 154) indicates that he regarded four bassoons, four horns and two cornets in unison as the equivalent of two tenor saxhorns (in unison).

The nearest present-day equivalents to saxhorns are to be found in British brass bands. This surprising circumstance is due to the influence of the Distin family, John Distin and his four sons, an English brass quintet who enjoyed only qualified success until they heard Sax's instruments at Berlioz's concert in February 1844 and asked Sax to equip them with saxhorns – whereupon they went from triumph to triumph, spreading their own and Sax's fame across Europe and the USA. Henry, one of the sons, set up an

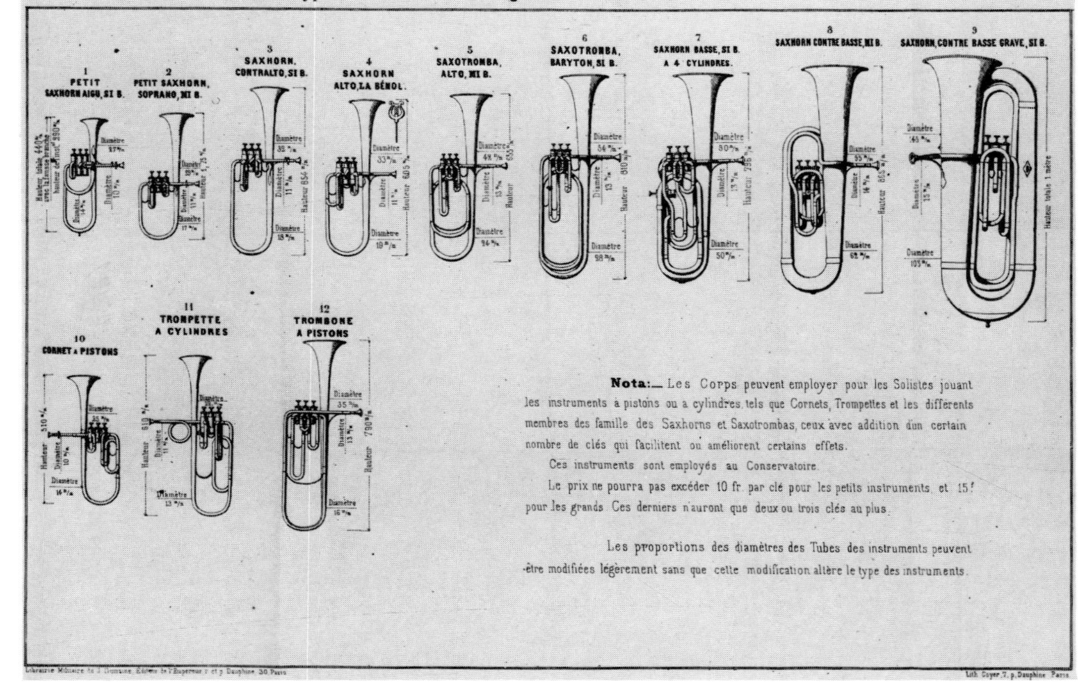


13 Saxhorns and saxtrombas, from A. Elwart, *Manuel des aspirants aux grades de Sous-Chef et de Chef de musique de l'Armée* (Paris 1861), Plate 2

agency for Sax's instruments in London in 1846. In 1853 he persuaded the Mossley Temperance Band to equip itself entirely with saxhorns; it promptly won the first Belle Vue brass band contest in Manchester that year and was responsible for the inclusion of saxhorns in all brass bands, a feature that has survived until this day – if with some modification. Players for the saxhorn parts in *Les Troyens* could therefore be found among the members of brass bands. Instrumental nomenclature has changed in the meantime but, as indicated by Horwood,[13] the following substitutes can be suggested (Berlioz's own alternatives are indicated in brackets):

| | |
|---|---|
| *Saxhorn soprano* | Soprano cornet in E flat (trompette à cylindres en Mi♭) |
| *Saxhorn contralto* | Flugelhorn (trompette à cylindres en Si♭) |
| *Saxhorn ténor* | E flat horn (cor à cylindres en Mi♭) |
| *Saxhorn contrebasse* | E flat bass (tuba en Mi♭) |

There is no direct descendant of the *petit saxhorn suraigu*, its nearest modern equivalent being the piccolo trumpet in B flat.

APPENDIX C

# *The printed vocal scores*

**HUGH MACDONALD**

By far the greater number of vocal scores of *Les Troyens* have been issued as of one or other of its two parts, *La Prise de Troie* or *Les Troyens à Carthage*. Berlioz's original vocal score of 1861 and a short-lived issue by Choudens in about 1889 are the only one-volume vocal scores of the complete opera to be found. The first printed vocal score of *Les Troyens* is one of the greatest of bibliographical rarities. Berlioz made the piano reduction and paid for the engraving himself. The engraver he engaged was Madame (Veuve) Ris and the cost of engraving 2289 francs. Engraving commenced in September 1860, some months after Berlioz had signed a contract with Carvalho for production at the Théâtre-Lyrique in 1862 and with rehearsals in prospect. In his correspondence he first mentions this edition on 2 January 1861:

> I have had mountains of proofs to correct for *Les Troyens*, and I have not been able to find a moment to continue work on the score of *Béatrice*. (CI, p. 271)

Six weeks later he wrote:

> Meanwhile the engraving of my score is getting on quietly; it will probably not be finished for three months. (CI, p. 275)

In June 1861 he gave his reasons for undertaking the edition. The Opéra had now scheduled *Les Troyens* for 1863:

> The score is being engraved, but not for publication, as you seem to think. It will be ready to appear, that's all. (SW, p. 119)

Fifteen copies were drawn on Berlioz's instructions, of which seven survive, all bearing autograph markings. The first two, both designated 'Épreuves', are the sole sources of the Sinon scene in Act I. The importance of this score rests on its direct provenance from the composer's hand and his careful supervision of its making; also on its presentation of the opera in its original form in five acts before the division of the work into two in 1863. The score has 451 pages and no plate number.

When Berlioz reported the decision to mount the second part only under the title *Les Troyens à Carthage* at the Théâtre-Lyrique, he said that the score would appear nonetheless as *Les Troyens* entire (LI, pp. 250–1). But on 22 July 1863 he signed a contract with Antoine Choudens selling the plates of *Les Troyens* to be published in two parts. The price was 15,000 francs, the vocal score of *Benvenuto Cellini* being included (Hopkinson, p. 139).

Thus the first scores of the opera to be offered to the public were Choudens's vocal scores of *La Prise de Troie* and *Les Troyens à Carthage*, both published in the autumn of 1863.

### Les Troyens à Carthage

To Berlioz's title page and 271 pages of music Choudens added a new title page, with appropriate vignette, and 25 pages of Prologue – the introductory section composed by Berlioz to replace Acts I and II for the Théâtre-Lyrique performances. The score thus comprised 296 pages and bore a plate number A.C.988. The three final acts of the opera were now divided into five, the *Chasse royale et orage* being assigned an act of its own, and the last act being divided into two. Since cuts were imposed in the theatre immediately after the first performance, the publisher attempted to abide by his claim on the title page that the edition conformed with the production. The complete unaltered form of this score is therefore very rare – only two copies are known. All later copies were cut or altered in different ways, so that as many as eight different states of this edition are found. Most copies show one or more of the following alterations:

1. 63 bars from the *Marche Troyenne* in the Prologue – cut.
2. The repeat on p. 69 (in No. 19) – not shown.
3. The Anna–Narbal duet (Nos. 30–1) – cut.
4. Iopas's song (No. 34) shown as an optional cut.
5. The six bars on p. 194 originally concluding the Septet (No. 36) are replaced either by a longer passage of seventeen bars or by a cadential close in F major.
6. Mercury's entry (on p. 203) reduced to show twelve bars after the change of key, not fourteen.
7. The sentinels' duet (No. 40) – cut.
8. The Dido–Aeneas duet (No. 44) – cut.
9. Certain pages are lithographed, not engraved.

These alterations were effected in various combinations, and cannot be arranged in any clear sequence of issue. According to his *Memoirs*, Berlioz consented to these extensive cuts out of stupefaction at the way Carvalho was treating the opera on the stage. To see the vocal score similarly interfered with caused him the bitterest distress:

> But oh, the agony of seeing a work of this kind laid out for sale with the scars of the publisher's surgery upon it! A score lying dismembered in the window of a music shop like the carcass of a calf on a butcher's stall, and pieces cut off and sold like lights for the concierge's cat! (*Mem.*, p. 604)

He was continually drawing Choudens's attention to mistakes. He complained at length on 2 April 1865:

> You ask me if the copy of *Les Troyens* [*à Carthage*] is in order, and I am forced to reply: no. You have only reinstated two duets; the other (the Anna–Narbal duet) is still missing, although listed in the Table on p. 1. Furthermore there are two major faults on p. 154, faults made by your engraver, because it's one of his plates.
>
> If you want this put right you will do me justice and a favour, if a musical matter can do me any favour at present. A score is a book that many people like to read and consult, and you have unfortunately dissatisfied several of your customers who would have liked to have my work as I wrote it, not mutilated.
>
> (*Rivista Musicale Italiana* (1913), p. 290)

Three 'Airs de ballet' and twelve 'Morceaux séparés' were issued in 1863, some transposed down for lower voices. Iopas's song, for example, was put down a tone 'for mezzo-soprano'.

Sometime before 1874 Choudens tidied up the disorder by issuing a '2ème édition' of the vocal score of *Les Troyens à Carthage*, presented as an opera no longer in five acts but in four. It still used Berlioz's original plates but now numbered only 206 pages. No less than nine numbers were cut from the main text, although they were given in a 59-page supplement.

Next from Choudens was a 'Nouvelle édition', still in four acts, issued for the Opéra-Comique revival of *Les Troyens à Carthage* in 1892. The original plates were still in service, though many had by now been re-engraved. All cuts were restored from the supplement except the Anna–Narbal duet and the Dido–Aeneas duet, of which no mention is made; the *Chasse royale et orage* was misplaced after, not before, the scene in Dido's garden, an error that has persisted in vocal scores to this day, causing wide misunderstanding. This score had 249 pages. The twelve 'Morceaux séparés' were re-issued at this time with some new transpositions and one substitution.

Finally, Choudens issued a new edition in 1899, with a different piano reduction, possibly made by the L. Narici responsible for the piano arrangement of *La Prise de Troie* at the same time. The plate number was now A.C.11258 and there are 353 pages. This score is still in print today, although the following errors should be observed:

1. The modern title page states, incorrectly, that the piano transcription is by Berlioz himself.
2. The Prologue, mis-titled 'Prélude', includes only the *Lamento* and lacks the entry of the Rapsode and the *Marche Troyenne*.
3. The *Chasse royale et orage* is misplaced after, not before, the garden scene.
4. The division into four acts differs from Berlioz's division into five.

This score has also been reprinted by Edwin Kalmus (New York), with French text only.

Among miscellaneous vocal scores of *Les Troyens à Carthage* are: (1) an English version 'arranged as a dramatic cantata' by H. E. Krehbiel for performance in New York in 1887; (2) a pocket edition of the 1892 score showing just the vocal line without accompaniment; (3) an edition with Italian and German words only, issued for the 1890 performances in Karlsruhe (the Italian title is given as *Didone abbandonata*); and (4) a Russian edition published by Bessel for the Moscow performances of 1899.

### La Prise de Troie

Choudens's 1863 edition was published from Berlioz's own plates with an extra title page (with vignette) and a plate number of A.C.987. It contained 179 pages, and was divided into three acts with a division and scene change inserted between Nos. 3 and 4. It was unusual and commendable to publish such a score with no concurrent performances, and because there was no production there were no complications in the text. In 1879, when *La Prise de Troie* was first given in concert form, two extracts, the *Air de Cassandre* (No. 2) and the *Air de Chorèbe* (from No. 3 - much cut), were issued separately. Later they were re-issued each with two alternative transpositions.

Choudens's next edition was published to coincide with the Paris Opéra's staging of *La Prise de Troie* in 1899. A new piano reduction was made by L. Narici. This score bore the plate number A.C.11312 and filled 257 pages. It is still in print today and is generally free from error, except for a notorious E flat (for E natural) in bar 34 of the *Marche et Hymne* on p. 71. It has also been reprinted by Edwin Kalmus (New York), with French and German text.

An edition of Act II under the title *The Fall of Troy* (Nos. 4–11) with English text was published by Schirmer for the New York performance of 1882.

### Les Troyens (complete)

Apart from the 1861 scores, the only one-volume vocal score of the entire opera to be published was an edition put out by Choudens in about 1889, not apparently in conjunction with any performances and perhaps in an altruistic attempt to restore the original opera. Paris performances of the separate parts in 1892 and 1899, however, were to lead to the re-issue of each part. The score comprised 443 pages and used most of Berlioz's original plates, bearing the numbers A.C.987 and A.C.988. The *Chasse royale et orage* is treated as the second *Tableau* of Act III rather than the first *Tableau* of Act IV, but otherwise the score is remarkably faithful to Berlioz's whole design. Cuts indicated in the autograph full score are shown in a supplement.

A vocal score conforming with the *New Berlioz Edition* text of the full score (Vol. 2a–b) and containing French and German texts is available on hire from Bärenreiter-Verlag.

APPENDIX D

# *Select list of performances (Staged and concert)*

**LOUISE GOLDBERG**

| *Date* | *City* | *Opera Company/Theatre* | *Version* |
|---|---|---|---|
| 4.XI.1863 | Paris | Théâtre-Lyrique | II, cut |
| 7.XII.1879 | Paris | Concerts Pasdeloup/ Cirque d'Hiver | I, concert |
| 7.XII.1879 | Paris | Concerts Colonne/ Théâtre du Châtelet | I, concert |
| 6.V.1882 | New York | Thomas's May Festival/ 7th Regiment Armory | I Act 2, concert |
| 26.II.1887 | New York | Chickering Hall | II, cut, concert |
| 6–7.XII.1890 | Karlsruhe | Grossherzogliches Hoftheater | I+II |
| 28.I. or early II.1891 | Nice | Grand Théâtre Municipal | I, excerpts from II |
| 9.VI.1892 | Paris | Opéra-Comique/Théâtre-Lyrique | II, cut |
| 29.I.1893 | Munich | Munich Opera/Kgl. Hof- und Nationaltheater | II |
| 17, 24.III.1895 | Munich | Munich Opera/Kgl. Hof- und Nationaltheater | I+II |
| 30.III.1897 | Liverpool | Royal Liverpool Philharmonic Society | II, cut, concert |
| 2.XII.1897 | Manchester | Hallé Orchestra/Free Trade Hall | II, cut, concert |
| 30–1.III.1898 | Cologne | Kölner Stadttheater | I+II |
| 15.XI.1899 | Paris | Opéra | I |
| 23.XI.1899 | Milan | Teatro Lirico | I |
| 26.XII.1899 | Moscow | Imperial Opera | II |

| *Language* | *Conductor* | *Cassandra* | *Dido* | *Aeneas* |
|---|---|---|---|---|
| Fr. | Adolphe Deloffre | – | Anne Charton-Demeur | Jules Monjauze |
| Fr. | Ernest Reyer | Anne Charton-Demeur | – | Stéphani |
| Fr. | Edouard Colonne | Leslino | – | Piroia |
| Engl. | Theodore Thomas | Amalie Friedrich-Materna | – | Italo Campanini |
| Engl. | Frank van der Stucken (?) | – | Marie Gramm | Max Alvary |
| Germ. | Felix Mottl | Luise Reuss-Belce, Zdenka Mottl-Fassbender | Mailhac | Oberländer, Gerhäuser |
| Fr. | Warnots | Tylda | Vaillant-Couturier | Saléza |
| Fr. | Jules Danbé | – | Marie Delna | Emmanuel Lafarge |
| Germ. | Hermann Levi | – | Milka Ternina | Heinrich Vogl |
| Germ. | Hermann Levi | Emanuela Frank | Milka Ternina | Heinrich Vogl |
| Engl. | Frederic Cowen | – | Marie Duma | Edward Lloyd |
| Engl. | Frederic Cowen | – | Marie Duma | Edward Lloyd |
| Germ. | Arno Klessel | Olive Fremstad | Bertha Pester-Prosky | Klemens Kaufung |
| Fr. | Paul Taffanel | Marie Delna, Meyrianne Heglon | – | Lucas |
| It. | Edouard Colonne | Armanda Bourgeois | – | ? |
| Russ. | ? | – | Carri | Koshits, Donskoi |

| *Date* | *City* | *Opera Company/Theatre* | *Version* |
|---|---|---|---|
| 27.VI.1900 | Leipzig | Neues Stadttheater | I |
| 24.X.1900 | Leipzig | Neues Stadttheater | II |
| 9.XII.1903 | Leipzig | Neues Stadttheater | I |
| 9.XII.1904 | Regensburg | Stadttheater | II |
| 26.V.1905 | Munich | Kgl. Hof- und Nationaltheater | I |
| 5.VIII.1905 | Orange | Concerts Colonne/Théâtre Antique | II |
| 26–7.XII.1906 | Brussels | Théâtre Royal de la Monnaie | I+II, some cuts |
| 29–30.X.1907 | Munich | Kgl. Hof- und Nationaltheater | I+II |
| 20.III.1908 | Boston | Jordan Hall | Act IV, Scene 2 |
| 5.VI.1908 | Munich | Prinzregententheater | I+II |
| 18.V.1913 | Stuttgart | Kgl. Hoftheater (Grosses Haus) | I+II, condensed |
| 5.VII.1919 | Nîmes | Paris Opéra/Les Arènes | II |
| 6.II.1920 | Rouen | [Paris Opéra version]/ Théâtre des Arts | I+II, condensed |
| late 1920 | Strasbourg | Théâtre Municipal | II |
| 10.VI.1921 | Paris | Opéra | I+II, condensed |
| 2.VIII.1921 | Vichy | Grand Casino | II |
| 23.III.1928 | Lyons | Opéra de Lyon/Grand Théâtre | II |
| 1.XI.1928 | Manchester | Hallé Orchestra/Free Trade Hall | II, concert |
| 15.II.1929 | Paris | Opéra | I+II, condensed |
| 15.VI.1930 | Berlin | Staatsoper/Preussisches Staatstheater | I+II, condensed (Kapp) |
| 3.VIII.1931 | Orange | Concerts Colonne etc./ Théâtre Antique | I+II, condensed |
| 22.XI.1932 | Geneva | Orch. de la Suisse Romande/ Grand-Théâtre | I |

| *Language* | *Conductor* | *Cassandra* | *Dido* | *Aeneas* |
|---|---|---|---|---|
| Germ. | Gorter | Eibenschütz | – | Moers |
| Germ. | Gorter | – | Doengas | Moers |
| Germ. | Hagel | Korb | – | Untucht |
| Germ. | Philipp Hofmann | – | Böling | Grusin |
| Germ. | Felix Mottl | Preuse-Matzenauer | – | Knote |
| Fr. | Edouard Colonne | – | Félia Litvinne | Rousselière |
| Fr. | Sylvain Dupuis | Charles-Mazarin | Claire Croiza | Léon Lafitte |
| Germ. | Felix Mottl | Preuse-Matzenauer (also sang Anna) | Fassbender | Buysson |
| Fr. | Albert Debuchy | – | Nora Burns | Clarence Shirley |
| Germ. | Felix Mottl | Preuse-Matzenauer (also sang Anna) | Fassbender | Buysson |
| Germ. | Max von Schillings | L. Hoffmann-Onegin | Sofie Palm-Cordes | Rudolf Ritter |
| Fr. | François Ruhlmann | – | Josée Gozatégui | Paul Franz |
| Fr. | Paul Sonnier | Hélène Duvernay | Comès | Cochera |
| Fr. | Paul Bastide | – | Mancini | M. Verdier |
| Fr. | Philippe Gaubert | Lucy Isnardon, Yvonne Courso | Josée Gozatégui, Germaine Grialys | Paul Franz, John Sullivan, M. Verdier |
| Fr. | Paul Bastide | – | Josée Gozatégui | M. Verdier |
| Fr. | Valcourt | [Cast included MM Forti, Laskin, Mestrallet, Calbet, Marcotti, Genelis, Alté; Mmes Frozier, Marot, Montazel, Zavoli] | | |
| Engl. | Sir Hamilton Harty | – | Tatiana Makushina | Francis Russell |
| Fr. | Philippe Gaubert, Henri Busser | Germaine Lubin | Marisa Ferrer, Georgette Caro, Lucienne De Méo | Paul Franz, Georges Thill |
| Germ. | Leo Blech | Karin Branzell | Frieda Leider | Helge Roswaenge |
| Fr. | François Ruhlmann | Jane Cros | Marisa Ferrer | José de Trevi |
| Fr. | Albert Paychère | Marisa Ferrer | – | José de Trevi |

| *Date* | *City* | *Opera Company/Theatre* | *Version* |
|---|---|---|---|
| 22.XI.1932 | Nantes | Grand-Théâtre | II |
| 18–19.III.1935 | Glasgow | Grand Opera Society/ Theatre Royal | I+II, a few cuts |
| 31.VII.1938 | Orange | Paris Opéra/Théâtre Antique | I |
| 1940 | Brno | | II (?) |
| 3.VI, 2.VII.1947 | London | Royal Philharmonic/ BBC broadcast/recorded | I+II, some cuts, concert |
| 13.X.1948 | Birmingham | Midland Music Makers/ Birmingham & Midland Institute | I+II, condensed |
| 29.XI.1950 | Oxford | Oxford University Opera Club | I+II, cut |
| 19.VII.1951 | Naples | Auspices of Teatro San Carlo/Teatro di Pompeii | II |
| 22.XI.1951 | Paris | Orchestre de la Radio-lyrique/RTF broadcast | I, concert |
| 24.III.1952 | Capetown | Van Riebeck Festival | II |
| 10.V.1952 | Paris | Orchestre de la Société des Concerts du Conservatoire/ Palais de Chaillot/recorded | II, concert |
| 11.XII.1953 | Paris | Opéra | excerpts, concert |
| 1954–5 | Marseilles | Opéra | II |
| 27.III.1955 | Boston | New England Opera Theater | I+II, cut |
| 6.VI.1957 | London | Royal Opera/Covent Garden | I+II, a few cuts |
| III.1958 | Stockholm | Royal Opera | I+II, cut |
| 14.VI.1958 | Lyons | Opéra de Lyon/Théâtre Antique | I+II, condensed |
| 29.XII.1959, 12.I.1960 | New York | American Opera Society/ Carnegie Hall | I+II, concert |
| 29.IV.1960 | London | Royal Opera/Covent Garden | I+II |
| 27.V.1960 | Milan | La Scala | I+II, cut |
| VII.1960 | Nice | Opéra de Lyon/Arènes de Cimiez | I+II, condensed (Bruder) |
| late 1960 or 1961 | Strasbourg | Opéra de Strasbourg | I+II, condensed (Bruder) |

| *Language* | *Conductor* | *Cassandra* | *Dido* | *Aeneas* |
|---|---|---|---|---|
| Fr. | Simon Borelli (?) | – | Georgette Frozier | Lapelleterie |
| Engl. | Erik Chisholm | Jenny Black | Dorothy Pugh | Guy McCrone |
| Fr. | Philippe Gaubert | Marisa Ferrer | – | José de Trevi |
| ? | Rafael Kubelik | – | ? | ? |
| Fr. | Sir Thomas Beecham | Marisa Ferrer | Marisa Ferrer | Jean Girardeau |
| Engl. | Arthur Street | Kathleen Green | Hilda Miller | Leslie Deathridge |
| Fr. | Sir Jack Westrup | Barbara Rawson | Arda Mandikian | John Kentish |
| It.(?) | André Cluytens | – | Elsa Cavelti | Tyge Tygesen |
| Fr. | Henri Tomasi | Marisa Ferrer | – | Georges Jouatte |
| Engl. | Erik Chisholm | – | Emilie Hooke | Ernest Dennis |
| Fr. | Hermann Scherchen | – | Arda Mandikian | Jean Girardeau |
| Fr. | Georges Sébastian | – | Suzanne Juyol | Raoul Jobin |
| Fr. | ? | – | ? | ? |
| Engl. | Boris Goldovsky | Eunice Alberts | Mariquita Moll | Arthur Schoep |
| Engl. | Rafael Kubelik | Amy Shuard | Blanche Thebom | Jon Vickers |
| Swed. | Herbert Sandberg | Kjerstin Dellert | Kerstin Meyer | Set Svanholm |
| Fr. | Paul Cabanel | Régine Crespin | Régine Crespin | Richard Martell |
| Fr. | Robert Lawrence | Eleanor Steber | Regina Resnick | Richard Cassilly |
| Engl. | John Pritchard, Muir Matheson | Amy Shuard | Kerstin Meyer | Jon Vickers |
| It. | Rafael Kubelik | Nell Rankin | Giuletta Simionato | Mario del Monaco |
| Fr. | Edmond Carrière | (Simone Couderc?) | Simone Couderc | Louis Roney |
| Fr. | Fréderic Adam | Lucienne Delvaux | Rita Gorr | Louis Roney |

| *Date* | *City* | *Opera Company/Theatre* | *Version* |
|---|---|---|---|
| 17.XI.1961 | Paris | Opéra | I+II, condensed |
| 5.V.1963 | Oxford | Chelsea Opera Group/ Town Hall | I, concert |
| 5.V.1964 | Buenos Aires | Teatro Colón | I+II, condensed (Bruder) |
| 10.V.1964 | Cambridge | Guildhall | II, concert, ballets cut |
| 11.III.1965 | Paris | Radio broadcast | I+II, condensed, concert |
| 25.III.1965 | London | New Philharmonia Orch./ Royal Festival Hall | I, concert |
| 14.IX.1966 | London | New Philharmonia Orch./ Royal Albert Hall | I, concert |
| 4.XI.1966 | San Francisco | San Francisco Opera/ War Memorial Opera House | I+II, condensed (Bruder) |
| 13, 16.XII.1966 | London | London Symphony Orch./ Royal Festival Hall | I+II, concert |
| 4.III.1967 | Stuttgart | Stuttgart Opera/ Württembergisches Staatstheater | I+II, condensed |
| 13.IX.1967 | London | London Symphony Orch./ Royal Albert Hall | II, concert |
| 24.II.1968 | Lisbon | Teatro Nacional de S. Carlo | I+II, condensed (Bruder) |
| 1.IX.1968 | London | London Symphony Orch./ Royal Albert Hall | I+II, uncut, concert |
| 15.IX.1968 | San Francisco | San Francisco Opera/ War Memorial Opera House | I+II, condensed (Bruder) |
| 10, 17.IV.1969 | Manchester | Hallé Orchestra/Free Trade Hall | I+II, concert |
| 3.V.1969 | Glasgow | Scottish Opera/King's Theatre | I+II, uncut |
| 29, 31.V.1969 (or 30–1) | Rome | RAI Orchestra/RAI broadcast | I+II, concert, no ballets |
| 17.IX.1969 | London | Royal Opera/Covent Garden/recorded | I+II, uncut |
| 19.XI.1969 | Paris | Opéra | I+II, condensed |

| *Language* | *Conductor* | *Cassandra* | *Dido* | *Aeneas* |
|---|---|---|---|---|
| Fr. | Pierre Dervaux | Geneviève Serrès | Régine Crespin, Marguerite Mas | Guy Chauvet |
| Engl. | Colin Davis | Josephine Veasey | – | Richard Gandy |
| Fr. | Georges Sébastian | Régine Crespin | Régine Crespin | Guy Chauvet |
| Fr. | Colin Davis | – | Josephine Veasey | Alberto Remedios |
| Fr. | Pierre-Michel Le Conte | Berthe Monmart | Berthe Monmart | Marcel Huylbrock |
| Engl. | Colin Davis | Josephine Veasey | – | Ronald Dowd |
| Engl. | Colin Davis | Janet Baker | – | Ronald Dowd |
| Fr. | Jean Périsson | Régine Crespin | Régine Crespin | Jon Vickers |
| Engl. | Colin Davis | Kerstin Meyer | Evelyn Lear | Ronald Dowd |
| Germ. | Wolfgang Rennert | Grace Hoffman | Hildegarde Hillebrecht | Mario del Monaco, Robert Thomas |
| Engl. | Colin Davis | – | Evelyn Lear | Ronald Dowd |
| Fr. | Edmond Carrière | Suzanne Sarroca | Suzanne Sarroca | Guy Chauvet |
| Engl. | Colin Davis | Amy Shuard | Josephine Veasey | Ronald Dowd |
| Fr. | Jean Périsson | Régine Crespin | Régine Crespin | Guy Chauvet |
| Engl. | Maurice Handford | Anne Pashley | Anita Vallki | Alberto Remedios |
| Engl. | Alexander Gibson | Ann Howard | Janet Baker | Ronald Dowd |
| Fr. | Georges Prêtre | Marilyn Horne | Shirley Verrett | Nicolai Gedda |
| Fr. | Colin Davis | Anja Silja | Josephine Veasey (Janet Baker) | Jon Vickers (Ronald Dowd) |
| Fr. | Pierre Dervaux | Lyne Dourian, Nadine Denize | Josephine Veasey, Berthe Monmart | Guy Chauvet, Jean Bonhomme |

| *Date* | *City* | *Opera Company/Theatre* | *Version* |
| --- | --- | --- | --- |
| 4.II.1971 | Augsburg | Augsburg Opera | I+II, some numbers shortened |
| 9.II.1971 | New York | New Jersey Symphony/ Carnegie Hall | I, excerpts, concert |
| 3–4.II.1972 | Boston | Opera Co. of Boston/ Aquarius Theater | I+II, uncut |
| 17.III.1972 | New York | Pro Arte Festival Orch./ Carnegie Hall | I+II, uncut, concert |
| 24.VIII.1972 | Edinburgh | Scottish Opera/King's Theatre | I+II, uncut |
| 16.IX.1972 | Wiesbaden | Hessisches Staatstheater | I+II, condensed |
| 21.IX.1972 | London | Royal Opera/Covent Garden | I+II, some cuts |
| 22.X.1973 | New York | Metropolitan Opera | I+II, a few cuts |
| IX.1974 | Geneva | Grand Théâtre | I+II |
| 17.X.1976 | Vienna | Wiener Staatsoper | I+II, some cuts |
| 3.X.1977 | London | Royal Opera/Covent Garden | II |
| 23.V.1978 | Marseilles | Opéra de Marseille | I |
| 30.VI–1.VII.1978 | Chicago | Chicago Symphony/Ravinia Festival | I+II, uncut, concert |
| 20.IV.1980 | Marseilles | Opéra de Marseille | II |
| 18, 20.IX.1980 | Lyons | Opéra de Lyon | I+II, 'semi-staged' |
| 4.V.1982 | Milan | La Scala | I+II, some cuts |
| 10.X.1982 | Hamburg | Staatsoper | I+II |
| 26.IX.1983 | New York | Metropolitan Opera | I+II, uncut |
| 18.XII.1983 | Frankfurt | Oper Frankfurt | I+II, uncut |
| 15.VI.1986 | Portsmouth | Bournemouth Symphony | I+II, uncut concert |

| *Language* | *Conductor* | *Cassandra* | *Dido* | *Aeneas* |
| --- | --- | --- | --- | --- |
| Germ. | Hans Zanotelli | Linda Karén | Anita Salta | Voijslaw Vujacic (Ronald Dowd) |
| Fr. | Henry Lewis | Marilyn Horne | – | omitted |
| Fr. | Sarah Caldwell | Maralin Niska | Régine Crespin | Ronald Dowd |
| Fr. | John Nelson | Clarice Carson | Evelyn Lear | Richard Cassilly |
| Engl. | Alexander Gibson | Helga Dernesch | Janet Baker | Gregory Dempsey |
| Germ. | Heinz Wallberg | Liane Synek | Ella Lee | Gene Ferguson |
| Engl. | Colin Davis | Jessye Norman, Josephine Veasey | Josephine Veasey, Janet Baker | Jon Vickers (Marshall Raynor, Alberto Remedios) |
| Fr. | Rafael Kubelik, John Nelson | Shirley Verrett | Christa Ludwig (Shirley Verrett) | Jon Vickers |
| Fr. | John Nelson | [Cast included Evelyn Lear, Gisela Schröter, Anne-Marie Blauzet, Michèle Vilma, Guy Chauvet, Robert Massard, John Macurdy, Jules Bastin]. | | |
| Fr. | Gerd Albrecht | Helga Dernesch | Christa Ludwig | Guy Chauvet |
| Engl. | Colin Davis | – | Yvonne Minton, Josephine Veasey | Richard Cassilly |
| Fr. | Diego Masson | Nadine Denize | – | Guy Chauvet |
| Fr. | James Levine | Nadine Denize | Shirley Verrett | Guy Chauvet |
| Fr. | Diego Masson | – | Nadine Denize | Guy Chauvet |
| Fr. | Serge Baudo | Nadine Denize | Margarita Zimmermann | Stan Unruh |
| Fr. | Georges Prêtre | Nadine Denize | Dunja Vejzovic | Alexey Steblianko |
| Fr. | Sylvain Cambreling | Karan Armstrong | Hanna Schwarz | Guy Chauvet |
| Fr. | James Levine | Jessye Norman, Gwynne Cornell | Tatiana Troyanos, Jessye Norman | Placido Domingo, William Lewis |
| Germ. | Michael Gielen | Anja Silja | Rachel Gettler | William Cochran |
| Fr. | Roger Norrington | Jo Ann Pickens | Eiddwen Harrhy | Stuart Kale |

| *Date* | *City* | *Opera Company/Theatre* | *Version* |
|---|---|---|---|
| 27.XI.1986 | Leeds | Opera North/Grand Theatre | I, with first perf. of Sinon scene |
| 28.II.1987 | Cardiff | Welsh Opera/New Theatre | I + II, uncut |
| 18.IX.1987 | Leeds | Opera North/Grand Theatre | II, uncut |
| 19.IX.1987 | Lyons | Opéra de Lyon | I + II, uncut (incl. Sinon scene) |

| *Language* | *Conductor* | *Cassandra* | *Dido* | *Aeneas* |
|---|---|---|---|---|
| Engl. | David Lloyd-Jones | Kristine Ciesinski | – | Ronald Hamilton |
| Engl. | Charles Mackerras | Anne Evans | Della Jones | Jeffrey Lawton |
| Engl. | David Lloyd-Jones | – | Sally Burgess | William Lewis |
| Fr. | Serge Baudo | Jo Ann Pickens | Kathryn Harries | Gary Lakes |

# *Notes*

Works referred to in the text or in the Notes by abbreviation, author, or by author and title only are cited in full in the Bibliography.

### 2 Biographical introduction

1 See Condé, p. 296.
2 *Journal des Débats*, 3 February 1857
3 *Mem.*, p. 610
4 Richard Wagner: *My Life*, trans. Andrew Gray and ed. Mary Whittall (Cambridge 1983), p. 559
5 CG V 2327
6 See April FitzLyon: *The Price of Genius* (London 1964), pp. 345–62.
7 T. J. Walsh: *Second Empire Opera: The Théâtre-Lyrique, Paris 1851–1870* (London 1981), p. 111. Much of the information in this chapter is drawn from this book.
8 Bibliothèque Nationale: *Berlioz* (exhibition catalogue) (Paris 1969), p. 110
9 NL, pp. 154–5
10 LI, p. 261
11 Hugh Macdonald: 'Les Troyens at the Théâtre-Lyrique', *Musical Times*, 110 (September 1969), pp. 919–21
12 Wagner, *My Life*, p. 520
13 *A travers chants*, pp. 321–3 (review of Wagner's 1860 concerts in Paris)
14 *Mem.*, p. 539
15 Claude Rostand, in a review of the Philips recording in *Le Figaro Littéraire*, 21–7 September 1970, p. 5: translated by David Cairns in his essay 'Les Troyens and the Aeneid', *Responses* (London 1973), pp. 88–110

### 4 Composition

1 *Journal des Débats*, 17 April 1855
2 *Mem.*, p. 596. See also the dedication of the score, NBE Vol. 2a, p. [2].
3 Peter Cornelius: *Literarische Werke* (Leipzig 1905), Vol. 1, p. 223
4 Charavay Catalogue No. 697, June 1957
5 They are fully examined in Macdonald: 'A Critical Edition', pp. 131–55.
6 The original version of this passage is given in NBE Vol. 2c, pp. 940–2.

7 No letters from the Princess to Berlioz have survived. This one was apparently sixteen pages long (CG V 2165).
8 *Die neue Rundschau*, June 1907, p. 724
9 See NBE Vol. 2c, pp. 931–4.
10 See Hugh Macdonald: 'Berlioz's Self-borrowings', *Proceedings of the Royal Musical Association*, 92 (1965–6), pp. 27–44
11 LI, p. 227
12 *Mem.*, p. 369
13 *Journal des Débats*, 3 February 1857
14 *Ibid.*, 9 November 1863
15 Private collection
16 The celebrated actress Rachel had died seventeen days before.
17 *Le Guide Musical*, 29 November 1903

**5 Berlioz the poet?**

1 Letter to Carvalho, 15 July (1863). NL, pp. 240–1
2 Sainte-Beuve: *Vie, poésie et pensées de Joseph Delorme*, ed. G. Antoine (Paris 1957) p. 147. All translations are my own.
3 Victor Hugo: *Préface de Cromwell*, in *Victor Hugo, Œuvres complètes. Critique* (Paris 1985), p. 27
4 He is named in the manuscript of Adèle Hugo: *Victor Hugo raconté par un témoin de sa vie* (Paris 1985), p. 459: 'Chaque ami particulier de l'auteur avait des amis. Chacun de ses amis particuliers présenta à Victor Hugo une liste nominative d'individus dont il répondait. Cet ensemble formait des escouades ayant chacune un chef de file, Berlioz, Geraldi, Nousseau. . .'. This implies that Berlioz was a 'chef de tribu', which would mean that he attended several performances, taking other young friends and supporters with him.
5 Théophile Gautier: *Histoire du romantisme* (Paris 1911) p. 111
6 Quoted in *Victor Hugo. Cromwell. Hernani.* (Paris 1912) p. 714
7 Hugo, *Préface de Cromwell*, p. 29
8 CG V 2380: 'Je marchais tout vivant dans mon rêve étoilé' – clearly one of Berlioz's favourite quotations, taken from *Ruy Blas*, Act III Scene 4, where the Furne edition (1841) reads: 'Donc je marche vivant dans mon rêve étoilé!' One may consider that Berlioz's memory has actually improved the line.
9 NL, p. 156
10 References in brackets are to Berlioz's numberings (see Synopsis). Quotations have been checked against the autograph libretto (F-Po, Rés.589) and may therefore differ from the libretto in the Philips recording, in which the lines of verse are often not detectable.
11 This is a direct translation from the *Aeneid* (2.354): *Una salus victis nullam sperare salutem*. Delille has: 'Tout l'espoir des vaincus est un beau désespoir.'
12 See Antoine Reicha: *Art du compositeur dramatique ou cours complet de composition vocale* (Paris 1833), Vol. 1, p. 14: 'De la versification lyrique sous le rapport de la musique'.

13 See also Julian Rushton: 'Berlioz' roots in 18th century French opera', *Berlioz Society Bulletin*, 50 (April 1965), pp. 3-10. This article shows how Marmontel's libretto for Piccinni's *Didon* contains some 'verbal anticipations' of *Les Troyens*, thus reinforcing from a different angle my point about neo-classical language. Rushton's evaluation, however, differs from mine: 'It is everywhere obvious that Berlioz' words. . .have more richness and strength.'

14 See the article by E. F. entitled 'Des poèmes d'opéras' in *La Revue musicale*, 25 September 1830.

15 Deschamps is singled out by L. de M. (Lucas de Montigny?) for his translation of *Don Juan* in an article entitled 'Du Style et de la poésie des opéras français' (*Revue et Gazette musicale de Paris*, 13 December 1835, pp. 405–6), whose thesis is that present-day opera *lacks* poetry. In the present context another of the writer's remarks may appear prophetic: 'Aujourd'hui, les théâtres veulent à tout prix en avoir fini avec les pièces de Shakespeare; on prétend qu'il n'y a point de musique en ce puits merveilleux, parce que des hommes de peu de talent n'ont pas su creuser assez à fond pour en trouver. Mettez Berlioz à l'œuvre, et vous verrez si l'urne ne sera pas remplie jusqu'aux bords à l'heure où vous lui demanderez compte de sa journée.'

16 Castil-Blaze: *Sur l'opéra français, vérités dures mais utiles* (Paris 1856), p. 18: '. . .une mixture, un pudding de mots coupés, brisés, parfaitement inintelligibles même pour un auditoire parisien'.

### 6 Berlioz and Virgil

1 This essay is a shortened version of 'Les Troyens and the Aeneid', *Responses* (London 1973), pp. 88–110.

2 A possible influence here is Piccinni's *Didon*, which Berlioz had got to know during his student days. Much of the action in Marmontel's libretto is concerned with Iarbas and his unsuccessful wooing. There are also verbal similarities between the two librettos in the later scenes, where Marmontel stays closest to Virgil.

### 7 *Les Troyens* as 'grand opera'

1 Hugh Macdonald: 'Music and Opera', in D. G. Charlton (ed.): *The French Romantics* (2 Vols., Cambridge 1984), Vol. 2, pp. 353–81. See also David Charlton: 'Grand opéra', in Gerald Abraham (ed.), *New Oxford History of Music*, Vol. 9 (in preparation).

2 *Richard Wagner's Prose Works*, trans. and ed. William Ashton Ellis (London 1892–9), Vol. 7, p. 193

3 Jeffrey Langford: 'Berlioz, Cassandra and the French Operatic Tradition', *Music and Letters*, 62 (July–October 1981), pp. 310–17

4 Preface to libretto of *Fernand Cortez* (Paris 1809)

5 An alternative view, centring on a comparison between *Les Troyens* and Wagner's *Der Ring des Nibelungen*, may be found in the chapter headed 'Operatic Epic and Romance' in Peter Conrad's *Romantic Opera and Literary Form* (Berkeley and Los Angeles 1977). See also Paul Robinson:

*Opera and Ideas* (New York 1985), and Jane Fulcher: *The Nation's Image: French Grand Opera as Politics and Politicized Art* (Cambridge 1987).

**8 On the nature of 'grand opera'**

1 Marie-Antoinette Allevy: *Le Mise en scène en France dans la première moitié du dix-neuvième siècle* (publications de la Société des Historiens du théatre, Vol. 10) (Paris 1938)
2 Daguerre was employed part-time by the Opéra for two years, where his notable joint creation was the brilliant *Aladin* with music by Nicolo Isouard (1822), the first opera to use gas stage lighting. See H. and A. Gernsheim: *L. J. M. Daguerre* (2nd edn New York 1968), pp. 11–12.
3 Nicole Wild: 'La Recherche de la précision historique chez les décorateurs de l'Opéra de Paris au XIXème siècle', in *International Musicological Society: Report of the Twelfth Congress, Berkeley, 1977*, ed. Daniel Heartz and Bonnie Wade (Kassel etc., 1981), pp. 453–63
4 H. Robert Cohen: 'On the Reconstruction of the Visual Elements of French Grand Opera', in *ibid.*, pp. 463–80
5 Catherine Join-Dieterle, '*Robert le Diable*: le premier opéra romantique', *Romantisme*, 28/29 (1980), p. 161
6 Karin Pendle: *Eugène Scribe and French Opera of the Nineteenth Century* (Ann Arbor 1979), pp. 33–4 *et passim*. This largely replaces W. L. Crosten's *French Grand Opera: An Art and a Business* (New York 1948).
7 See Steven Huebner: 'The Second Empire Operas of Charles Gounod' (unpublished dissertation, Princeton University 1985), pp. 155ff.
8 Pendle, *Eugène Scribe*, p. 388
9 Ludwig Finscher: 'Aubers *La Muette de Portici* und die Anfänge der Grand-opéra', in *Festschrift Heinz Becker*, ed. Jürgen Schläder and Reinhold Quandt (Laaber-Verlag, n.p., 1982), pp. 87–105
10 D. G. Charlton: 'Religious and Political Thought', *The French Romantics*, Vol. 1, p. 58
11 I have paraphrased these definitions from Pendle, *Eugène Scribe*, pp. 85ff.
12 See Jean R. Mongrédien: 'Variations sur un thème: Masaniello', in *Jahrbuch für Opernforschung*, 1985, ed. Michael Arndt and Michael Walter, pp. 90–121.
13 The printed libretto of *La Muette de Portici* (Paris 1828) reads at this point: 'Parvenue au haut de la terrasse, [Fenella] contemple cet effrayant spectacle [i.e. of the first flames from the volcano] . . . lève les yeux au ciel et se précipite dans l'abîme . . . au même instant le Vésuve mugit avec plus de fureur; du cratère du volcan la lave enflammée se précipite. Le peuple épouvanté se prosterne.'
14 Carl Dahlhaus, in *Realism in nineteenth-century music*, trans. Mary Whittall (Cambridge 1985), p. 83, citing only *Le Prophète*, ignoring that work's tendency towards the epic, and selecting his evidence, manoeuvres himself into the position of saying the work is 'political opera born from an unpolitical spirit'.

### 9 The unity of *Les Troyens*

1 *Mem.*, p. 603
2 Jasper Griffin: 'Introduction' to *Virgil: The Aeneid*, trans. C. Day Lewis (Oxford 1986), p. xxiii
3 See Basil Deane: 'The French Operatic Overture from Grétry to Berlioz', *Proceedings of the Royal Musical Association*, 99 (1972–3), pp. 67–80. Deane refers to Lacépède's (in *La poétique de la musique*, Paris 1785) division of the operatic overture into five types, the fifth consisting of there not being any. No examples of this type before *Les Troyens* are known.
4 NBE, p. 840

### 10 The Musical Structure

1 See Julian Rushton: 'The Overture to *Les Troyens*', *Music Analysis* 4 (1985), pp. 119–44. In this article I have already broached many of the questions with which the present chapter is concerned. Inevitably some of the same details and conclusions appear again; but I have not reproduced the tables of data which form the bulky appendices to the article, and to which the reader is invited to refer. Instead I have tried to integrate my results into a wider argument.
2 Herbert Lindenberger: *Opera: the Extravagant Art* (Ithaca 1984), pp. 75ff
3 Letter to Liszt: see p. 51.
4 Berlioz's own views on key-character refer specifically to the violin (see his *Grand traité*, p. 33). F major in *Les Troyens* is nearly always a key of calm, often with pastoral associations (Coroebus's Andante in No. 3; Nos. 25, 36, and the Andante of No. 41, however, are not pastoral, while Iopas's song, No. 34, is a pastoral *divertissement*). Passing references to F are not necessarily calm: No. 16 (p. 218), No. 46 (p. 687), the climax of No. 47, p. 707 bar 41. Such contradictions, between substantial areas in a key and passing references in which the key's significance may lie in its relationship with its surroundings, will always arise in studies of this phenomenon. Hugh Macdonald asserts that certain very flat keys are present in *Les Troyens* for colouristic rather than structural reasons (*Berlioz*, p. 199); this is probably true in general, but see Rushton, 'The Overture to *Les Troyens*', pp. 121 and 124, and App. 1 and 2.
5 A flat is used for the ritual despair of No. 14; but in No. 15 for a message of hope (p. 246), although Cassandra knows it is not for her; then in No. 16 for the death-devoted hymn ('Complices de sa gloire'), later repeated in A. Aeneas's No. 41 ends in A flat, but in despair; Dido's farewell (No. 48) is also in A flat. This complex of death and resignation is confirmed by passing references such as the A flat at 'Strange destiny' (p. 399) and Dido's prophecy of Hannibal (p. 732). The latter, a prophecy of victory by one about to die, is exactly analogous to Cassandra's situation in No. 15; both passages turn from A flat to C flat (p. 247, 'Une nouvelle Troie'; p. 734, 'son nom vainqueur'), although with Dido the orchestral burst of C flat moves at once to G flat.
6 Beginning Act II in the same key suggests that no interval need be made

at this point. As it happens, Act III, although set in distant Carthage some years later, follows easily from Act II; No. 17 is in the relative major (E flat from C minor) and its arpeggiated melody sounds familiar: 'De Carthage les cieux' (p. 298) is a major version of 'Aux chemins de l'Ida' (p. 290), so that the first melodic idea of Act III closely resembles the last vocal melody to arise in Act II. Tonal links are not pursued between the later acts but there is a motivic connection (of equally unfathomable significance) between the end of Act III (p. 441, basses) and the opening of the *Chasse royale*, while the call of 'Italie' which ends Act IV is soon taken up in Act V.

7 Aeneas's *andante* is analysed in Rushton: *The Musical Language of Berlioz*, p. 160.

8 To the four melodic images in Table 10.1 may be added:

D Melodies made of semitonal descent over a considerable range (No. 8, countersubject, p. 131 bar 12; No. 12, speech of Hector's ghost; No. 50, Dido's final entrance: all evidently associated with death and mourning).

E A swaying third, usually minor and also mournful, mysteriously included in No. 4 (p. 96, horns); also in No. 8 (p. 149, wind); No. 12, the opening bar of Act II (Ex. 10.10, trombones); major third, vocalised 'O–a', *Chasse royale*, p. 470.

F The conventional musical sign for a serpent, dragon, or monster; evidently illustrative in No. 7 (p. 126: cf. the dragon motive of *Das Rheingold*) and No. 8 (p. 82: 'monstres hideux'); perhaps symbolic of cunning in the Sinon scene.

G Relationship between the funeral rituals Nos. 6 and 49, and bass motives in Nos. 16 and 50, the latter taken from 49; see Rushton, 'The Overture to *Les Troyens*', p. 121.

H A melodic curve which unrolls a dominant seventh from the root down to the leading note, a conventional shape which, however, always stands out: all the following instances refer directly to Aeneas's destiny except the last two, which he sings himself (referring to Dido). Like 'Italie', this is a vocal motive: No. 15 (p. 247) Cassandra: 'Une nouvelle Troie' – see Ex. 10.15A; No. 27, four instances: (p. 396) Ascanius: 'un chef pieux', (p. 397) Ascanius referring to Helen's veil, (p. 397) Panthus on Aeneas's duty: 'rendre aux siens une patrie', (p. 400) Dido: 'Qui n'admire ce prince'; No. 28 (p. 425) Aeneas to Panthus: 'Où la gloire vous appelle'; No. 41 (pp. 632–3) Aeneas: 'Reine adorée', 'Ame sublime' – see Ex. 10.15B.

Ex. 10.15A

Ex. 10.15B

9 It may be objected that the diminished seventh is ubiquitous in Berlioz's music, but there are places in *Les Troyens* where it comes close to acting as a reference-point, so indeterminate is the tonality: No. 3, bars 165–84; No. 42; the opening of No. 50 (passages not readily connected but all of the highest significance to the characters involved).
10 The 'death' rhythm is discussed as a traditional motive by Frits Noske: 'The Musical Figure of Death', *The Signifier and the Signified* (The Hague 1977); see also Rushton, 'The Overture to *Les Troyens*', p. 125. Berlioz used it in an early version of the love-duet (No. 37, p. 940); it occurs when Dido accuses Aeneas of coldness. Perhaps Berlioz felt the verbal irony was sufficient.
11 On Mercury's entrance, see Rushton, 'The Overture to *Les Troyens*', p. 122 and App. 2.
12 On the relation of Cassandra's motive to Dido's prophecy, and to the preceding No. 1, see *ibid.*, pp. 130–1.
13 Ernest Newman, *Opera Nights* (London 1943), p. 316
14 This idea, which spells BACH in Ex. 14A bars 40–2, is also, in the version in No. 3, exactly like the meeting of Tristan and Isolde in Act II of Wagner's opera (written contemporaneously with *Les Troyens*): see the 2/4 section, 'Bist du mein?', 'Hab' ich dich wieder?' The gulf separating Wagner from Berlioz at this time is epitomized here: what in Berlioz serves a complex, tragic purpose is used by Wagner (admittedly accelerated) for exuberant happiness.

### 11 Commentary and analysis

1 For a detailed discussion see Macdonald, 'A Critical Edition', pp. 190–2.

### 12 *Performance history and critical opinion*

1 See Appendix D for an abbreviated list of productions. Details of each production from 1863 to 1973 may be found in Goldberg. Listed for each production are pertinent data such as dates, version performed, conductor and cast; included also for each are selections from and a bibliography of reviews and writings.
2 Albert Soubies: *Histoire du Théâtre-Lyrique, 1851–1870* (Paris 1899), p. 39
3 David Cairns discussed this problem in '*The Capture of Troy*: Royal Festival Hall, 25th March 1965', *Berlioz Society Bulletin*, 51 (July 1965), p. 13.
4 Richard Capell: 'Berlioz's *Trojans*', *Musical Times*, 7 (1 January 1929),

pp. 17–19. In his synopsis the *Chasse royale* is after the duet. In a letter in the 1 February 1929 issue (p. 154), Tom Wotton indicated where the scene should be.

5 The synopsis is given in Julius Kapp: 'Einführung in das Werk', *Blätter der Staatsoper und der Städtischen Oper*, 10 (June 1930), pp. 6–8. Reprinted in Goldberg, pp. 274–8.

6 For further discussions of the staging, see Emily Coleman: '*The Trojans*, Covent Garden; Staging Notes with Press Comments', *Theatre Arts*, 41 (August 1957), pp. 23–4; Blanche Thebom, '*The Trojans* – Backstage View', *New York Times*, 16 June 1957, Section 2; and 'TV and Tape Recorders Aid *The Trojans*', *Daily Telegraph* (London), 7 June 1957.

7 The 1964 Buenos Aires production, for example, omitted ten of the first sixteen numbers (Acts I and II) entirely, and made cuts in three of the remaining six. Cassandra was the only cast member of the first two acts.

8 Many excerpts from his columns in the *Sunday Times* (London) on *Les Troyens* are reprinted in his *Berlioz, Classic and Romantic*, ed. Peter Heyworth (London 1972), pp. 197–233.

9 Valuable discussions of the reviews of the première can be found in Alfred Ernst: *L'Œuvre dramatique de H. Berlioz* (Paris 1884), pp. 251–87, in Hugh Macdonald: '*Les Troyens* at the Théâtre-Lyrique', *Musical Times*, 110 (September 1969), and in T. J. Walsh: *Second Empire Opera: The Théâtre-Lyrique, Paris 1851–1870* (London 1981), pp. 165–71.

10 From Auguste de Gasperini: 'Théâtre-Lyrique Impérial. *Les Troyens*', *Ménestrel*, 30 (8 November 1863), p. 391, and '*Les Troyens* de Berlioz; la partition', *ibid.* (15 November 1863), p. 400

11 Gustave Bertrand: *La Crise musicale; à propos des 'Troyens' de M. Hector Berlioz* (Saint-Germain 1863), pp. 10–11. This article first appeared in *La Revue Germanique*, 1 December 1863.

12 Georges de Massougnes: *Berlioz; son œuvre* (Paris 1870), pp. 24–5

13 Léon Kerst: 'Théâtre National de l'Opéra-Comique', *Petit Journal*, 8 June 1892

14 Camille Bellaigue: 'Théâtre de l'Opéra-Comique, *les Troyens* de Berlioz', *Revue des deux mondes*, III, Vol. 112 (15 July 1892), p. 460

15 Julien Tiersot: '*Les Troyens à Carthage*, de Berlioz, à l'Opéra-Comique', *Ménestrel*, 58 (12 June 1892) p. 187

16 Adolphe Jullien: '*Les Troyens* de Berlioz à Carlsruhe', *Revue d'art dramatique*, 21 (January–March 1891), pp. 65, 67. The article was reprinted in Jullien: *Musiciens d'aujourd'hui* (Paris 1892), pp. 10–21.

17 Paul Dukas: 'Académie Nationale de Musique: *La Prise de Troie*', *Revue Hébdomadaire*, 8 (2 December 1899), p. 126

18 Reynaldo Hahn: 'Opéra: *Les Troyens*', unidentified Paris newspaper, 11 June 1921

19 Ernest Closson: '*Die Trojaner*', *Signale*, 65 (9 January 1907), pp. 46–8

20 Raymond Bouyer: 'La Physionomie des *Troyens* en 1920', *Ménestrel*, 82 (20 February 1920), p. 78

21 Ernest Newman: 'Berlioz and *The Trojans*', *Sunday Times* (London), 19 June 1921

22 Ernest Newman: '*The Trojans*; Glasgow's brave effort', *Sunday Times*, 24 March 1935

23 Donald Francis Tovey: *Essays in Musical Analysis, 4* (London 1937), p. 89
24 Mosco Carner: '*The Trojans*: Covent Garden', *Time and Tide*, 38 (15 June 1957), p. 747
25 Clarendon: '*Les Troyens* à l'Opéra', *Figaro* (Paris), 20 November 1961
26 David Cairns: 'Berlioz's Lyric Tragedy', *New Statesman*, 22 September 1967, p. 375
27 Jacques Bourgeois: 'Covent Garden. *The Trojans* (A French Critic's Opinion)', *Opera*, 8 (September 1957), p. 585
28 Robert Collet: 'The Trojans', *Score*, 20 (June 1957), p. 67
29 Winton Dean: '*The Trojans*', *Opera*, 8 (June 1957), pp. 341–2
30 Winton Dean: 'Readers' Letters. *The Trojans*', *Opera*, 11 (July 1960), p. 515
31 Alan Levitan: '*Les Troyens*: Romantic as Classicist', *Boston after Dark*, 15 February 1972
32 Gasperini: 'La partition', p. 400

### *Appendix B* Antique and obsolete instruments

1 NBE, p. 757
2 James Blades: *Percussion Instruments and their History* (London 1984, rev. edn), p. 288, which includes illustrations
3 Karl Peinhofer and Fritz Tannigal: *Handbook of Percussion Instruments* (New York 1976), which also describes the modern orchestral darabucca (pp. 105–7) and sistrum (p. 157)
4 See also Bryan Whitton: 'The Derabucca', *Drum and Percussion*, September 1974, pp. 14–17, which includes illustrations.
5 Wally Horwood: *Adolphe Sax 1814–1894: His Life and Legacy* (Baldock, Herts. 1983). See pp. 76–7, 90, 121 and 135.
6 Jürgen Eppelsheim: 'Berlioz' "Petit saxhorn suraigu"', *Gesellschaft für Musikforschung. Bericht über den internationalen Musikwissenschaftlichen Kongress Berlin 1974*, ed. Hellmut Kühn and Peter Nitsche (Kassel 1980), pp. 586–91
7 Malou Haine and Ignace de Keyser: *Catalogue des instruments Sax au Musée instrumental de Bruxelles* (The Brussels Museum of Musical Instruments): Bulletin, ed. René de Maeyer, 9 (1/2 1979) and 10 (1/2 1980), p. 9
8 *Grand traité*, p, 285
9 Haine and de Keyser, *Catalogue*, pp. 136–7
10 Malou Haine: *Adolphe Sax, sa vie, son œuvre, ses instruments de musique* (Brussels 1980), p. 145
11 *Grand traité*, p. 285
12 Also illustrated in Eppelsheim. Haine and de Keyser include two of the three plates of saxhorns in Kastner's *Manuel général* and photographs of instruments (including a sopranino saxhorn) in the Brussels collection.
13 Horwood, *Adolphe Sax*, pp. 57–77 and 153–63

# *Select bibliography*

Works referred to in the text or in the Notes by abbreviation, author, or by author and title only are cited in full in the Bibliography that follows. This is limited to material of relevance to the present book and may be supplemented by reference to material cited in the Notes. An extensive Berlioz bibliography is contained in the revised reprint of Hugh Macdonald's *New Grove* entry: *The New Grove Early Romantic Masters 2* (London 1985), pp. 181–95.


**Music and writings by Berlioz**

NBE (New Berlioz Edition) *Hector Berlioz: New Edition of the Complete Works.* Vol. 2: *Les Troyens* (Bärenreiter, Kassel 1969), ed. Hugh Macdonald. Vols. 2a and 2b comprise the full score (Acts I and II; III, IV and V); Vol. 2c is the Supplement (Foreword and Critical Notes, and various Appendixes which include the discarded Sinon scene, the Prologue composed for *Les Troyens à Carthage*, the simplified orchestration of the *Chasse royale et orage* and the original Finale, as well as rejected music, several sketches and details of the cuts made for the 1863 performances). Vols. 2a and 2b are reprinted under one cover as a miniature score (Eulenburg, London 1974).

This is the only published edition of the full score and the only reliable edition of the opera as a whole. References in the present book to the music of the opera are to page numbers in NBE, the pagination of which is continuous. A second number after a page number indicates a bar number. Music examples in vocal score are taken or adapted from Berlioz's own privately printed vocal score (see Appendix C).

H. D. Kern Holoman: *A Catalogue of the Works of Hector Berlioz*, NBE Vol. 25 (Kassel 1987). Definitive; includes all Berlioz's known music and writings.

*A travers chants* [1862], ed. Léon Guichard (Paris 1971).

SW *Briefe von Hector Berlioz an die Fürstin Carolyne Sayn-Wittgenstein*, ed. La Mara (Leipzig 1903). Letters (in French) written by Berlioz during and after the composition of the opera.

Condé *Cauchemars et passions*, ed. Gérard Condé (Paris 1981). The only available selection from Berlioz's feuilletons.

CG *Correspondance générale* (Paris 1972– ); Vol. 1, 1803–32, ed. Pierre Citron; Vol. 2, 1832–42, ed. Frédéric Robert; Vol. 3, 1842–50, ed. Pierre Citron; Vol. 4, 1851–5, ed. Pierre Citron, François Lesure and Hugh Macdonald; Vol. 5 is in the press. Vol. 6 will be the last in this edition of the complete correspondence, which is rendering other collections obsolete. In the present book references are to CG letter numbers.

CI *Correspondance inédite* (Paris 1879). The first published collection of Berlioz's letters.

*Grand traité d'instrumentation et d'orchestration modernes* [1843; 2nd edn 1855, reprinted Farnborough 1970].

*Les grotesques de la musique* [1852], ed. Léon Guichard (Paris 1969).

LI *Lettres intimes* (Paris 1882). Letters to Berlioz's lifelong friend Humbert Ferrand.

LT 'Lettres de Berlioz sur *Les Troyens*', ed. Julien Tiersot, *La Revue de Paris*: Vol. 4, 1 August 1921, pp. 449–73; Vol. 4, 15 August 1921, pp. 749–70; Vol. 5, 1 September 1921, pp. 146–71. Includes many letters not in SW.

*Mem.* *The Memoirs of Hector Berlioz* [1870], trans. and ed. David Cairns (2nd edn London 1970).

NL *New Letters of Berlioz 1830–1868*, trans. and ed. Jacques Barzun (New York 1954).

*Les soirées de l'orchestre* [1852], ed. Léon Guichard (Paris 1968).

**Writings by other authors**

Jacques Barzun: *Berlioz and the Romantic Century* (Boston 1950; London 1951; rev. edn Boston 1969).

Etiénne Destranges: *Les Troyens de Berlioz: étude analytique* (Paris 1897). Contemporary opinion.

Louise Goldberg: '"Les Troyens" of Hector Berlioz: A Century of Productions and critical reviews' (unpublished dissertation, University of Rochester 1973).

D. Kern Holoman: *The Creative Process in the Autograph Musical Documents of Hector Berlioz c.1818–1840* (Ann Arbor 1980).

Cecil Hopkinson: *A Bibliography of the Musical and Literary Works of Hector Berlioz* (Edinburgh 1951; 2nd rev. edn, Richard Macnutt, Tunbridge Wells 1981).

Hugh Macdonald: *Berlioz* (London 1982).

'A Critical Edition of Berlioz's *Les Troyens*' (unpublished dissertation, University of Cambridge 1968).

Brian Primmer: *The Berlioz Style* (2nd edn London 1975).

Julian Rushton: *The Musical Language of Berlioz* (Cambridge 1983).

# *Discography*

## BY MALCOLM WALKER

all recordings in stereo unless otherwise stated

*symbols*

Ⓜ mono recording (4) cassette version (CD) Compact Disc version
* 78rpm record

*D* Dido; *A* Aeneas; *C* Cassandra; *Cor* Coroebus; *An* Anna; *N* Narbal; *As* Ascanius; *I* Iopas; *P* Priam; *M* Mercury; *H* Hecuba; *Hy* Hylas; *Pa* Panthus; *TS* Trojan Soldier; *GC* Ghost of Cassandra; *Hel* Helenus; *GP* Ghost of Priam; *GH* Ghost of Hector; *SH* Spirit of Hector; *Gr* Greek Chieftain; *FS* First Sentry; *SS* Second Sentry

**Complete**

1970s Veasey *D*; Vickers *A*; Lindholm *C*; Glossop *Cor*; Begg *An*; Soyer *N, SH*; Howells *As*; Partridge *I*; Thau *P, M, TS*; Bainbridge *H, GC*; R. Davies *Hy*; Raffell *Pa*; Lennox *Hel*; Herincx *GP, FS*; Wicks *GH, Gr, SS* / Wandsworth School Boys' Ch.; Royal Opera House Chorus and Orch. / C. Davis Philips 6709 002 (4) 7699 142 (CD) 416 433-2PH4

**Incomplete**

1947 (broadcast performances) Ferrer *D, C*; Giraudeau *A*; Cambon *Cor, N*; Corke *An, H, GC*; Joachim, Braneze *As*; Vroons *I*; Joynt *P, GP, SS*; S. Scott *M*; Cunningham *Hy, Hel*; C. Paul *Pa*; Dowling *TS, Gr*; Frank *GH, FS*; BBC Theatre Chorus; Royal PO / Beecham
Melodrum Ⓜ MEL303(5)

*Les Troyens à Carthage*

1952 (concert performance) Mandikian *D*; Giraudeau *A*; Dépraz *N*; Rolle *As*; Gallet *I, Hy*; Dran *M, SS*; Abdoun *Gr, FS*; Paris Vocal Ensemble; Paris Conservatoire Orch. / Scherchen
Ducretet-Thomson (UK) Ⓜ DTL93001/3

**Excerpts/Highlights**

1965 Crespin *D, C*; Chauvet *A*; Vernet *N*; Berbié *As*; Dunan *I*; Hurteau *M, Pa*; Paris Opéra Fanfare, Chorus and Orch. / Prêtre
EMI 2C 181 16395/6
Angel SBL3670

*Act 5 – 'Inutiles regrets!'*

1934 Thill *A*; orch. / Bigot EMI (m) 2C 061 12154M (4) 112154-4
EMI (m) HLM7004

1961 Chauvet *A*; orch. / Etcheverry
Polaris (m) L80.007

1960s (live performance: Italian) Del Monaco *A*; orch.
Levon (m) ML1003

*Act 5, Scenes 2 and 3*

1969 Baker *D*; Greevey *An*; Howell *N*; Erwen *I*; Ambrosian Opera Chorus; London SO / Gibson
EMI SXLP30248 (4)
TC-SXLP30248
Angel S-36695

*Act 5, Scene 2 – (a) 'Je vais mourir. . .' (b) 'Adieu, fière cité'*

1957 Gorr *D*; Philharmonia / Collingwood
EMI (m) HLP23
RCA (US) LM6153

1960 Gorr *D*; RTF Radio Lyrique Orch. / Le Conte
Chant du Monde (m)
LDX78762/3 (4) K478.762/3

1968 Veasey *D*; Royal Opera House Orch. / Kubelik
Decca (4) 417 174-4DA
London OSA1276

1979 Takács *D*; Hungarian State Opera Orch. / Patane
Hungaraton SLPX12391

1903 (b) Litvinne *D*; pno
IRCC 200*
Rococo (m) R38

1920s (b) Frozier-Marrot *D*; orch.
EMI W1032*

# Index